AF361403

STAGING THE TRIALS OF MODERNISM

Testimony and the British Modern
Literary Consciousness

DALE BARLEBEN

Staging the Trials of Modernism

Testimony and the British Modern Literary Consciousness

UNIVERSITY OF TORONTO PRESS
Toronto Buffalo London

© University of Toronto Press 2017
Toronto Buffalo London
www.utppublishing.com

ISBN 978-1-4875-0107-5

Library and Archives Canada Cataloguing in Publication

Barleben, Dale, 1972–, author
Staging the trials of modernism : testimony and the
British modern literary consciousness / Dale Barleben.

Includes bibliographical references and index.
ISBN 978-1-4875-0107-5 (cloth)

1. English literature – 20th century – History
and criticism.   2. Law in literature.   3. Trials in literature.
4. Culture in literature.   I. Title.

PR478.L37B37 2017   820.9′35540904   C2016-907362-9

University of Toronto Press acknowledges the financial assistance to its
publishing program of the Canada Council for the Arts and the Ontario
Arts Council, an agency of the Government of Ontario.

Contents

Acknowledgments

I dedicate this work to Natasha and my parents, Marie and Irwin.

My parents made me who I am.

Natasha makes me better.

I am very grateful for funding from the Social Sciences and Humanities Research Council of Canada, the Ontario Graduate Scholarship Fund, the University of Toronto Fellowship Fund, the University of Toronto Department of English, the Modernist Studies Association, the Office for the Advancement of Research at John Jay College, and PSC-CUNY, which have made my research possible.

I face a tricky task in paying Linda Hutcheon a compliment; I feel the severe crush of the anxiety of influence upon me. She has guided, so graciously, so many. Making things worse, it is equally daunting to encapsulate, in a few words, the immeasurable support she has given me throughout this project. Though my comments, like mimeograph, might sound commonplace, and though I will surely do injustices by my omissions, I will try, in brief, to thank her for what she has done for me in lengthiness. Linda's energy is incalculable. She has never once uttered: "I'll get to it," or, "it has to wait." Instead, I assume, she sacrifices sleep. But with this sacrifice never comes a *sense* of sacrifice; no matter what the task, Linda delivers on requests with untold speed, acumen, and a smile on her face. And her smiles are legendary. Whether in her class, in an oral exam, or in a job talk, a smile and a nod from Linda Hutcheon quiets the nerves. She supports unselfishly. She is fair and she is elegant.

Greig Henderson is not elegant, but his words are. A philosopher and a poet, conversations with Greig are never boring, never hollow. At times of philosophical crisis, and these are many, when arguments jumble and ideas swirl, passing them through the filter of Greig's gifted intellect always results in clarity. His mind, a fully indexed anthology of English literature, is an invaluable resource and, unlike the Robarts Library, it is never closed. He and Erica make the miles from home seem only minutes away. He is forthright and he is considerate.

Mary Nyquist considers. Her mind is crystalline. Her scholarly accomplishments do nothing to diminish her intellectual curiosity. Each meeting with Mary means a flurry of new ideas and a focusing of old ones. She reads with critical precision and she comments with meticulous lucidity. She rouses intellectual enthusiasm by example. She is wise and she is inspiring.

Alysia Kolentsis inspires, too; she walks in quiet distinction. She is a sounding board that endures unnatural wear and tear. She bears everyday rants and quells daily episodes of doubt. She suffers my hardships as if they were her own. She is the mitochondrion of my intellectual cytoplasm.

Allison Pease critiques with scholarly shrewdness and laughs with abandon. From the Hutcheon school of academic generosity, she gently guides scholarly pursuit while making the process delightful. She is sagacious and she is buoyant.

Finally, the anonymous readers at the University of Toronto Press were constructively critical. They helped refine the structure of the text and sharpen the arguments within. My editor, Daniel Quinlan, was heroic in the ways he navigated this manuscript through the various stages of publication. My copy editor, Barry Norris, was meticulous and brought his keen eye and sense of style to the text. The production folks at UTP, and especially Wayne Herrington, were wonderful.

To each of you I give my sincere thanks.

STAGING THE TRIALS OF MODERNISM

Testimony and the British Modern
Literary Consciousness

Turning and Turning: The Gyres of Modern Law, Culture, and the Interiority of the Civil Subject

Finally, he was a quartered. This last operation was very long, because the horses used were not accustomed to drawing; consequently, instead of four, six were needed; and when that did not suffice, they were forced, in order to cut off the wretch's thighs, to sever the sinews and hack at the joints.

After these tearings with the pincers, Daimens, who cried out profusely, though without swearing, raised his head and looked at himself; the same executioner dipped an iron spoon in the pot containing the boiling potion, which he poured liberally over each wound. Then the ropes that were to be harnessed to the horses were attached with cords to the patient's body; the horses were then harnessed and placed alongside the arms and legs, one at each limb.

Monsieur Le Breton, the clerk of the court, went up to the patient several times and asked him if he had anything to say. He said he had not; at each torment, he cried out, as the damned in hell are supposed to cry out, "Pardon, my God! Pardon Lord." Despite all this pain, he raised his head from time to time and looked at himself boldly. The cords had been tied so tightly by the men who pulled the ends that they caused him indescribable pain. Monsieur le Breton went up to him again and asked him if he had anything to say; he said no. Several confessors went up to him and spoke to him at length; he willingly kissed the crucifix that was held out to him; he opened his lips and repeated: "Pardon, Lord."

> – *Gazette d'Amsterdam*, 1 April 1757; quoted by Foucault, *Discipline and Punish*

The barristers came first. They wore their wigs and gowns without exception, partly as a tribute to the importance of the occasion, or the perhaps to secure themselves against the inconvenient possibility of being denied admittance. They came not [as] single spies, but whole battalions. And, so far as they were permitted, they took possession of every seat which seemed capable of accommodating their persons. They sat in the barristers' seats; they sat in the solicitors' seats; they sat in the witnesses' seats; they sat in the ushers' seats; and excepting the Bench, they sat in all the other seats which they could capture. And when the seats were all used up, they stood, a serried mass of voluble, grey-wigged, black-gowned humanity, in the gangways and approaches of the court. The only serious rivals to the barristers were the reporters. All the seats that were not occupied by briefless barristers contained reporters. What few remaining places were not occupied by the reporters were filled by an eager, struggling crowd of lookers-on, who had succeeded, in ways on which it were rash to speculate, in prevailing upon the janitors to grant them entrance. Up above, the public proper looked down on the battling crowd beneath.

– M. Holland, The Real Trial of Oscar Wilde

The Science of Dissection: X-Rays and Invasive Legal Procedures

The first Nobel Prize in physics was awarded to Wilhelm Conrad Röntgen in 1901. It recognized his outstanding achievement for discovering a new form of radiation in 1895. When Röntgen wrote a preliminary report and submitted it to the Würzburg Physical-Medical Society journal, he called the unknown new radiation "X." The discovery occurred when he noticed a green iridescent glow on a wall. Between the wall and his primitive cathode ray generator was a pile of books. Placing a number of other objects between the generator and the wall, Röntgen, quite by accident, saw the outline of the bones in his hand.[1]

Oscar Wilde's trials also occurred in 1895, but he died in 1900. In less time than it took for Röntgen to rise to the heights of scientific glory, Wilde fell from literary and social grace. While the X-ray penetrated flesh and allowed medical science new insights into the physical interiors of human beings, the British legal system found new ways to penetrate flesh and access the mental and moral culpability of the civil subject.

Modernist writers' preoccupation with interior mental states emphasizes the mistrust with which they approach objectivity, especially as it touches identity. The modernists' concerns are analogous to the developing of jurisprudence not just at the same time, but decades later. Reading the trials of the British moderns traces the evolution of legal thought and uncovers the ways the moderns helped influence how we understand interior mental states. By reading the legal and literary production in concert, we can appreciate what each field brings to the table and the symbiotic relationship they form.

Torture, Spectacle, and the Trial Process

Stately, plump Oscar Fingal O'Flaherie Wills Wilde arrived at the courtroom wearing a winged collar on which a black tie and diamond-sapphire pin lay tossed.[2] A loose frock-coat, buttonhole-less, was accented gently by his sombre grey suede gloves.[3] The atypi-cally demure dress and the urgency with which he pushed his way through the crowd reflected a different Wilde, a man whose life had already changed a great deal over the past few months. Though he was, in fact, the plaintiff in the action for libel against the marquess of Queens-berry, his solicitors had recently informed him of the defence filed by Queensberry's solicitors. The defence of justification alleged a great many acts of "sodomy and other acts of gross indecency and immoral-ity" with a great many of Wilde's "victims" (M. Holland 287). Queens-berry had been privately and publicly insulting and threatening Wilde, shortly after Wilde began his relationship with Queensberry's son, Lord Alfred Douglas. The note Queensberry left for Wilde at the Albemarle Club, addressed "To Oscar Wilde Posing Sodomite," became the catalyst in the legal action Wilde initiated and then later abandoned.[4] This action, in turn, became the vehicle for Wilde's fall from late Victorian grace. Queensberry's defence became the necessary information leading to the Crown's prosecution of Wilde for gross indecency in two subsequent tri-als. Wilde's story attracts attention not simply for its sensationalism, but also for its value as a record of the culture that made the literary crown prince of Aestheticism, literally the lowly pauper of Reading Gaol.

Wilde's experience, moreover, serves as a catalogue of discourses working at the turn of the twentieth century. The criminal action he commenced precipitated a criminal action against him; each was a trial not only of his actions, but also of his literature and his reputation. The press coverage of these affairs was extensive, and contributed further to Wilde's vilification. His conviction resulted in his incarceration, bank-ruptcy, and literary ruin. He served two years' hard labour. After his release from prison he lived in disgrace in France under the pseudonym "Sebastian Melmoth," until his death three years later. At the centre of the cultural denigration of Wilde, directing its players and asserting its morality, was the legal machinery of trial. While lawyers strove for his confession, Wilde resisted pointed cross-examination with devilish acumen. His linguistic acrobatics frustrated his accusers and troubled contemporary theories of confession, leaving viewers with anything but an "authentic" experience of speaking guilt.

The first epigraph at the head of this chapter, a press report quoted in Michel Foucault's *Discipline and Punish*, emphasized the nature of torture in eighteenth-century European legal cultures that relied upon pain, suffering, and spectacle as both punishment and deterrent. Foucault's discussion evidences what he sees as the "disappearance of the spectacle and the elimination of pain" in these penal systems over the past two hundred years (11). He argues that, although these public elements of torture have been suppressed, they remain, undisclosed, in the criminal justice system, exacerbating any judgment a justice of the court might pass. The system gives medical experts, prison officials, and educators the power to inflict further punishment that a judge did not necessarily contemplate in sentencing (14–24). With these specific arguments I agree, but I disagree that these developments have led to the "disappearance of the spectacle and the elimination of pain." Although Foucault deals only with post-trial punishment – specifically, in this case, execution – I assert that any examination of punishment in modern liberal democratic states must also look closely at the trial apparatus that brings the accused to judgment.

The second epigraph also comes from a newspaper account: the *Westminster Gazette*'s of Wilde's first appearance at the Old Bailey in March 1895. On the face of this description, there seem to be clear parallels between the spectacles of execution detailed in the *Gazette d'Amsterdam* and of courtroom proceedings as reported by the *Westminster Gazette*. The accused is put in a position of shame, elevated physically, exposed to public scrutiny. The mob awaits the performance of a death sentence or throngs for a vantage point from which to follow trial proceedings. In both an execution by torture and civil or criminal trial procedure, the accused and, often, the accuser are subjected to a system that privileges ceremony, tradition, and spectacle. The act of giving testimony becomes a performance; the performance, public in nature and relying on the adversarial process, becomes a spectacle.[5]

For my purposes, however, I do not limit "spectacle" to the proceedings of the court or even to the kind of post-trial punishment Foucault suggests. I wish also to track the interplay among the litigants as they moved from incidents to the courts to the press. Adding complexity, I relate these forms of spectacle to the literary production of the British moderns who became all too familiar with these courts. Rather than limiting these interactions to the authors themselves, I focus on conversations among the era's literary, legal, and press narratives to draw some more general conclusions about the dependence of one discipline upon another.

In so doing, I hope also to propound a limited theory of the poetics of law and literature that brings together British modern thinking and what I call cultural and critical legal studies (CCLS).[6] In a sense, the ways today's leading literary and legal scholars interpret and theorize the relationships among discourses grew from approaches such as Mark Kelman's early *Guide to Critical Legal Studies*,[7] which nicely situates how lawyers, jurists, and other scholars began focusing on what he calls a "self-critical assessment of certain recurring themes in CLS writing on law and legal discourse" from the early years of the movement (2). Concomitantly, literary theory was reinventing how we read literary discourse. CLS and literary theory both influence current cultural studies, where leading critics such as Peter Brooks, Peter Goodrich, Desmond Manderson, and Austin Sarat, among many others, are seeking to complicate the relationship between literature and the law beyond its original and ineffectual "law in literature" and "law as literature" dichotomy.

Having practised in and become familiar with both disciplines over the past few years, I have developed a concern for the ways legal and literary scholars seem at odds when discussing the usefulness of one discipline to the other. Competing discourses seem to fall into a chasm, with little intermingling beforehand. By investigating some of the British moderns, I hope to reduce that gap and create an opportunity for further debate about the issues facing law, literature, and culture.[8] Catherine MacKinnon, in *Towards a Feminist Theory of the State*, her treatise exploring liberal democratic notions of human rights law, argues that "a jurisprudence is a theory of the relation between life and law" (237).[9] Wallace Stevens, in the poem "Men Made Out of Words," suggests: "Life consists of propositions about life" (76). In effect, the words we invoke to describe life become part of the very fibre of life itself; the law as an act of speech is, then, like life itself, circular and self-referential. Given the law's reliance on precedent, tempered by its mandate to change as society changes, its study depends upon exchanges not just within the legal world, but also in the world at large. I am working towards a theory of relations among life, law, literature, and the media that presupposes their porosity and throws into high relief the notion that spectacle and violence fuelled ideas of justice in the society of the British moderns. The focus of these arguments is to rethink the differences among law, custom, and morality. As Peter Fitzpatrick suggests, "law, in short, constituently combines a self-grounding with grounds other to it. It is this explicit combining which, in various neo-sacral manifestations, provides the operative ground of law in modernity" (12). By comparing the wisdom of the British moderns and the legal writings of the time, it becomes impossible to abandon the idea of the reasonable individual. A way must be found to redefine the individual free from prejudice, however difficult this might be, as the discipline of cultural studies has discovered. One must then also define "reasonableness," a project with which the law has struggled for centuries. Together, these definitions should inform our cultural debates.

I am most interested in presenting the ways legal cases emphasize the composed nature of legal identity. In my discussions of Wilde, Joseph Conrad, Ford Madox Ford, and James Joyce, I trace the ways each author interacted with and wrote about the law and its formation of identity. I argue that the law's requirement of *viva voce* testimony necessarily provides challenges to the ontological certainty of individual identity.[10] These authors represent not just modernist sensibilities, but also the era's increasing interest in interiority. Indeed, as I see them, Wilde, Conrad, Ford, and Joyce fall along a spectrum of interiority – different in degree, but not in kind. One hundred years later, they present as a quartet of modernists who sought to subvert the conventions of their time. At the heart of their "newness" was their focus on mental processes, which seemed sophisticated then in ways we take for granted today. In *Kangaroo Courts and the Rule of Law*, Desmond Manderson maps a particularly eloquent history of the stakes of modernist poetics in the seminal year of 1922. While cataloguing the factors that influenced modernist production and their associated responses, he notes:

> Now the response of artists and thinkers to these transformations and doubts was not uniform. For some this shattering of established ways of knowing or being was a matter of description, for others it provoked invention or celebration, mourning, fear or nihilism. The expressionists seem to respond with despair to this new world; the futurists and the constructivists embraced it as a land of unfettered imaginative possibility; the dadaists, cubists and modernist writers with a certain whimsy. But regardless of their affective orientation, certain key features emerge. Modernism signifies a commitment to individual over social good, a sense of rootlessness and exile, and, coupled with an emphasis on the varieties and uncertainties of individual subjectivity, the most comprehensive critiques of representation and the most radical experiments in form. Again

> Rimbaud presaged much that was to follow when he wrote Je est un autre.
> The fractured subjectivity, the formal inventiveness, the linguistic restless-
> ness, the uncertain searching that lies close to the heart of all his poetry
> seems not far from the mark. (26–7)

Ironically, the legal demand for ontological certainty – for a definite, concrete, and unwavering identity – privileges the position that there is, at its heart, some resolute form of individual identity. As one traces the stylistic shifts from Wilde and Conrad to Ford and Joyce, an inward turn is evident in the ways these writers thought about the civil subject. A continuum demonstrates the ways the moderns prefigured some of the complex ways we think about the individual and the mental aspects of identity. By recognizing the moderns' contribution to the dialogue of subjective interiority, we see that issues such as rights and autonomy, which figure so prominently in liberal jurisprudence, were also key to the philosophical foundations that many of the moderns championed. Perhaps more ironically, it becomes evident that the law's mission of challenging individual identity habitually manufactures guilt. An examination of trial representations reveals that, frequently, the mental state of an individual who is on trial changes, with the accused, whether innocent or not, often taking on the identity impelled by the law.

These kinds of ontological challenges integrate legal identity with personal identity. Assertions made in the search for epistemological certainty at law necessarily influence the self-image of the civil subject. When the law ascribes legal identity to the subject, it affects the ontology of the subject and alters self-perception. If the law refuses to recognize legal subjectivity, this is an even more serious affront to the individual's ontological status. The hyper-conflicted nature of the individual at trial suggests that "individualism" itself is necessarily a legal fiction. Liberal positivist jurisprudence, however, requires individualism to operate. At its core, and as interpreted by H.L.A. Hart, legal positivism allows shifts in interpretation through philosophical inquiry. This inquiry is the purview of legal philosophers, judges, and lawyers, who argue about the normative structures of the law. A pure form of positivism could result in injustice, but only if the law itself were unjust. Each individual, however, must be treated on the basis of moral equality, which has little to do with morality; rather, this is the premise that the law should correct for differences of birth, be they physical, mental, social, or some other form of inequity. This insistence on the production of the individual does not trump liberal cornerstones of rights, autonomy, and justice. If we acknowledge that these concepts are also structures, and that we must think of them as ideals to strive for, then they cannot be gutted from the liberal project of legal equality.[11]

We must preserve the liberal idea of individualism simply because we cannot discard responsibility at law. If cultural factors determine all actions, legal accountability becomes moot. Therefore, the idea of a reasonable person must also continue so that we might foster equality. Although it is true that a major re-theorization is necessary, and that this reform must include conceptions of ethnicity, religion, gender, nationality, and economics, the project cannot be abandoned simply because of its complexity. The British moderns faced the same struggle. Through their literary texts, the moderns uncovered problems with how the law of their time treated autonomy, rights, and the individual. If we compare these writings to contemporary cultural and legal criticisms of the law, we see their integrated nature – not as mutually exclusive, but as championing the same project. Many of the discussions the moderns raised prefigured contemporary jurisprudence, but they served as common ground from which cultural critics and legal scholars might push for legal reform. Robert Cover famously wrote:

> Legal interpretation takes place in a field of pain and death. This is true in several senses. Legal interpretive acts signal and occasion the imposition of violence upon others: A judge articulates her understanding of a text, and as a result, somebody loses his freedom, his property, his children, even his life. Interpretations in law also constitute justifications for violence which has already occurred or which is about to occur. When interpreters have finished their work, they frequently leave behind victims whose lives have been torn apart by these organized, social practices of violence. Neither legal interpretation nor the violence it occasions may be properly understood apart from one another. (1601)

In short, this project uses the British moderns to help understand how scholarship in cultural and critical legal studies can continue to reinterpret the field of pain and death as we know it.

Legal Narrative, Machinery, and Identity

I begin, in Chapter 1, with a history of the Criminal Law Amendment Act of 1885, inquiring into the purported intentions of this legislation and some of its consequences, including the trials of Oscar Wilde. In relating the historic justification for this legislation to its drafting and its application and interpretation by the courts, some serious questions arise about the workings of the liberal democratic judiciary and its ability to both uncover the "truth" and dispense "justice." I draw on Wilde's courtroom proceedings to illustrate the law's difficulty in pursuing two related but seemingly competing projects: searching for the truth, and probing the credibility and identity of the individual. That is to say, the law, in a situation that demands testimony, also requires epistemic certainty from the subject it puts on trial. It requires truthtelling. Yet it concurrently allows legal counsel to question the validity of the individual's testimony, thus manufacturing ontological uncertainty, both for the trier of fact and for the person on trial. This sets up my discussions in later chapters of Peter Brooks and Shoshana Felman, and grounds understanding of the legal practices at play in the legal documents of the era.

Closely related to these issues are the ways the British law of the time began thinking about the interiority of the civil subject.[12] Until the nineteenth century, criminal law focused upon proof of the commission of the act and, in many cases, on the character of the accused. In the Anglo-Saxon era, for example, the judge used character to determine not only guilt, but also the severity of the sentence imposed. In many cases, court proceedings became a battle of witnesses and the amassing of the greatest number to either affirm or refute the accused's moral character.[13] There were still remnants of this practice in the courts of the British moderns, as there are today, but these procedures frequently were being eclipsed by the determination of the accused's intentions, rather than character.[14] Mapping these legal developments, there is a connection between the legal and literary discourses of the time, including their concomitant shifts to the interiority of the civil subject. The styles for which modernism became most famous, including direct and indirect interior monologue,[15] are closely connected to this discursive shift in thinking about the internal workings of the mind and identity politics. Freud's work, for instance, was then gaining popular appeal, and did not so much begin as become fascinated with the relationship between identity and interiority. Correspondingly – and of increasing importance after the turn of the twentieth century[16] – to be convicted of a criminal offence the accused needed to satisfy two elements of criminality: the *actus reus*, or guilty act, and the *mens rea*, or guilty mind. For a court to determine the latter element of guilt, then, it became necessary to shift the focus of courtroom proceedings towards intent.

Confession: Ontological and Epistemological Trauma

To illustrate further the connection between legal and literary concepts of intent, in Chapters 2 and 3 I explore the legal proceedings in which Wilde, Conrad, Ford, and Joyce contributed to the critical legal discourse of their epoch. Continuing my comparison of their literary output to the actual cases in which they were involved, I propose that these authors began a project similar to that of cultural studies scholars in the ways they uncovered and demonstrated the inherent traumas associated with giving sworn testimony.[17] What I call an "ontological trauma" is the result of what Peter Brooks identifies as the exceptional position of the testifying subject. When the state obliges an individual's testimony, claims Brooks, the forced act of testifying on the stand does violence to the accused, because it requires public performance, and thereby intensifies feelings of guilt in both the guilty and the innocent alike (21–2). The accused is left in the exceptional circumstance of having only limited knowledge of the facts, yet still being required to discover the truth, leading to a challenge to the ontological position of the testifying subject. "Western literature," Brooks posits, "has made the confessional mode a crucial kind of self-expression that is supposed to bear a special stamp of sincerity and authenticity and to bear special witness to the truth of the individual personality" (18). My discussion attempts to redefine classic definitions of trauma theory to incorporate shifting subject positions, and thereby to add nuance to Brooks's notion of trauma and testimony. That is to say, giving forced sworn testimony always results in some form of trauma, but this does not necessarily create a victim in the common sense that trauma theory posits. Rather, challenges to identity often cause an individual to change his or her idea of self. The disturbance of a testifying individual's position is a traumatic event that creates real shifts in the subject's interiority.

Although confession and, more broadly, public testimony bear this special mark of authenticity in a Brooksian sense, the court must still weigh each piece of testimony and then pronounce sentence. In essence, the court either confirms or refutes the subject's confessional authenticity, and pronounces the accused either guilty or not guilty. The power in this pronouncement diverges somewhat from Brooks's arguments. He describes the ways guilt, through confession, produces further guilt in the confessor. My contention here is that, although the speech act "I confess," as Brooks describes it, is undoubtedly instrumental in the production of guilt, the speech act "you are guilty," when associated with the court's final pronouncement, confirms and reiterates this confession while branding the accused with the indelible mark of criminality. If the accused has not confessed, the court's pronouncement trumps the accused's testimony of innocence.

My modification to the Brooksian pronouncement potentially carries many dire consequences. Not only does the judgment affect the body of the accused, in the sense of the possibility of incarceration and further physical trauma, but the words used to render the verdict also brand the individual a criminal, a tortfeasor, a liar, a pervert, or a reprobate. The force of these words lies not only in their public pronouncement, but also in the mental harm they can inflict. Working with some of the foundational principles of speech act theory in J.L. Austin and John R. Searle and later interpretations of these concepts in Jacques Derrida and Judith Butler, I aim to create a further medium for debate about the real trauma enacted in the re-enactment of events through trial testimony. Comparing these speech act theories and concepts of trauma to both the real-life and fictive accounts of the trials of the British moderns, I hope to bridge some of the gap between current scholarship in legal cultural studies and liberal jurisprudence. Drawing on these fictional accounts as a lens through which one might conceive the trial process as always a harm-provoking event, I aim to strengthen the voice of literary discourse in the dialogue between cultural and jurisprudential perspectives.

As well, I attempt to affirm an interpretation of the British moderns as intrinsically connected to their historical moment through their interaction with the law. Many early critics in modernist scholarship privileged an authorial position of exteriority with respect to the societies in which the authors of high modernist texts lived because of their measured and intense exploration of the interiority of the mind. Joyce, for instance, was often satirized for what people took as his neutrality towards the First World War.[18] Tom Stoppard captures this prevailing attitude in his play, *Travesties*, where a fictionalized Henry Carr, in a dream, performs "a masterly cross-examination" on Joyce in the witness box, and finishes his questioning with a query about what Joyce did during the Great War, to which Joyce replies, "I wrote *Ulysses*, ... what did you do?" (65). Yet, as the past two decades of historicist criticism can attest, the connection between authors and culture is perhaps one of the most fertile grounds for critical investigation.[19] My examination of the legal and literary texts produced between 1890 and 1922 explores further the association between authors and their culture at the locus of legal procedure – procedure that both interprets statute and reinterprets precedent. The deeply troubling trial situations that the moderns reconstruct in their works are both evidence of their strong connection to their social system and a testament to the effects of the legal system on the political climate of their epoch.

The British Moderns: Style and Interiority

In Chapter 2 I specifically link my discussions of jurisprudence and the contemporary law of the moderns to the literary production of Wilde and Conrad. I begin with an examination of style, arguing that the shift towards interiority of the focalized narrative is coeval with the shift in the judicial turn towards increasingly complex ideas of *mens rea*. *De Profundis*, Wilde's epistolary prose poem to Douglas, is thematically and stylistically different from his more celebrated works, and takes serious aim at the law in both its legislative and executive forms. I trace Wilde's style and use of interiority to argue that his was one of the first modernist criticisms of law to go beyond satire and, additionally, to call for legal reform. This kind of writing, which mixes creative artistry and real social criticism, differed from Victorian, Romantic, or even Early Modern and Enlightenment criticisms of the law, as modernist accounts focused on the internal and psychological violence of legal proceedings. *De Profundis* was published five years after Freud's *The Interpretation of Dreams*, though both works were written at roughly the same juncture. This kind of thinking about the interiority of human identity politics influenced fiction, science, and law, and made the spaces for speaking about relationships between these disciplines more porous. Situating my discussion in the context of Felman's work on testimony, I argue that courtroom exposure changed Wilde's ontology. Looking at the rift that Lisa Rodensky posits between nineteenth-century and modernist authors, the stylistic shifts we observe are part of a continuum along which Wilde, Conrad, Ford, and Joyce are situated. Using Butler's ideas to criticize previous speech act theory, CCLS might help to reinterpret both the way the British moderns represented trial proceedings and the ways liberal jurisprudence might think about individuals.

Taking Wilde's style as my point of departure, I further contextualize his writing within the events of the trials that precipitated his incarceration. Emphasizing as it does the heteronormativity of the law, Wilde's case nicely demonstrates the failure of liberal jurisprudence to hold to its principles of the rule of law, rights, autonomy, and justice. Through all of this, however, Wilde refused to confess – at least in the legal or Brooksian sense. Taking up the scholarly debate about confession surrounding Wilde, I argue that what many see as confession is, rather, censorial prose directed at the legal system and its machinery.

Connecting Wilde to Conrad and placing them on a continuum of narrative interiority, I see both authors' styles as heralding the more famous high modernist styles of Ford and Joyce. Wilde's style is a foretaste of indirect interior monologue, and in outlining the publication history of *De Profundis* I endeavour to show the links between this history, Wilde's writing, and the kinds of writing about law we see in works by later modernist authors. Like Wilde, Conrad connects late Victorian writing to the modernist canon, drawing from both. In this way Conrad reworks Victorian sensibilities, and, in *Lord Jim*, mixes omniscient and first-person narration to juxtapose and emphasize the distinction between exterior and interior narrative forms. A further connection between Conrad's style and the nautical influences from which he drew is his serious fascination with the trial process, and especially his familiarity with the law surrounding the admiralty and the colonies, that drives much of the novel. The raging debates surrounding the validity of colonial law and the application of English common law to the seas contextualize the real-life narrative of the *Jeddah*, a vessel towed to port after the crew abandoned its sinking human cargo. I link the media coverage of this event to Conrad's depictions of it in *Lord Jim*, and argue that Conrad's novel stands as an archival legal record, much as do the newspaper reports and trial transcripts. Emphasizing Linda Hutcheon's theory of historiographic metafiction, *Lord Jim* continues the conversation among literature, law, and the press surrounding the *Jeddah*.

From these discussions of style and context, I move to arguments surrounding the specific trial episode in *Lord Jim*. Jim's situation is distinct, as he approaches the stand with the full intention of telling the "truth" insofar as he has access to it. Unfortunately for Jim, Conrad's narrative underlines the inherent competition between epistemological and ontological motives in trial procedure. While Jim struggles to tell the "truth," he realizes that this is sometimes an impossible project, due to his limited access to what the law calls "facts." Moreover, the character assassination so common in cross-examination becomes another focal point from which Conrad's narrative accentuates Jim's ontological crisis, begun by his dereliction of duty and exacerbated by the trial process. Brooks's work factors importantly here, as I explore the ways the law manufactures Jim's guilt.

Taking Wilde and Conrad as the immediate precursors of the styles more commonly associated with modernist writing, such as indirect or direct interior monologue, I begin Chapter 3 by comparing these stylistic insignia to the approach Ford uses in *The Good Soldier*. Placing the need for knowledge and the narrator's inability to attain it in the foreground, Ford creates a narrative focused upon the broken reminiscences of a defeated cuckold. The self-reflexivity and the self-doubt in Dowell's narration are continually revealed throughout the narrative, as he tries to get the facts straight. He goes over them in his head, and repeats episodes in an effort to tell an accurate tale. Recognizing his fallibility, however, leads him to offer alternative and often competing perspectives of the narrative's events. In this way, he mirrors the legal trial.

Building on this style of telling and retelling with contextual blocks, we can trace Ford's writing within his legal life and within the work of Dimock, Brooks, and Aristodemou. Ford was involved in court proceedings on many occasions, and from an early age grew to understand the trauma associated with appearing in court. Cited for contempt twice and convicted once, Ford learned that the law of his day did not abide impudence, and his effrontery landed him in prison for a short time. His experiences in court arising from his courtship of Elsie Martindale were reported in both the press and in legal reporting series.[20] In fact, Ford's reporting to the press of the original court proceedings brought the press in as co-defendants in the judge's contempt proceedings. Since the judge had elected to hold the original proceedings in private, the media, through its second-hand reporting, also breeched this judicial decision. The media, in these ways, played an even more active role in the triangle of discourse, creating a powerful voice that reported the interplay between the author and the court of law. The dialogue among the press, literature, and the law in this instance flowed naturally from these events into Ford's depiction of Edward Ashburnham, a gentleman accused of sexual assault, tormented and broken, at least in part, by the lingering effects of trial and public humiliation. Tracing Ford's real-life court proceedings, press coverage, and ultimate fictional representation of the trauma associated with trial, I further my argument that the interiority that was becoming ever more important in findings of criminal liability was reflected in, and influenced by, the literary and press dialogues in which the law engaged. The traumas of ontology and epistemology are pronounced in Ford's work, and they reveal the law's ability to alter human perception and manufacture *mens rea*.

In the second section of Chapter 2, I introduce Joyce into the culture of jurisprudence, legislation, literature, and the press. *Ulysses* offers a veritable profusion of material for discussions of law and culture, linking nationalism, publication history, sexual mores, and legal proceedings at the locus of its textuality. Even though I omit completely from this discussion the book's banning and eventual vindication at the hands of the law (on this, see Barleben), the years leading to its publication are rich with historical insights into the conceptions of interiority and the individual that were developing in and alongside the works of Wilde, Conrad, and Ford. The focus is on "Circe," the episode of *Ulysses* that traces the wanderings of Bloom and Stephen in the Dublin red-light district of "nighttown" and continues with Bloom's surrealist trial. Starting with a brief explanation of style and how I believe it works to set off the "Circe" episode from the rest of the text, we see that Joyce's experiences with the law allowed him an acute understanding of its polyphony. Robert Spoo nicely argues the ways this episode sounds in this polyphony; I further this argument to include the voice of law. For Joyce the law was at once an indigenous and colonial presence. The mix of cultures plays out in both colonial domination and Irish resistance to the laws and the machinery in place to ensure its operation. For Joyce every Irish legal proceeding entailed a clash between colonial and indigenous Irish ideology.

Playing this out in the language of "Circe," Joyce creates a parodic *roman à clef*, where British subjects and officials come under attack for their brutal and crass exercises of colonial authority. The style of drama in this episode differs from the previous fourteen episodes, and emphasizes the multiplicity of voices at play, especially in the legal framing of the episode. Added to this, Joyce revisions Jewishness, nationalism, and sexuality within the confines of the law, which I discuss in the context of Ann Ardis's theories of sexuality and Linda Hutcheon's theories of parody. Each of these positions becomes a site for scrutiny, and Bloom, the object of all of these attacks, suffers the onslaught and defends himself as best he can. But Joyce is doing far more than creating a parody of the law and colonial practice in Ireland. Rather, he is representing a culture that insists upon a multiplicity of voices and a legal structure that searches for the unitary.

The polyphony in Joyce's "Circe" undercuts the law's insistence on epistemological certainty. Unlike the singular, though changeable, perspective afforded by Dowell's narrative voice, the multiplicity of perspectives in "Circe" flows through a multiplicity of voices. Joyce thus refutes the dominating presence of colonial law. Far from the situation of Edward Ashburnham, where we struggle with our sympathies and ultimately feel justified in his condemnation, the situation of Bloom is that of a man compromised by the law for his heritage, his sexuality, and his nationality. It is here that we feel law's bias at its worst, and it is from here that we might begin to question the legal framework that allows such devastating attacks while utterly disregarding the individual, rights, autonomy, and justice.

The ultimate goals of this book are threefold. First, my analysis of select British moderns points to a similarity between literary interpretations (or at least representations) of the law and cultural studies interpretations. In each instance, the relationship between law and life is filtered through the lenses of authors and scholars who write about the inherent difficulties with doctrines of liberal jurisprudence. In essence, literature provides the groundwork for many of the criticisms of the law that CCLS has recently levelled.

Second, I endorse the premise that one difficulty inherent in the British legal system is its adherence to spectacle and violence during the trial process. By tracing some of the relationships among the literature, authors, media, and judicial procedures of the time, I hope to illuminate this somewhat macabre element of the modern British trial process, which is still enacted in the contemporary judicial systems of many Commonwealth countries. This process, ironically, manufactures guilt.

Finally, I hope to reduce some of the tension that persists between liberal legal jurisprudence and cultural studies – tension that comes from what Peters recognizes as "interdisciplinary longing" (451). Rather than using one school's critique of the other to acknowledge and strengthen weaknesses in their respective theoretical frameworks, in current practice criticism often becomes terminal, with little cooperative interplay between these modes of critical inquiry even in joint law and humanities initiatives. Liberal literary and cultural perspectives, on the surface, are so at odds with each other – each seeing the other as of very little interpretive use – that there is very little common ground on which they can converse. Yet each school has much to offer the other. Although I espouse the view that liberal jurisprudential philosophy might guide a useful conception of the law, I believe that cultural studies reworks some of the tenets of this liberal tradition. I am in no way suggesting that my discussion will decide the arguments in question; rather, I hope that it might provide some ground on which a more profitable dialogue might continue.

Modernist culture's multifarious connections to the law are prophetic indicators of the ways we *still* engage with ideas of the law. But they also underscore the serious problems in delineating what we mean by the "law."[21] Like Auden's poem, "Law Like Love," we might trace a lineage from natural law to inherited law, to canon or ecclesiastical law, to the common law, to academic interpretations of the law, to nihilist interpretations of the law, to the law surrounding partisan politics or popular consciousness, and, finally, individualism. In each instance, one movement builds on the last, rather than superseding it. In effect, these traditions are credentials for what we think the law *can* or *cannot* do, and manifestations of our desires for things we wish the law *could* do.

At the root of these historical and current debates about the possibility and propriety of the law lies a basic dichotomy between descriptive and normative interpretations of legal systems. Although it is undeniable that the law infiltrates both our bodies and our minds and that we, in turn, secrete the law in our own actions, a general confusion results from a position that holds that "the law is what the law is to me." If scholarship focuses on descriptive argumentation about law, it unquestionably will gravitate towards the critical interpretation of both the system and its repercussions. That is to say, the claustrophobic feelings that flow from recognizing that the law subconsciously affects our every move are very real, but these feelings are the ripples from throwing the stone of the legal system in the societal pond. Since these ripples cannot return to the rock, but disperse and eventually lose their force, to mitigate such dispersion and attenuation I try to interpret not only the normative intentions of the rock of the legal system itself, but also the descriptive ripples that flow from it, along with the waves that result once these ripples collide with other objects floating on the pond[22] – including the individuals, groups, and institutions over which the law holds power. The waves sent back from these objects, in turn, affect the ways we need to interpret the law.

In short, although the liberal tradition of jurisprudence proves deeply flawed in practice, the critical interpretations of this practice must offer something to the normative understanding of the object of law; otherwise, the law is a dead ideological state apparatus, not a living practice in our lives. Furthermore, the need to understand the law as a system of norms, flawed as it might be, opens the possibility for interpretive dialogue that might more effectively implement any given liberal legal system within its social framework. But we still need to conceptualize the rock. If we allow the rock to disintegrate the minute it strikes the pond, we lose our referent. The free interplay between the system and its subjects is doomed to nihilist paralysis.

Peters imagines the death of interdisciplinarity resulting in a study that asserts the hyper-reality of the objects under study, but then posits this hyper-real space as the means by which we still might affect change. Even though we know that the hyper-real does not exist, it becomes a site for change in the real. We see that, in a similar manner, to treat the law as a system, in full knowledge of the system's porosity, is the only way to improve the system. Many think this approach desperately optimistic; yet, when we consider the grave importance of the law in all aspects of our lives, can we afford to be otherwise?

Scholars such as Desmond Manderson use tenets of liberal jurisprudence to configure their conceptions of modernist poetics. For example, as he grounds the structure of his work on that of D.H. Lawrence, he argues that we must focus on the rule of law and its particular aspects that show us "the notion of how judicial decision-making should be understood, the extent to which and in what ways we are right to think of it as constrained, and whether 'the rule of law' thus furthers or, on the contrary, inhibits the realisation of justice" (1–2). We see leading thinkers of modernist law and literature such as Manderson seeking to redefine, reinterpret, refigure, and yet still preserve liberal notions like the rule of law. We cannot start afresh, in other words, but we can build on the past, rather than eviscerating it.

Violence and trauma in the trial process, as the British moderns interpreted it, reflect the exigencies of a court system in need of reform. In many modernist works, legal depictions act as satire by which we might gain an understanding of the underpinnings of public discourse and the law. But it is not this satire that is the major contribution of the modernist canon to the legal thinking of its age; rather, it is the interplay between legal and literary discourses about the interiority of the civil subject that provides the most fertile ground for analysing the liberal tradition of trial and testimony.[23] Placing these discourses alongside some of the press coverage of the day, I hope to open a discussion that emphasizes the relationships among the law, government policy, and literary production, and the British moderns who acted within the confines of these systems.

Legal Reforms, the Blackmailer's Charter, and Oscar Wilde's Trials: The Legal Stage of Modernism

Critical to the three trials of Oscar Wilde was the Criminal Law Amendment Act of 1885. Wilde's courtroom experience illustrates one of the law's paradoxes: its pursuit of the truth while challenging the credibility and identity of the individual. In this chapter I trace the conversations between the legal developments and the literary discourses of the time, including their shifts to the interiority of the individual. Modernism's styles have become famous, especially for direct or indirect interior monologue, and these are closely connected to the discursive shift in thinking about the internal workings of the mind and identity politics. As noted, criminal offences required two elements: the *actus reus*, or guilty act, and the *mens rea*, or guilty mind. Accordingly, I provide a brief history of *mens rea* and its evolution alongside modern thinking. I also uncover the movement towards defining intent in criminal procedure in the *Tyrell* and *Munslow* cases, and I relate Wilde's trials to some of the ways constitutional issues surrounding citizenship intersect with the concept of rights. I link rights within British liberal democracy to Wilde's trial transcripts and his post-trial writing to demonstrate the imperative for legal reform.

The Criminal Law Amendment Act: Paternalism Redefined

Section 11 of the Criminal Law Amendment Act (CLAA), headed "Outrages on decency," deals neither with women and girls nor with their protection. Instead, it reads: "**11.** Any male person who, in public or private, commits, or is a party to the commission of, or procures or attempts to procure the commission by any male person of, any act of gross indecency with another male person, shall be guilty of a misdemeanour, and being convicted thereof shall be liable at the discretion of the court to be imprisoned for any term not exceeding two years, with or without hard labour." The Crown used this section to arrest and indict Wilde, ten years after the Eliza Armstrong "white slavery" scandal. By this time the CLAA was known as the "blackmailer's charter," as its vague language had vast application for extortion (Holland xii).

Section 11 of the CLAA amended its predecessor in the Offences Against the Person Act of 1861, which read: "**61.** Whosoever shall be convicted of the abominable Crime of Buggery, committed either with Mankind or with any Animal, shall be liable, at the Discretion of the Court, to be kept in Penal Servitude for Life or for any Term not less than Ten Years." This section was itself an amendment of an amendment, within a legal tradition outlawing sodomy that began with Henry VIII and his Buggery Act of 1533. Sodomy, before this date, was outlawed by ecclesiastical courts and included such punishments as live burial, but the 1533 Act was the first to carry Royal Assent (Bailey 145). The Buggery Act made penalties for bestiality and homosexuality equivalent, and carried punishments including death and forfeiture of property. Over the next three centuries, these anti-homosexual punishments were repealed and re-enacted over and over again; after 1533, however, homosexuality was always considered criminal behaviour, and only after 1861 was it no longer a capital offence.[1]

"Gross Indecency": Homosexual Catchall

This legislative genealogy illustrates that Parliament, having suffered ridicule for persecuting women under the Contagious Diseases Act and now in the guise of protecting women from the perils of prostitution, again enacted legislation that served only to further the persecution of a different group. The wording of section 11 broadened the scope of the offence from what had been the clearly defined act of buggery in precedent, to the vague language of "gross indecency," which left the courts open to define as far short of penetrative homosexual sex. The wording's ambiguity allowed criminals to blackmail men they accused of having engaged in indecent relations, and because little proof was necessary, the accused often paid even if innocent. The law, enacted with the broadest of possible interpretations, thus left citizens with only a faint idea, or perhaps no idea at all, of how the courts might proceed. Moreover, the law willingly privileged one moral group over another – with heterosexual morality used to criminalize homosexual behaviour – rendering ambiguous any talk of rights or autonomy, since legal definitions of these concepts rely foundationally on the rule of law. This arbitrariness, indeed, became more clearly apparent as the Act was used more to apprehend and prosecute homosexuals than to protect women. The history of the Act as the "blackmailer's charter" reached its climax with the arrest of Oscar Wilde in 1895.

In 1885, while the Armstrong scandal raged under the direction of *Pall Mall Gazette* investigative journalist W.T. Stead and the CLAA was passed, Oscar Wilde was, ironically, employed by the *Gazette* as a reviewer (Hyde 47). Since his review and editorial work did not provide Wilde sufficient means to support his family, he turned to stage writing in the late 1880s and early 1890s as a potential source of income. His first successful play, *Lady Windemere's Fan*, came in 1892. At the time of his arrest both *The Importance of Being Earnest* and *An Ideal Husband* were playing to great acclaim (Hyde 49). In retrospect, however, it seems that the arrest was at least as much a product of Wilde's pride as it was any sort of legal imperative. To understand the significance of Wilde's actions in the legal context of his era, it is useful to review, however briefly, some specific circumstances leading up to and including the trial proceedings in which he found himself involved. Although these have received ample treatment in Wilde scholarship over the years, some important details have been either ignored or treated with what I feel is unjustified terseness. To these circumstances I now turn.

Wilde v. Queensberry: Trial One and the Legal/Literary Conversation

Lord Alfred Douglas was an ass. Introduced to Wilde by a mutual friend in 1891, he had read *The Picture of Dorian Gray* and, himself an aspiring poet, looked to Wilde as a mentor and cultural sophisticate. The two soon became lovers, much to the dismay of Douglas's father, the hunting, boxing Marquess of Queensberry. Douglas, affectionately called "Bosie," was, at twenty-one, rebelling against his overbearing father and envisioning a romantic life as a poet without paternal interference. Queensberry, in contrast, became increasingly outraged at his son's behaviour, and began a series of malicious attacks upon Wilde. The first salvos came in missives directed from Queensberry to Douglas, which Douglas promptly showed to Wilde. After many of these went unheeded, Queensberry, on 1 April 1894, wrote:

> Your intimacy with this man Wilde must either cease or I will disown you
> and stop all money supplies. I am not going to try to analyze this intimacy,

and I make no charge; but to my mind to pose as a thing is as bad as to be it. With my own eyes I saw you both in the most loathsome and disgusting relationship, as expressed by your manner and expression. Never in my experience have I seen such a sight as that in your horrible features. No wonder people are talking as they are. Also I now hear on good authority, but this may be false, that his wife is petitioning to divorce him for sodomy and other crimes. Is this true, or do you not know of it? If I thought the actual thing was true, and it became public property, I should be quite justified in shooting him at sight. (Hyde 71)

To this, Douglas replied by telegram: "What a funny little man you are," thereby incensing his father to further and more serious acts of hatred towards Wilde (Hyde 71).

One such act was calculated to spoil the opening of *The Importance of Being Earnest* on 14 February 1895. Queensberry arrived with a "grotesque bouquet of vegetables" with which he planned to create a disturbance (M. Holland xix). Wilde got wind of his plan, however, and managed to deny Queensberry entry and save the opening. Four days later, Queensberry left a visitor's card with his name in typescript and a handwritten note for Wilde at the Albemarle Club, of which they were both members. The note read either "For Oscar Wilde, posing as a somdomite [*sic*]" (Foldy 1; Hyde 76) or "For Oscar Wild, posing somdomite [*sic*]" (M. Holland xix). As I suggested in my introduction, Queensberry's hand was amorphous at best, and either interpretation reveals the inherent homophobia and hatred he felt for Wilde. Yet it is the second interpretation that I find more convincing as played out in the circumstances of the first trial, to which I move momentarily.

The card Queensberry left for Wilde was finally retrieved ten days hence. Wilde's tolerance had reached its end. On 28 February he wrote to his first homosexual lover, Robert Ross: "I don't see anything now but a criminal prosecution. My whole life seems ruined by this man" (Hyde 77). Douglas, with characteristic juvenile, glib pugnacity, goaded Wilde into proceeding with his litigious inclinations. In his explanation of these circumstances, Montgomery Hyde focuses on Queensberry's moral obligation to his son and, ignoring Douglas's contribution to the proceedings, even goes so far as to proclaim: "Wilde must now be considered as a pathological case study" (50). Although Hyde indeed mentions Douglas's inane insistences, there is less commentary about the ways young Douglas victimized Wilde and more about what Hyde sees as the innate genealogical and parental reasons Wilde was gay.[2]

Michael Foldy's account significantly updates this atavistic imagining, while concentrating on the cultural production of homophobia and his exploration of heterosexism.[3]

When Queensbury was arrested and charged with criminal libel, he immediately began mounting his defence, which, he knew if conducted with utmost diligence, could itself become the imputing document for Wilde's arrest for "gross indecency." By the time Queensberry made it to magistrate's court, his private investigators had amassed enormous evidence confirming Wilde's sexual proclivities.

When Wilde's barrister, Sir Edward Clarke, opened his case for the prosecution of Queensberry, he noted that any mention of the word "sodomite" in relation to a gentleman would inflict the utmost injury upon his reputation. He went further to state, repeatedly, that this accusation was one imputing the "gravest of offences" (M. Holland 26). The tactic in Clarke's opening statement was to convince the jury that even the lightest accusation of sodomy was enough to convict Queensberry, but this, in hindsight was an ill-fated and fatal rhetorical move. By arguing that the card might read "posing as a somdomite [*sic*]," he focused the gravity of the issue upon the seriousness of Queensberry's libel in its softest form, thus also increasing the importance of Wilde's statements to the contrary being equally true. In effect, Clarke conceded that Queensberry's libel rested on Wilde's "posing as a sodomite," rather than being a "posing sodomite." While trying to convince the jury of the gravity of even a slight suggestion of sodomy, Clarke did not foresee the ways this would make Wilde's prosecution simpler under section 11 of the CLAA. Queensberry need find evidence only that Wilde involved himself in situations of "gross indecency" – that is, homosexual encounters short of sodomy – in order to acquit himself of the libel charge. Yet these findings, under the amended legislation, would also serve as damning evidence for Wilde's own prosecution. Clarke, of course, was operating under the mistaken assumption that Wilde had told him the truth.

Although this might be a somewhat trifling point, especially when considering the monolith of evidence assembled against Wilde, it was essential in that it set Wilde upon a pedestal of moral impeccability. Not only was Wilde *not a sodomite*, argued Clarke, but also *any suggestion* that attributed even a pose as such was worthy of sanction for libel. Therefore, after Queensberry admitted both his writing on the card and also that there was a suggestion of sodomy in it, there was nothing left for the prosecution to do. The trial shifted completely towards

Queensberry's defence of justification, and Wilde became the focus of the court's scrutiny. This amounted to a shift in the burden of proof; in effect, Wilde proved the writing on the card was Queensberry's, but now Queensberry must prove his innocence in the libel action through the plea of justification. He was no longer presumed innocent of the charge, but must prove his innocence.

I deal most significantly with the apparatus of trial and testimony in the next chapter, but some points of concern are of direct relevance here. Edward Carson began his cross-examination of Wilde with questions about his acquaintance with Douglas, but it swiftly turned into a debate on literary principles. Carson began asking Wilde about articles that both he and Douglas had submitted to *The Chameleon*, citing them as instances of homosexually themed work (M. Holland 68–76). He then moved to criticism of *The Picture of Dorian Gray*, censuring Wilde's work with grave aplomb: "The story, which deals with matters only fitted for the Criminal Investigation Department or a hearing *in camera*, is discreditable alike to author and editor." Further: "Mr. Wilde has brains and art and style, but if he can write for none but outlawed noblemen and perverted telegraph boys, the sooner he takes to tailoring (or some other decent trade), the better for his own reputation and the public morals" (M. Holland 77). Using the courtroom as a forum for established public opinion and popular criticism by the press, Carson began the assassination of Wilde's character. The attack was brilliantly plotted. It began with examinations of passages of Wilde's work and demands that Wilde defend his aesthetic opinions. "Carson's tactic of removing Wilde's statements from their intended aesthetic context, and reading them instead in relation to the 'real' world," argues Foldy, "proved to be highly effective. No matter how clever, witty, and entertaining Wilde's responses were, they could not substantively counter the insinuating thrusts of Carson's questions" (8).

The effect of this questioning further illustrates the interconnectivity of the legal and literary discourses at the site of trial. Although the defence of justification was to alleviate Queensberry of the charge of libel, it also served as a censor for Wilde's literary work. While censuring Wilde's sexual conduct, the trial also became a venue for declaring Wilde's novel and plays works of obscenity – that is, the trial should be understood as an act of shaming, as a public humiliation that went far beyond proving Wilde's guilt within the specific confines of the legislation or precedent commencing an action. Having passages of Wilde's work read in open court was setting legal precedent for the obscenity trials of Radclyffe Hall's *The Well of Loneliness* and James Joyce's *Ulysses*, although this was clearly nowhere within the purview of Wilde's claim of libel against Queensberry.[4] These lines of questioning spoke as much to the intrinsic heterosexual morality of the law that underpinned them as they did to Queensberry's defence of justification.

The questioning then moved on to letters between Wilde and Douglas, which were sufficiently inflammatory. At the beginning of the third day of trial, Carson addressed the court with his opening statement for the morning:

> If your lordship pleases, gentlemen of the jury: yesterday when it came to the usual time for adjourning the court, I had dealt as fully as I intended to deal with the question of Mr Wilde's connection with the literature that has been produced in this case and also with the fact of those letters, one of which was produced by him and one of which was produced by us, and I almost hoped that I had sufficiently demonstrated upon those that so far as Lord Queensberry is concerned, he was absolutely justified in bringing to a climax in the way he did, this question of the connection between Mr Oscar Wilde and his son. I have unfortunately a more painful part of the case now to approach. I have to comment upon the other evidence which is supplemental to what I may call the clear and admitted facts. It will be my painful duty to bring before you these young men one after the other to tell their tale. It is, of course, even for an advocate, a distasteful task, but gentlemen of the jury, let those who are inclined to condemn these men for allowing themselves to be dominated, mislead, corrupted by Mr Oscar Wilde, remember the relative positions of the two parties, and remember that they are men who have been more sinned against than sinning. (M. Holland 273)

Carson's comments here mirror his approach to the questions he levelled at Wilde and his literary work: on both occasions he sought to impeach Wilde as a purveyor of distasteful, insidious, irregular, and immoral lifestyle practices. Carson's defence of Queensberry wanted not only to uncover proof positive to the claim itself, but also to vilify Wilde as a dangerous criminal, set on tainting the minds of his readers and his sexual "victims."

Carson began crafting a narrative that highlighted the young, uneducated, and poor men with whom Wilde had sexual relations, while painting Wilde as the antithesis of all of these characteristics. Those "innocent" male prostitutes, some of whom were blackmailing Wilde, never took the stand, as Clarke wisely discontinued the lawsuit and made the following statement:

> My lord, I think it must have been present to your lordship's mind that those who were representing Mr Oscar Wilde in this case had before them a very terrible anxiety. They could not conceal from themselves that the judgement that might be formed of that literature and of conduct which has been admitted, might not improbably induce the jury to say that when Lord Queensberry used the words "posing as sodomite," he was using words for which there was sufficient justification to entitle a father, who used those words under these circumstances, to the utmost consideration and to be relieved from a criminal charge in respect of that statement ... I feel that he could not resist a verdict of "not guilty" in this case – "not guilty" having reference to the words "posing as." (M. Holland 280–1)

Here, Clarke returned to his opening concession, now as a scapegoat to try and curtail Wilde's impending cross-examination into criminal malfeasance for sodomy. In an effort to protect his client from the more serious "is," Clarke conceded that there was enough evidence to justify the words "posing as." Again, the catalogue of young men with whom Wilde allegedly had relations, the catalogue that Carson enumerated in open court, took Clarke completely by surprise. To protect his client and save his credibility as an advocate, he had no choice but to discontinue the case in the face of this insurmountable pejorative evidence. The court found Queensberry not guilty, and directed Wilde to pay the costs of the action.

The trial left Wilde notably and understandably shaken. At its opening, Wilde playfully engaged in repartee with Carson, often causing laughter in the courtroom:

> CARSON: "Have you ever known the feelings you describe here?"
> WILDE: "I have never allowed any personality to dominate my art."
> CARSON: "The passage I am quoting says, 'I quite admit that I adored you madly.' Have you ever had that feeling?"
> WILDE: "I have never given admiration to any person except myself. [Laughter] The expression was, I regret to say, borrowed from Shakespeare." [Laughter] (Foldy 11)

But by the end of Carson's probing and punctilious cross-examination, Wilde was upset and demoralized. After Carson asked whether it was the ugliness of one of the young men that caused Wilde not to kiss him, Wilde, on the verge of tears, engaged in a number of short flippant responses, culminating in his blurting reply: "You sting me and insult me and try to unnerve me – and at times one says things flippantly when one ought to speak more seriously. I admit it" (Foldy 17). Wilde's measured, witty responses became defensive, capitulating blurting. This degeneration of Wilde's ability to testify to his own actions and intentions is the starting point for my discussion of the inherent trauma in trials. I pursue this shortly, but my immediate discussion of Wilde's subsequent two criminal trials requires that I introduce more fully what I define as the epistemological and ontological traumas that accompany the act of courtroom testimony.

The obsession with knowledge and its unavailability is what I call *epistemological trauma* in the courtroom context. That is, how can the judge or jury – or we, as secondary readers of trial events – be certain about either the acts or the mental states of the actors? To pursue this question, we must also inquire into what I call *ontological trauma* in trial procedure. That is, in what ways are the very existence and identity of an accused formulated within the context of the testimony narrative? The law's insistence upon truth-telling, while allowing legal counsel to question the individual's credibility, also manufactures ontological uncertainty for the judge, jury, and, most remarkably, the person on trial. In effect, the public humiliation that often occurs in giving testimony amounts to a reworking of the individual's idea of the self. This process relies on the individual's limited knowledge of "the facts" and the concurrent and constant accusations directed at the individual's character.

This raises the question of how one might assert one's individual rights or autonomy when the very foundations of one's identity are under attack. The liberal tradition of protecting the individual from harm by others or by the state seems compromised, as the law itself allows these harms to continue within the courtroom context. Again, the question of why the law fails to protect turns on the specific circumstances of each case at bar. In Wilde's litigation, critics such as Hyde have considered Carson's cross-examination "brilliant" because it exposed Wilde's dishonesty. But it went much further: it put at issue Wilde's personal life, not only in the context of his sexual preferences and actions, but also in the realm of his art. Carson used every means available to him to show Wilde's immorality, gross indecency and perhaps even sodomy, though the latter was never broached before Clarke abandoned the action. Yet these "crimes" are all conditions of the pervading morality in 1895. The CLAA codified that morality, and made homosexuals a degenerate group of individuals. Yet it was not until his public humiliation on the stand that Wilde felt the full crushing force of the law.

This first trial marked the onset of Wilde's ontological trauma. Though he had always been subjected to the homophobic and discriminatory culture of Victorian England, he still managed to attain literary, dramatic, and social acclaim thanks to his work. His sexual practices, absent Queensberry, would have remained relatively unknown, if much suspected. It took Carson's cross-examination to eviscerate Wilde's will, Wilde's ego. The paradoxes for which he was so famous, in law, became sites of inconsistency. His oral virtuosity, exuding aphorism and witticism in the legal context, became his way to prove his hostility towards the court and the law itself. His acuity and ability to defend himself became, in the courtroom, uncooperativeness, deceitfulness.[5] By these comparisons I aim to show the ways courts subject all forms of discourse to their own linear epistemological narrative of causality. Ironically, the epistemological trauma of the accused rests on his or her inability to uncover facts that satisfy this narrative. In effect the problems associated with speaking truthfully while satisfying both a logical and causal chain of events vitiate the accused's sense of having access to the truth in an arena of competing truths. Wilde's trial transcripts provide evidence, for example, that he was vilified not so much for dishonesty as for the ideological risk he posed to the heterosexual normative framework of Victorian culture.[6]

These legal proceedings further emphasize the difficulty of balancing the social need to regulate an individual's conduct against the individual's need to act without governmental or personal interference. The legal system's failure to protect Wilde emanated from the legal bias against homosexual conduct. In many of Carson's remarks during his cross-examination, comments intended to justify Queensberry's claim of "posing sodomite," Wilde was painted as both immoral and infectious. But Carson also spoke about the harm Wilde had wreaked, and would continue to cause, should his conduct go without censure. This type of prosecution goes to the criminal nature of the offence.[7] The distinction is significant here because a civil claim, like the tort of libel, allows for a remedy for one individual as against another. It designates a private harm, not necessarily important to social order. This speaks more directly to the underlying principle that the balance between social regulation and individual rights comes from the law's reliance on the harm principle in civil litigation.[8] Yet Carson's remarks clearly were directed towards Wilde's acts being of a criminal nature. That is, his malfeasance, in Carson's narrative, threatened the very underpinnings of social order in late Victorian society.

Whether Wilde was harming the young men with whom he had sexual relations turns on whether the definition of harm in operation was either a civil or a criminal standard. Yet all this seems severely incongruous with the ultimate aim of determining whether Wilde was harmed by Queensberry's card. In other words, Wilde's private life was relatively private until the apparatus of trial, which was supposed to aid him in his suit against Queensberry, ironically made him and his private affairs matters of great public importance.[9] In Victorian England, under the CLAA, the acts Wilde committed were, in fact, crimes – though this was not determined until his subsequent trials. Yet the problems this fact raises, in turn, revolve around justifications for this particular law as an instrument of state power. Hence there seems to have been an irresolvable circularity in the law's project of protecting the individual and its unlimited scope in uncovering facts. Epistemological uncertainty, again, resulted in epistemological trauma for the accused. Rather than attempting a provisional response here, I move instead to Wilde's subsequent criminal prosecution, in order to explain and explore the issue of Wilde's refusal to submit to laws he thought were unjust.

Mens Rea: A History in Brief

To gain a more sophisticated appreciation of the differences among civil and criminal procedure, the criminal libel trial of Queensberry, and the subsequent criminal trials of Wilde, I want to elucidate a key distinction. Aside from the social versus private division I have already mentioned, the element of intent also plays a crucial role in determining the seriousness of an offence.[10] In civil cases generally, and in Wilde's criminal case specifically, intent can manifest itself in the arguments of both the plaintiff and the defendant. Wilde hoped to prove that Queensberry intentionally published an untrue statement about him, thus injuring his reputation and causing him damage. Queensberry, in contrast, argued that it was never his intent to injure Wilde, but merely to get Wilde away from his son. These issues became of little importance to the proceedings, of course, once Queensberry's attorneys uncovered sufficient evidence that buttressed the truth of his written statement.

Once this statement was found to carry ample truth of its contents, intent became a rather secondary issue.

The first surviving reference to *mens rea* in an English law book occurs in *Leges Henrici Primi*, from circa 1109 (Sayre 983–4). Yet this same tract advocated absolute liability for most criminal actions. Only in the case of perjury did the law state *"reum non facit nisi mens rea"* (a guilty mind was required). Later, however, canonist influence connected crime more and more with sin. For example, between 1220 and his death in 1268, Henry Bracton, a justice of the King's Bench and a clergyman, helped write *De Legibus et Consuetudinibus Angliæ*, one of the first treatises on English common law. The work contained many conflations of legal and religious doctrines, although even at this early point in England's legal history there are hints that these discourses are not the same. "There are several kinds of homicide," Bracton stated, "for one is spiritual, the other corporal, but of spiritual homicide we have nothing to say here at the moment" (2: 340). Although this appeal to the division of homicide along spiritual and corporal grounds appears, perhaps, like a precursor to ideas of legal positivism, this dichotomy, in fact, is nothing of the sort. As Bracton went further to explain:

> Corporal homicide is where a man is slain bodily, and this is committed in two ways: by word or by deed. By word in three ways, that is, by precept, by counsel, and by denial or restraint. By deed in four ways, that is, in the administration of justice, of necessity, by chance and by intention. In the administration of justice, as when a judge or officer kills one lawfully found guilty. But it is homicide if done out of malice or from pleasure in the shedding of human blood [and] though the accused is lawfully slain, he who does the act commits a mortal sin because of his evil purpose. But if it is done from a love of justice, the judge does not sin in condemning him to death, nor in ordering an officer to slay him, nor does the officer sin if when sent by the judge he kills the condemned man. (2: 340)

The explanation of justification for corporal homicide in this passage is rife with paradox. Leaving aside the commissions by word, the deeds Bracton enumerated under this heading turn very much on matters of intention. Here, however, intention is equivalent to psychological motivation, which, in turn, rests wholeheartedly upon canonical ideas of good and evil. The conflation of legal justice with psycho-spiritual condition is a reflection of the medieval belief in natural law. For Bracton, any separation of moral and legal was simply impossible, as intention is tantamount to virtuousness or sinfulness. By attempting to assert the law's dominion over the affairs of England, Bracton, instead, reasserted the hold of canonical discourse over its citizens.

But this is precisely the reason I find it difficult to attribute any serious weight to arguments for a modern definition of *mens rea* this early in British legal history.[11] Although talk of a judge's evil or just intention in putting to death an accused might be a precursor to modern ideas of *mens rea*, the religious implications are also evidence of the academic approach Bracton took in his ponderings of the law. This, then, troubles how the law in theory compares to the law in practice. Bracton reflected on the laws as he saw them, and as he thought they should be. How accurately his account holds to the ways judges then actually decided cases is debatable. Few records exist of cases decided during this period; of those available, *mens rea* is mentioned only in cases of treason (Baker 427–8). Perhaps of more import, there was little reason to delve into the mental element of a crime when, for example, in the case of homicide, capital punishment attached itself to any and all killings, regardless of intent, and differentiating between murder and manslaughter was therefore a moot consideration. In these circumstances, only a king's pardon could save the convicted.[12]

Mens rea became of much greater importance during the Early Modern period, and, as Sayre reports, "we can trace the changed attitude in new generalizations concerning the necessity of an evil intent which are found scattered through the Year Books in the remarks of judges and counsel and which later make their appearance as settled doctrines in the writings of Coke and Hale during the seventeenth century" (989).[13] For the most part, criminal law in this period concerned itself particularly with defining felonies, for which the punishment was death. The mental element in most felonies was sometimes implied (as in cases of burglary or rape), which led to "courts tend[ing] towards restrictive rather than equitable exposition," because of the seriousness of the capital offence (Baker 426; Sayre 988). In other words, the courts were concerned more with defining exactly what constituted felonious activity than with finding equitable solutions to the situations of murder, larceny, or arson. In so doing, however, they often discussed intent for malfeasance. Where the courts of the thirteenth, fourteenth, and fifteenth centuries were little concerned with differences between murder and manslaughter, Early Modern courts began dealing with such distinctions.[14]

Even in less serious cases, such as theft, courts were becoming more concerned with the mental intent to commit the crime. Coke's *Institutes of the*

Laws of England, for example, demonstrates the ways courts began demarcating boundaries of mental culpability. Coke points to what Sayre calls "a revolutionary change in meaning" in his discussion of larceny (999). Coke writes: "First, it must be felonious, *id est cum animo furandi* [that is, with the intention of stealing], as hath been said, *Actus non facit reum nisi mens sit rea* [an act does not make a defendant guilty without a guilty mind]. And this intent to steal must be when it cometh to his hands or possessions; for if he hath the possession of it once lawfully, though he hath *animum furandi* afterward, and carryeth it away, it is no larceny" (107). The crucial distinction here is between the morality associated with canonical law texts and the attempt to define a specific intent at a specific moment. There is little evidence that, until the seventeenth century, anything but moral turpitude was considered in determining mental guilt in felonious endeavours. That is, the distinction between people who were innately good or bad carried the day.

This turn in judicial thinking during the seventeenth century – from bearing in mind general moral odiousness to considering specific mental intent – was the most fundamental shift in thinking about *mens rea* since the trial process began,[15] but it was perhaps more a result of changing attitudes towards criminality than a revolution in jurisprudential thinking. The era saw a growing class of legal professionals and the increasing significance of the Inns of Court in legal culture. But neither of these shifts was as important as the changing views about the threat of criminality. As John Briggs writes, "[b]y 1660 the perception of crime had changed. More and more, disorder among and crimes by the common people were seen as threats to society, what they called the common weal or commonwealth; it was not just the monarch who felt threatened, but also the aristocrats, gentry and merchants" (17). Briggs goes further to argue that, as a result, "order" and "privilege" in society became synonymous and symbiotic, and that the criminal law was thus more and more an instrument of class dominance (17). Perhaps Briggs's class theory of criminal law and Sayre's jurisprudential theory of criminal law of the same era are pieces of the puzzle picture, rather than whole pictures on their own. In any case, I believe that both these lines of critical inquiry are important to understanding the shift in legal discourse concerned with mental aspects of criminality two hundred years later and the resulting difficulties in legislating and enforcing these ideas.

Writing in 1932, Sayre's conclusion about the jurisprudential ideology of his contemporary culture was that the cultural model, similar to the one Briggs outlines, was increasingly directing jurisprudential thinking about *mens rea*:

> Our modern objective tends more and more in the direction, not of awarding adequate punishment for moral wrongdoing, but of protecting social and public interests. To the extent that this objective prevails, the mental element requisite for criminality, if not altogether dispensed with, is coming to mean, not so much a mind bent on evil-doing as an intent to do that which unduly endangers social or public interests. As the underlying objective of criminal administration has almost unconsciously shifted, and is shifting, the basis of the requisite *mens rea* has imperceptibly shifted, lending a change to the flavor, if not to the actual content, of the criminal state of mind which must be proved to convict. (1017)

These statements speak to a changing attitude about the interiority of the civil subject at the turn of the century and in the immediate decades following. Although *mens rea* was already a prominent ethical characteristic of modes of criminal inquiry for English courts as far back as the sixteenth century, it was the movement towards delineating, with some specificity, the interiority of the civil subject on trial with which modern courts, and concurrently modern writers, became so preoccupied. Sayre's analysis argues the unconscious and imperceptible shifts in thinking about the administration of justice and requisites for *mens rea*; his comments illustrate the pertinence of these minute shifts and, moreover, the sum total effect of many of these shifts over time. Whether an accused's intent is morally good or bad falls away from criminal inquiry, and English judges began questioning, instead, the state of mind present at the time the accused committed the criminal act.[16]

The Queen v. Tyrrell and *The Queen v. Munslow*

Just before returning to Oscar Wilde's criminal trials to further explore these concepts, I think it pertinent to survey two other particular cases that underscore the importance of these changing attitudes and that act as prologue to Wilde's involvement with criminal trial procedure. The first concerns another perversion of the Criminal Law Amendment Act, while the second deals with the specific *mens rea* for libel. Each case merits comment both because they represent the cultural moment from which they came, and because they link to the trial situations in which Wilde found himself and of which he later wrote.

The 1894 decision in *The Queen v. Tyrrell* dealt with section 5 of the CLAA, which provided for protection against "defilement of girl[s] between thirteen and sixteen years of age." The section made it a misdemeanour offence punishable by not more than two years, with or without hard labour, for any person who:

> (1.) Unlawfully and carnally knows or attempts to have unlawful carnal knowledge of any girl being of or above the age of thirteen years and under the age of sixteen years; or
>
> (2.) Unlawfully and carnally knows, or attempts to have unlawful carnal knowledge of any female idiot or imbecile woman or girl, under circumstances which do not amount to rape, but which prove that the offender knew at the time of the commission of the offence that the woman or girl was an idiot or imbecile.

In these two subsections, the *mens rea* element of crime became conflated with the more colloquial meaning of "carnal knowledge." That is to say, the import of carnal knowledge in this instance was euphemism for rape, while the actual *mens rea* for the offence was evidence showing that the accused either knew or ought to have known that the girl was mentally incompetent according to subsection 2. Subsection 1 was silent about intent, unless the reading of the section stretched to "carnal knowledge" as not merely a euphemism for a sexual act, but as both that act and the intention of committing that act with a minor by this same statutory definition. It is immediately apparent that the CLAA, like all legislation, had inherent gaps and problems with interpretation. Yet the *Tyrrell* case took these problems to an even more ludicrous level.

Jane Tyrrell was tried and convicted of "having unlawfully aided and abetted, counselled, and procured the commission by one Thomas Ford of the misdemeanour of having unlawful carnal knowledge of her whilst she was between the ages of thirteen and sixteen," and on a second count of "having falsely, wickedly, and unlawfully solicited and incited Thomas Ford to commit the same offence" (710). The case went to appeal, where counsel for the defendant argued, on the basis of *mens rea*, against the ridiculousness of convicting a girl for aiding and abetting in the crime based on a section of the Act headed "Protection of Women and Girls" (711). Counsel's main argument was as follows:

> A girl under sixteen is treated as of so immature a mind as not to be capable of consenting. The Act assumes that she has no mens rea, and she cannot,

therefore, be treated as capable of aiding and abetting. If a girl is liable to be convicted of aiding and abetting an offence under s. 5 she is also liable to conviction for aiding and abetting the felony made punishable by s. 4, and she would then be liable to be sentenced to penal servitude for life, because an accessory before the fact to a felony may be punished as a principal. The result would be to render the Act inoperative, because girls would not come forward to give evidence. (711)

Here, the *mens rea* element of the crime, according to counsel for the defence, was irrelevant when applied to Tyrrell because the very criminal statute that made it an offence to "attempt carnal knowledge" stripped girls between ages thirteen and sixteen of the requisite mental ability to consent. Moreover, if the Crown's reasoning was accepted, as it was at trial, then the same could be applied not only to the misdemeanour under section 5, but also to the felony under section 4, which used similar language to describe sexual acts with a girl under thirteen. Defence counsel's argument underscored the twisted reading of the Act that was not only argued by Crown counsel, but accepted at the trial level. Chief Justice Lord Coleridge, siding with the defence, held: "The Criminal Law Amendment Act, 1885, was passed for the purpose of protecting women and girls against themselves" (712). He did not mention defence counsel's reasoning based on *mens rea*, but focused instead on the pith and purpose of the Act. His reading of "protection," of course, seems rather perverse itself. No section of the Act, in my estimation, stated or even hinted that the Act had been passed to protect women and girls from "themselves."

As this was the same legislation that resulted from Stead's antics and the Armstrong case, the goals, it seems, should have been squarely directed against men who committed acts of child rape or who procured such acts on behalf of others. Coleridge's reading, much in the vein of the Contagious Diseases Act and, taking some of Crown counsel's arguments, redirected blame from the paternal target of the legislation to the female victims.[17] That is to say, Justice Coleridge agreed with the Act's purpose of protecting women and girls, but shifted the blame from their male oppressors to themselves. Girls, to him, were to blame for the problem, but they did not attract the retributive hand of the law because of their mental incapacity. In this way, Justice Coleridge also agreed with defence counsel, although he did not state this explicitly.

In this case, however warped the judge's reasoning, Tyrrell's conviction was quashed. Yet this judicial decision became yet another document that attests to the predisposition and prejudice within the law at this cultural moment. Even when *mens rea* was considered a specific legal form – that is, a specific intent, not a moral disposition – courts often gave themselves the privilege of using moral disposition synonymously with intent in interpreting the statute in question whenever they saw fit. Although defence counsel rightly argued about the presence or absence of specific *mens rea*, Justice Coleridge chose to base his decision on protecting women against themselves, a bastardized reading of the Act in almost any estimation. I offer these observations as a preface to a reading of Wilde's trials, as I want to illustrate the often broad gap between legal theory as it advances and legal practice as it resists advancement.

The Queen v. Munslow, rather than ignoring the shift to specificity in criminal *mens rea*, shows the value some English justices placed on moving from this kind of concept of motive to a concept of intent – that is to say, it evidences a shift from moral value judgments of the individual to specific evidence of the accused's mental state at the time of the commission of the act. George Munslow was convicted of criminal libel under section 5 of the Libel Act, 1843: "If any person shall maliciously publish any defamatory libel, every such person, being convicted thereof, shall be liable to fine or imprisonment or both, as the court may award, such imprisonment not to exceed the term of one year." The indictment on which Munslow was convicted omitted the word "maliciously" from the charge. Munslow's solicitors argued that the indictment was void because of this omission, but Munslow was convicted nonetheless. On appeal, his solicitors repeated their defence, and added that it was essential that the word "maliciously" be included for indictments under section 5, as other sections of the Act used different language, such as "intent," which therefore made maliciousness a necessary, though not sufficient, condition of the indictment.

Chief Justice Russell stopped the prosecution after only a few sentences, as all five appellate justices agreed that the defence's arguments did not warrant quashing the indictment. Again, the term "maliciously" was the focus of judicial consideration. The justices were loath to deem the term a matter of the moral character of the accused; rather, they took it as a settled term of art in its common law context. That is, the term "maliciously" was an indicator of a possible defence to the charge of libel – that the publication of the material was innocent, or at least unintentional – not a personal characteristic of the accused. After deciding that section 5 of the Act neither created a new form of libel, apart from previous common law understandings of the crime, nor altered an existing idea of the offence, Chief Justice Russell held that "it provides for the application to that which was already an offence at common law of the appropriate punishment on conviction for that offence" (761). He then went further to find that the *mens rea* of the offence was one specific to the act of publishing defamatory material, and that the maliciousness of that intent was a matter of shifting the onus of proof:

> The word "maliciously" was introduced into the section in order to prevent the section working great injustice. Any one who publishes defamatory matter of another tending to damage his reputation or expose him to contempt and ridicule is guilty of publishing a defamatory libel, and the word "maliciously" was introduced in order to shew that, though the accused might be primâ facie guilty of publishing a defamatory libel, yet if he could rebut the presumption of malice attached to such publication he would meet the charge. (761)

Chief Justice Russell's discussion of the offence makes clear how important it was that malice attach itself not to the character of the individual, but to the individual's intention at the time of the offence. He stated, for example: "[the accused] may be able to avail himself of the statutory defence that the matter complained of was true, and that its publication was for the public benefit," thus discharging himself of the malicious intent required for conviction. This is the same scenario under which Queensberry was found not guilty of his libel against Wilde, although the court in that case never considered the defence of justification in quite so intricate a manner. Because Munslow's defence was so deeply predicated upon a challenge to the criminal libel legislation of the time and on its inherent reliance on the common law tradition of *mens rea*, this case is another milestone in the transformational emergence of criminal intent in the modernist era.

The specificity with which modern criminal courts have defined intent became ever more dependent upon the specific criminal offence to which it was attached. More important, and perhaps what made these shifts so different from initial Early Modern moves in this direction, was the tendency towards cataloguing and defining more of these specific offences and their associated intents within a statutory regime. The common law tradition based itself on precedent. Yet, by the turn of the twentieth century, the need to centralize and organize jurisprudential thinking made codification an ever-increasing legal reality. Although this did not diminish reliance on precedent in any way, it did make precise definition of terms within statutes a newly imperative issue. With the increasing shift to defining offences came an increasing shift to defining associated intents. With poorly defined statutes came robust bodies of case law that further attempted to resolve the ambiguities within the statutory definitions. Although this is commonplace in contemporary common law countries, it was during the last half of the nineteenth century and the beginning of the twentieth century that emerging statute-rich legal discourse began defining *mens rea* in the same precise fashion followed today.

I return now to Oscar Wilde's second and third trials, with a specific intention of my own – namely, to link these proceedings to the issues surrounding *mens rea* and the interiority of the civil subject on trial.

Wilde's Second and Third Trials: A Legal Witch Hunt

The information Queensberry's solicitors gathered for his defence of justification in the libel action brought by Wilde served as the foundation for Wilde's criminal prosecution. Rather than retrace the day-by-day accounts of the proceedings of these later legal events,[18] I want to focus on why Wilde's first criminal prosecution ended in a hung jury, while his second resulted in a conviction. At the centre of these events were counsel's tactical and rhetorical moves, and the distinctly different approach that was taken to criminal intent in the two trials.

Queensberry's trial for criminal libel opened on 3 April 1895 and ended two days later with Wilde's withdrawal of prosecution. At around six-thirty in the evening of that day, the police arrested Wilde at his lodgings. The next day, he and Alfred Taylor were charged on twenty-five counts of gross indecency and conspiracy to commit these acts under the Criminal Law Amendment Act. Wilde was denied bail, three times, and remained in custody by the order of the magistrate, Sir John Bridge, who reasoned: "I have to use my discretion according – in the words of a great judge – to the evidence given and the gravity of the accusation. With regard to the gravity of the case, I think there is no worse crime than that which the prisoners are charged. As to the evidence, all I shall say is that I do not think it slight, and I shall therefore refuse bail" (Hyde 157).[19] The first criminal trial began on 26 April under Justice Arthur Charles, and ended on 1 May with the jury unable to decide the guilt of the accused. Wilde was released on bail on 7 May, but returned to be tried on 22 May with a new judge, jury, and prosecutor. On 25 May Wilde and Taylor were both found guilty and sentenced to two years' imprisonment with hard labour. Wilde had already spent six weeks in remand, but that did not count. Most critics see the key difference between the two trials in the Crown's initial tactical decisions.[20] These bear some comment, as each also influenced the ways the court dealt with the *mens rea* issues at trial.

Sir Edward Clarke, Wilde's counsel for the libel trial, again offered his services, this time at no charge. His defence in the first criminal trial sought to impeach or discredit witnesses testifying for the prosecution. This he did with expert advocacy, illustrating the disreputable characters of the men who admitted homosexual relations with Wilde and their penchant for blackmailing men from whom they had allegedly received payment for sexual services. Clarke attempted to discredit the testimony of other witnesses by raising issues of memory or visual recognition, or by exploiting their tendency to confusion. This approach was extremely successful in the first trial, less so in the second. The Crown's three main tactical decisions, which shifted the opinion of the jury in the second trial to a verdict of guilty, related to the selection of the new prosecutor, the selection of the new judge, and the decision to sever the actions of Wilde and Taylor into separate trials.

A strange and particular rule of practice in this period allowed the solicitor-general – at the time Sir Frank Lockwood – to be appointed chief prosecutor in criminal matters. Exercising this option, the Crown brought in Lockwood to replace the original prosecutor, Charles Gill, who stayed on but no longer acted as lead counsel. Lockwood had a reputation as a merciless pedant,[21] so the substitution also let the Crown counsel make their final submissions last, a right that usually went to the defence counsel. This shift in rhetorical chronology troubled Clarke a great deal. He went so far as to suggest to Lockwood that he not exercise this right, as "[Clarke himself] when Solicitor-General never once exercised and will not exercise if ever [he] fill that distinguished position again" (Hyde 242–3). He also argued that Lockwood was overstepping his office in that he had "a responsibility more like the responsibility of a judge than like that of a counsel retained for a particular combatant in a forensic fray," while he also suggested "that [Lockwood] is not here to try to get a verdict by any means he may have, but that he is here to lay before the jury for their judgement the facts on which they will be asked to come to a very serious consideration" (Hyde 242). Lockwood ignored Clarke's suggestions, and proceeded to use his tactical advantage of the last word.

The second important change between trials was the Crown's replacing Justice Arthur Charles with Justice Alfred Wills. In the first trial,

Justice Charles found inadmissible most of the "literary" part of the case against Wilde that was read in from the Queensberry libel proceedings. In the second trial, Justice Wills, a seventy-seven-year-old expert on circumstantial evidence, among other prejudicial findings, allowed this evidence to be read to the jury.

The third difference that tactically prejudiced Wilde's case in the second trial was that, after the actions of Taylor and Wilde had been severed in two separate trials, Taylor's went first. His quick and stern conviction gained press headlines; few Londoners could have escaped the torrent of unfavourable coverage. Although the prosecution dropped all conspiracy charges, thereby reducing the number of counts in the action against Wilde from twenty-five to eight, Taylor's impending sentence was deferred until Wilde's trial was over.[22]

I in no way want to diminish the massive significance of these tactical manoeuvres for the outcome of Wilde's second trial: they were enormous and, in hindsight, insurmountable obstacles for defence counsel. I argue, however, that at the root of each was a new approach that changed the focus of the case away from the acts committed to the mental states that allegedly accompanied them. There is more to Lockwood's success in convicting Wilde, for example, than either his ruthlessness or his having the last word. Lockwood had the distinct advantage of reviewing the case materials, knowing that his predecessor, Gill, had focused on proving multiple accusations of "gross indecency" from multiple complainants.

Gill's tactic in the first trial was to have his witnesses give sworn testimony as to their sexual involvement with Wilde or their having seen Wilde involved in homosexual relations. For example, Charles Parker, the Crown's first witness, admitted to being in the St James's Restaurant in early 1893 when Taylor approached both him and his brother. He further admitted that, when Taylor eventually asked whether Parker would be agreeable to accompanying a man willing to pay for that company, Parker replied he would join "any old gentleman with money [who] took a fancy to [him]" (Hyde 170). After being introduced to Wilde and having dinner, Parker testified: "We had liqueurs. Wilde then asked me to go into his bedroom with him," and finally, that "[h]e committed the act of sodomy upon me" (Hyde 170).

The remainder of his testimony went on to the payment of £2 for this meeting, a subsequent similar meeting for which he received £3, and the presents of a silver cigarette case and a gold ring, which Parker eventually pawned. When Gill inquired into Parker's familiarity with some of the other witnesses to be called later for the prosecution, Clarke objected; Crown counsel did not press the matter (Hyde 170–1). Gill, it seems, hoped the actions would speak for themselves, and that the witnesses he called would stand up to cross-examination. Clarke's cross-examination, however, managed to dismantle Parker's credibility, first with accusations of blackmail, and then by proving that he had stolen clothes from his employer. In trying to establish the credibility of their witnesses as against the other side, neither side focused much on the mental elements of the alleged crimes. In effect, the trial's proceedings mirrored somewhat the medieval practice of a battle of witnesses, with the character of the accused, the prosecution hoped, proving both incredible and immoral by this battery of testimony.

Gill's cross-examination of Wilde, moreover, lacked the persuasive rhetorical force we commonly associate with pointed and direct questioning. Rather than offering Wilde only closed questions, requiring either a "yes" or a "no" in reply, Gill often let Wilde explain away what the prosecutor thought was *prima facie* evidence of sexual misconduct. On one occasion, Gill brought up Lord Alfred Douglas's poem, "Two Loves." Focusing on the line, "I am the Love that dare not speak its name," Gill asked Wilde: "What is the 'Love that dare not speak its name?'" (Hyde 200–1). Wilde was allowed to make a protracted and what some thought brilliant reply:

> "The Love that dare not speak its name" in this century is such a great affection of an elder for a younger man as there was between David and Jonathan, such as Plato made the very basis of his philosophy, and such as you find in the sonnets of Michelangelo and Shakespeare. It is that deep, spiritual affection that is as pure as it is perfect. It dictates and pervades great works of art like those of Shakespeare and Michelangelo, and those two letters of mine, such as they are. It is in this century misunderstood, so much misunderstood that it may be described as the "Love that dare not speak its name," and on account of it I am placed where I am now. It is beautiful, it is fine, it is the noblest form of affection. There is nothing unnatural about it. It is intellectual, and it repeatedly exists between an elder and a younger man, when the elder has intellect, and the younger man has all the joy, hope, and glamour of life before him. That it should be so, the world does not understand. The world mocks at it and sometimes puts one in the pillory for it. (Hyde 201)

Wilde's response provoked applause from the gallery. In it are many refutations of homosexual conduct, but just as many causes for further questioning. As he did on at least nine occasions, Gill failed to compel an admission of the guilty intent of Wilde's relations with young men. He failed to question Wilde so as to make out *mens rea*; instead he hoped that the mere repeated association with men and the giving of money and gifts might be sufficient evidence of sexual misconduct.

In the second trial, in contrast, Lockwood focused more on Wilde's attempts to conceal the acts than on the acts themselves. This, in itself, placed suspicion in the minds of the jury, as Wilde's testimony now often seemed much less persuasive than when Gill, in the first trial, had allowed his eloquent and winning prose to flow. Again, Wilde's counsel, Clarke, used what Foldy quite aptly calls his "sanity defence" (35), striving to show that Wilde's candidness and sincerity not just in the Queensberry libel action, but also in the present criminal proceedings, were proof positive of his innocence, as any guilty man would have fled to the continent. Clarke maintained that only an insane man would stay and suffer the slings and arrows of outrageous misfortune in the arena of criminal prosecution.

Lockwood, in stark distinction to Gill, would allow none of this to pass without cross-examination. Instead, he often forced Wilde into corners that exposed the rhetorical tactics the defendant had used to sidestep many of the most pressing issues of criminal intent in the case. For instance, on cross-examination about the "prose poem" letter Wilde had written to Douglas, Lockwood asked Wilde if the words "My own Boy" were meant as a mode of address, to which Wilde launched into what promised to be another shower of literary prose: "It does not seem to me to be a question whether a thing is right or proper, but of literary expression. It was like a little sonnet of Shakespeare." Lockwood quickly cut in: "I did not use the word proper or right … was it decent?" (Hyde 245). Wilde was clearly taken aback, and Lockwood succeeded in making him look at least confused and at worst mendacious. Wilde stumbled for answers. At each denial Lockwood berated him with further quotations from the letter, each extract making Wilde's denials more frivolous, each rhetorical manoeuvre forcing Wilde into positions of perpetual zugzwang.[23] Moving from the letters to the Queensberry case to the men Wilde entertained at dinner, Lockwood delved ever deeper into Wilde's intentions behind his actions:

> "Did you not pause to consider whether it would be the slightest service to lads in their position to be entertained in such style by a man in your position?"

"No. They enjoyed it as schoolboys would enjoy a treat. It was something they did not get every day. I don't suppose they would have cared to be entertained to a chop and a pint of ale – they were used to that."

"You looked on them as schoolboys?"

"They were amused by the little luxuries of Kettner's, the pink lamp-shades and so forth."

"Did you give them wine?"

"Yes. I certainly should not stint a guest."

"You would let them drink as much as they liked?" …

"I should not limit their consumption, … but I should consider it extremely vulgar for anyone to take too much wine at table." (Hyde 249–50)

These exchanges always made Wilde seem designing. Although he did his best to curtail the ends to which Lockwood pushed such statements, Wilde often made serious admissions, like those above, that prejudiced his innocence more than it made probative his etiquette. In this instance, the *mens rea* associated with allowing the witnesses to drink to excess seemed to overshadow Wilde's thinking it vulgar – the exact result for which Lockwood hoped.

In his closing remarks, Lockwood focused even more on Wilde's criminal intent. Speaking of the prose poem, he urged the jury to discount completely Wilde's explanations, and recommended a reading of the poem that suggested an attempt by Wilde to cover up what for Lockwood was a strikingly clear message. Referring to Wilde's remarks that some, if not most, would understand such lofty affection, Lockwood pronounced: "Gentleman, let us thank God, if it is so, that we do not appreciate things of this sort save at their proper value, and that is somewhat lower than the beasts" (Hyde 258). Here, again, Lockwood shifted the jury's perception of Wilde's letters as examples of criminal intent. He challenged Wilde's explanations of the accused's purported affection for Douglas, and replaced them with his own reading, with two results. First, he defied Wilde's reading; second, and more important, he undermined Wilde's innocence by pushing the jury towards perceiving Wilde as covering up the real *mens rea*.

Further in this line of argument, Lockwood produced one of his most damning submissions of all. The "sanity defence" that Clarke chose to argue was grounded foremost on Wilde's lack of *mens rea*. Again, no man could behave the way Wilde did unless he was innocent, went Clarke's argument. Yet this foundational argument crumbled when

Lockwood gave his own reading of Wilde's so-called openness around the witnesses who alleged to have seen him at the Savoy Hotel:

> The defendant has given no explanation of the discoveries made by the employees of the hotel. It is no conclusive answer to say that Mr Wilde did everything openly. If crime were always cautious, it would always go unpunished, and it is in moments of carelessness that crime is detected. Why was Lord Alfred Douglas, who slept in the next room, not called to deny the statements of the chambermaid? I maintain that she and the other witnesses from the Savoy Hotel could have no possible object in hatching up a bogus case. (Hyde 260)

Here, Lockwood turned Clarke's "openness" defence against Wilde, again, accusing him of criminal carelessness – another clear association with *mens rea*. To punctuate this claim, Lockwood stressed that the hotel employees had nothing to gain from their testimony and that Wilde, therefore, was again attempting to cover his actions in a thin veneer of openness, which, for Lockwood, lacked both credibility and persuasive force.

Justice Wills, in his summing up, was much less disposed to let the witnesses' testimony speak for itself. Just as Lockwood had given his opinions of Wilde's intentions to the jury, so too did Justice Wills interpolate his remarks within the discourse of the witnesses. Again, in reference to Alfred Douglas's two letters, Justice Wills remarked: "Is the language of those letters calculated to calm and keep down the passions which in a young man need no stimulus? … It is strange that it should not occur to a gentleman capable of writing such letters that any young man to whom they were addressed must suffer in the estimation of everybody, if it were known" (Hyde 262).

Mens rea, in this instance, appears most strongly in the justice's terms and phrases: "calculated," "calm and keep down the passions," and "it should not occur to a gentleman." In essence, the justice argued it was highly improbable that Wilde wrote the letters with the intention he stated. Instead, the judge portrayed Wilde as calculating to incite libidinous homoerotic impulse. Again, for Justice Wills, Wilde's standing as a gentlemen, rather than insulating him from these actions, makes the actions all the more unpalatable, as, in the justice's opinion, he would certainly have had the *mens rea* to commit the actions, though he should have had better sense. Justice Wills went further, directing the jury in what was irrefutably a prejudicial fashion for Wilde, when he later returned momentarily to the letters: "It is for you, however, to consider whether or not that letter is an indication of unclean sentiments and unclean appetites on both sides. It is to my mind a letter upon which ordinary people would be very liable to put an uncomfortable construction" (Hyde 264). Loading his statements with words such as "unclean," the justice made it difficult for the jury to find Wilde's state of mind, at the time of writing, anything but criminal. Yet unclean sentiments or appetites or, for that matter, unclean letters did not constitute, in itself, the crime of gross indecency. The most important aspect of Justice Wills's direction was that it persuaded the jury that Wilde would have had the requisite *mens rea* at the time the alleged actions took place.

Again, this was a species of character assassination on the part of Justice Wills. Yet it is just as important, for our purposes, to elucidate requisite *mens rea* as an idea separate and apart from motive. For instance, the justice invoked the very concept of motive in referring to some letters Wilde had written to Douglas, but which were in the possession of Wood, a known blackmailer. Wilde had the letters returned, but said the money he gave to Wood was to aid a man in need, not payment for blackmail. When talking about these letters, Justice Wills again directed the jury: "Do you believe that Mr Wilde was actuated by charitable motives or by improper motives?" (Hyde 264). At the same time, he warned, "Wood is a blackmailer," and told the jury not to act upon the evidence unless it was corroborated. But the question put to the jury was still only probative of *mens rea*, not a sufficient condition of criminal intent in and of itself. That is to say, motive is not *mens rea*, but shows that *mens rea* was present during the commission of the act. Again, in this case, whether or not the letters were bought back, Wilde's *mens rea* at the time of the act of gross indecency was, in fact, present.

The final aspect of difference on which I want to comment was the severing of the two actions between Taylor and Wilde, and what I see as the distinct effects on our understanding of *mens rea* at the time of the case. In the first criminal trial, Wilde and Taylor stood together on twenty-five counts under the CLAA, some of which alleged conspiracy. This made the issues at trial exceptionally complex, because it was with the introduction of the CLAA in 1885 that an accused could first give testimony. Section 20 read: "Every person charged with an offence under this Act … shall be competent but not compellable witnesses on every hearing at every stage of such charge, except an inquiry before a grand jury." But this section did not cover conspiracy, as criminal conspiracy was not contemplated within the framework of the CLAA. Therefore, Wilde and Taylor could give evidence of their own counts of gross indecency, but not on the counts that alleged conspiracy. Therefore, the jurors had to keep the testimonies of Taylor and Wilde separate, and they could not conflate them as one evidencing the guilt of the other for purposes of the conspiracy counts of the indictment. This, of course, led to confusion, and Clarke was loath to let this situation guide the proceedings, as he knew it was mentally impossible for the jury to prevent one person's testimony from incriminating the other. His objection at the beginning of the first trial, however, was overruled, and the Crown was allowed to proceed with the actions together (Hyde 166–8; Foldy 31–2).

On the fourth day of trial, after the parade of Crown witnesses and their examination and cross-examination and just before Wilde entered the witness box, Charles Gill dropped the conspiracy charges. The Crown was well within its rights to proceed as it decided, but this put a harsh burden on Wilde and his counsel, as the net effect was that restrictions were no longer placed on the testimony of Wilde or Taylor, as both were now charged only under the CLAA. Of course, while there were now fewer charges to answer, both Wilde and Taylor had already suffered the Crown's introduction of a good deal of evidence as to their conspiracy. Again, by the justice's direction, this was no longer to be a factor influencing the jury, but more realistically, how could it not? As Clarke pleaded, "My Lord, if those counts had been withdrawn in the first instance, I should have made an application to your lordship for the charges against the two prisoners to be heard separately" (Hyde 195).

But the defence suffered not just a tactical or technical disadvantage from this move; it shifted the focus from the *actus reus* to the *mens rea* of the offence. The Crown effected this shift by replacing the conspiracy counts with what might be most aptly called, by analogy, a Derridian trace. That is to say, the charge of conspiracy was in itself a *mens rea*–based offence. Unlike murder, for example, the conspiracy charge has little or no *actus reus*. First degree murder is killing someone with the intent to kill. Conspiracy is the intent to commit a criminal act, even though the act itself carries its own punishment. So it *should* follow that, by removing the charges of conspiracy, the Crown was actually shifting the focus of its case away from the *mens rea* and towards the *actus reus* of the offence. But this would only hold if the Crown had chosen this course at the outset of the proceedings, as Clarke argued it should have. Having led copious evidence into the conspiracy of Taylor and Wilde, and then having dropped the charges, the Crown now left this trace of the evidence within the minds of the jurors, although they were not supposed to consider this aspect of the case. The other aspect of this move was that, when the jurors were instructed in this manner, they undoubtedly would suffer further confusion in deciding just which testimony went to conspiracy and which went to the alleged acts of indecency. Regardless, the *mens rea* that so dominated ideas of conspiracy would always already be present in the minds of the jurors, thus prejudicing Wilde and Taylor.

The cumulative result of these tactical, rhetorical, and ideological shifts between the first and second trials took their toll on Wilde and his defence. Once the jury returned a verdict of guilty on seven of the eight counts of gross indecency upon Wilde, Taylor was brought back into the dock so that the prisoners could receive sentence. Justice Wills remarked: "Oscar Wilde and Alfred Taylor, the crime of which you have been convicted is so bad that one has to put stern restraint upon oneself to prevent oneself from describing, in language which I would rather not use, the sentiments which must rise to the breast of every man of honour who has heard the details of these two terrible trials" (Hyde 272). It was clear, at this point, that Wills intended no leniency towards either prisoner – indeed, it is most disturbing, but perhaps not surprising, given the severe prejudice against homosexual behaviour in these years, how the justice's rhetoric shifted from moderate impartiality to indignant censure. Here, the justice's speech in pronouncing sentence became a damaging punishment in and of itself. Regardless of whether we believe this was within the justice's purview or not, it is certainly difficult to understand what came next, when he said:

> It is no use for me to address you. People who can do these things must be dead to all sense of shame, and one cannot hope to produce any effect upon them. It is the worst case I have ever tried. That you, Taylor kept a kind of male brothel it is impossible to doubt. And that you, Wilde, have been the centre of a circle of extensive corruption of the most hideous kind among young men, it is equally impossible to doubt.
>
> I shall, under such circumstances, be expected to pass the severest sentence that the law allows. In my judgement it is totally inadequate for such a case as this. The sentence of the Court is that each of you be imprisoned and kept to hard labour for two years. (Hyde 272)

Wilde's public destruction was complete, or so he thought. His private mental and physical destruction was just beginning.

Considering the cases and legislation alongside the legal and artistic cultures of the *fin de siècle*, it seems liberal jurisprudence in practice again failed to protect all individuals. As with most legal failures of this sort, one group suffered at the hands of another, and the morality of the day ruled the law, much more so than the rule of law governed individual behaviour. The rights of private association of certain individuals counted far less, if at all, than did the public morality of the day. Individual autonomy, in this instance, did not extend so far as private acts of what was coined "gross indecency," and justice was also based firmly on the moral grounds of the time.

This is, perhaps, the most disturbing connection between life and law: in cases of failure to protect individuals, the law tends to follow blindly the morality of the day, rather than to prescribe ways to eliminate harm. Although differentiating between the two is often not an easy task, when morality becomes the driving force behind the law the legal system becomes one of majority rule, and cannot adequately protect those at the margins or outside the majority group from the harms of the many. It is these sorts of failures about which many British moderns spoke, and to which I now turn my attention.

Chapter Two

Law's Empire Writes Back:
Legal Positivism and Literary Rejoinder in Wilde and Conrad

In this chapter I connect jurisprudence and the contemporary law of the moderns to the writing of Oscar Wilde and Joseph Conrad. Starting with style, I argue that the shift towards interiority of the focalized narrative is coincident with the shift in the judicial turn towards increasingly complex ideas of *mens rea*. Wilde's style and use of interiority employed satire to compel legal reform; Shoshana Felman's work on testimony helps undergird Wilde's shifting ontology; Judith Butler's ideas of the speech act criticize previous speech act theory; and we see again that cultural and critical legal studies might help reinterpret both the way the British moderns represented trial proceedings and the ways liberal jurisprudence might think about individuals.

Taking Wilde's style and stressing the heteronormativity of the law, we see that Wilde's case reveals the failure of liberal jurisprudence to hold to its principles of the rule of law, rights, autonomy, and justice. Yet Wilde refused to confess, at least in the legal or Brooksian sense of the word. I take up the scholarly debate about confession surrounding Wilde, and argue that what many see as confession was, rather, censorial prose directed at the legal system and its machinery. Wilde and Conrad were antecedents to the styles of Ford and Joyce, so I place them on a continuum of narrative interiority. The publication history of *De Profundis* shows the links between publication, Wilde's writing, and the kinds of writing we see about law by later modernist authors. Conrad united late Victorian writing and the modernist catalogue, reworking Victorian sensibilities and, in the case of *Lord Jim*, mixing omniscient and first-person narration to juxtapose and emphasize the distinction between exterior and interior narrative forms. Linking press coverage of the *Jeddah* and Conrad's depictions of the event in *Lord Jim*,

I argue that Conrad's novel stands as an archival legal record, much as do newspaper reports and trial transcripts. Jim's situation is unique, as he tries to tell the "truth" as best he can. Yet we see again that Conrad's narrative proves the inherent competition between epistemological and ontological reason in trial procedure. Peter Brooks's theories help my argument as I explore Jim's manufactured guilt.

Testimony, Trauma, and Speech Acts in Western Literature

Wilde's courtroom appearances and experiences were unique in their respective frequency and severity. Yet it was an experience different in degree, not in kind, compared to that of many of his literary successors. Joseph Conrad, Ford Madox Ford, and James Joyce were all familiar with the inside of a courtroom. Although their trauma at the hands of the law was slight, especially when compared to Wilde's, it was trauma nonetheless. What these authors held in common, however, to a far greater extent than their trauma, was their literary representations of trial proceedings after their personal courtroom appearances. The ontological and epistemological trauma of court manifested itself very differently in each author's artistic vision, yet each representation also held with it the necessity of coming through an ordeal.

In this chapter I compare the legal exposure of Wilde and Conrad to their subsequent literary representations, drawing on Brooks's confessional theory and Felman's trauma theory. I pick up the ideas of epistemological and ontological uncertainty that I introduced in Chapter 1 regarding Wilde, and discuss my theory that no witness can escape the witness box without undergoing this kind of epistemological and ontological trauma. The grave effects of giving testimony and having a sentence pronounced inflict serious trauma on the identity of the accused. In effect, these kinds of legally sanctioned situations puncture any sphere of inviolability to which an autonomous individual might lay claim. Continuing this line of inquiry into the lives and works of my other chosen British moderns, I hope to develop my limited theory of the poetics of law and culture to emphasize their shared discursive frameworks, and to foster the argument that the conversation between legal and literary systems should be founded firmly in a cultural approach without abandoning ideas of legal positivism. For these purposes I examine Wilde's *De Profundis* and Conrad's *Lord Jim* in this chapter, and Ford's *The Good Soldier* and Joyce's *Ulysses* in the following chapter. In each case, I offer a reading of the cultural significance of the legal proceedings presented in their texts, and argue that the speech act of pronouncing sentence is key to understanding the trauma of giving legally compelled testimony in open court. I also offer a reading that links each author's style to that of the others on what I see as a continuum reflecting the turn towards interiority, both in literary and legal discourse. Wilde and Conrad began what Ford and Joyce brought to fruition. That is to say, I believe that the moderns, through their life experiences and connections to legal proceedings, among other influences, emphasized the shift towards ideas of interiority and the self, and that this is reflected in their literary styles. Contextualizing their literary production within a discussion of their styles and the historical moments in which they wrote, I hope to emphasize their interdependent relationships.

Before I present these arguments, Lisa Rodensky's work on interiority requires comment. Her *The Crime in Mind* posits a relationship between interiority and nineteenth-century writers such as George Eliot, arguing that it is the realist form that allows us to make connections between interior and exterior in ways similar to how the law regards *mens rea* and *actus reus*. She differentiates her ideas from those of other critics, such as Alexander Welsh, stating that "the central argument of his work is that the criminal law's preference for circumstantial evidence over testimony in the eighteenth and nineteenth centuries influenced the narrative practices of legal and literary texts of these periods: novels became narratives of circumstantial evidence, narratives in which external circumstances are arranged to tell a convincing story" (Rodensky 21). Rodensky disagrees with the way Welsh compares literary and legal texts. Her main concern is that Welsh "does not account for the way third person narration invites us into the mind of [Walter Scott's] Waverley" (21). Indeed, as I describe below, the shift was not a marked one: Victorian novels continued to turn inward, and characters and narratives increasingly concerned more sophisticated ideas of interiority. For Rodensky this becomes a problem when we consider the modernists. She questions the purchase of her argument beyond the realism of the Victorians. "The question," she wonders, "that the proceeding analysis of *Tess* raises for me is this: how would one carry forward the work I have done with the internal and external elements of crime beyond the realist novel?" (Rodensky 216). She continues with an example: "[My] analysis does not account for the way modern novels enter and represent the consciousness of their characters. Virginia Woolf's narratives of consciousness, for instance, allow readers direct access to the minds of her characters, access denied to us in law or in our everyday lives. Yet the kind of analysis I have pursued would be unproductive if applied to Woolf's work ... because her formal experimentations deny the separation of the internal from the external that plays so central a role in my study (217)." I lay out my answer to Rodensky's question over the remaining pages of this examination. In short, when we look at our texts we simply cannot allow "questions of responsibility [to be] emptied out," as she asserts postmodern literature often demonstrates, any more than we can give up on the project of law. I think that comparing Wilde's work at the *fin de siècle* and the modernists who wrote shortly after might help, at least in part, address Rodensky's concerns.

To begin looking at Wilde's literary work after his sentence and during his incarceration, one must first return to the ideas of Brooks and Felman. For Brooks, confession in Western literature "is supposed a special stamp of sincerity and authenticity and to bear special witness to the truth of the individual personality" (18). To illustrate this, Brooks employs J.L. Austin's discussion of speech acts in *How to Do Things with Words*. For Austin, language as much performs an action as it conveys information.[1] Austin is concerned, therefore, not merely with the structural aspects of language, or *langue*, but also with the intended utterance, or *parole*, behind the grammatical structures and symbols contained in the utterance.[2] Here, Austin inverts Ferdinand de Saussure's structuralist thinking about *parole* and *langue*. For Austin the extralinguistic functions that contribute to meaning always undergird the structure of language. From this, then, Austin delineates the distinction between the constative and the performative. Constative utterances describe or report, while performative ones are the actions themselves, or a least a part of that action. Using this as a foundational structure for his own theory, Brooks describes confession as inherently containing both types of utterance. In fact, he argues, one might produce the other: "the verbal act that begins 'I confess' entails guilt, which is already there in the act of confessing, so the referent – this particular guilt – may merely be a by-product of the verbal act" (21). It is this double character that exacerbates guilt, as "the confessional rehearsal or repetition of guilt is its own kind of performance, producing at the same time the excuse or justification of guilt (by the fact of confessing it) and the accumulation of more guilt (by the act of confessing it), in a dynamic that is potentially infinite" (22).

From these comments, I want to follow two lines of inquiry. First, I am interested in Wilde's confessional reticence while on the stand and in the dock, and in his contrasting literary production immediately following his conviction, which evidences a strong need to confess. Second, I want to propose that most of what Brooks holds as true of confession can also hold true of testimony in general. The first part of this first line of inquiry is fairly simple: Wilde never once confessed his legal "guilt" in any way while giving his testimony; he maintained his innocence throughout the three trials in which he was involved – at least, while he was in the witness box or in the dock. Although he freely admitted being in the company of the men with whom he was accused of performing acts of "gross indecency," he never once admitted any such act.

Montgomery Hyde, taking a story from Frank Harris's *Oscar Wilde, His Life and Confessions* and confirming these events by his reading of *De Profundis*, recreates the conversation between Wilde and Harris that allegedly occurred between the first and second trials for gross indecency. Harris tried to reassure Wilde, as he was convinced that Wilde's defence counsel would be able to punch further holes in the testimony of some of the leading witnesses. But Wilde instead confessed:

> "Oh Frank!" cried Wilde. "You talk with passion and conviction, as if I were innocent."
>
> "But you are innocent, aren't you?" asked Harris in amazement.
>
> "No, Frank," replied the other. "I thought you knew that all along."
>
> For some seconds Harris seemed stupefied by this confession. Then he said: "No, I did not know. I did not believe the accusation. I did not believe it for a moment." (Hyde 226)

I return to this momentarily in my examination of *De Profundis*, but for now I want to comment on both the probability and the significance of this reported conversation. In all likelihood, Wilde could have made this confession, though the print sources that might confirm it are somewhat sparse. Harris goes into great detail about this lunch conversation, and R.H. Sherard confirms these details in his accounts. Wilde's sexual preferences are no longer a subject of great debate, and the enormous evidence of his homosexual conduct is no longer any great surprise. What is most important in this line of inquiry is not whether Wilde had performed acts of "gross indecency" generally, but whether he did so with the specific men who gave evidence against him. In this line of questioning, "innocence" becomes a rather muddy idea. That is to say, even if this reported conversation were absolutely accurate, the concept of "innocence" here is far less firm. Wilde's ideas of his sexual conduct reveal a man with little shame for his actions. In fact, many of the speeches he gave on the stand about relationships between men being among the highest forms of human relations, though directed along intellectual lines, were also Wilde's opinions of homosexual culture. Even regarding his reported conversation with Harris, it is more difficult to argue that Wilde was confessing to the acts of which he was specifically accused than to argue that he was confessing to his sexual conduct generally. His ultimate conviction, likewise, seems much more a censuring of homosexuality generally than of the specific acts for which he was accused. We see the rule of law failing, again, while we concomitantly question the individual's autonomy and our ideas of justice. To pursue this further, I return to Brooks and his theory of confessor and confessant.

For Brooks the bond between confessor and confessant is fundamental to the production of confessions. The "affective bond ... contains, and activates, elements of dependency, subjugation, fear, the desire for propitiation, the wish to appease and to please. It leads to the articulation of secrets, perhaps to the creation of hitherto unrealized truth – or perhaps the simulacrum of truth" (35). Perhaps one of the most striking aspects of Wilde's steadfast denials at trial and his alleged confession to Harris is his lack of the elements of the affective bond Brooks describes here. Brooks posits the interrogation as the site of this affective bond, as he grounds this relation in such situations as religious or police-induced confessions. Yet Wilde's refusal to admit the alleged actions during trial denied this bond. Wilde refused to submit to the legal machinery that tried so vehemently to exact a confession. Instead, the only admissions of legal guilt come from sources outside the courtroom, in the situation of having lunch with friends. This was, perhaps, one of Wilde's greatest achievements in his ontological struggle: though he was well aware of his homosexual nature, he refused the law's censure of it, and admitted homosexual conduct only to those from whom he knew propitiation forthcoming. Harris, though surprised at Wilde's confession, only further supported his friend against the legal leviathan set on Wilde's destruction. In this way, the "unrealized truth" – or "simulacrum of truth," as Brooks terms it – hitherto not revealed at trial was Wilde's opinion that his homosexual acts were perfectly natural. Although he was guilty at law, paradoxically he was still innocent within his own social code of conduct. Wilde resisted confessing to the law's attempt to create a simulacrum of truth that would make his actions both unnatural and a danger to society.

I want to argue, further, that what Brooks says about the performance of guilt in the act of confession is also true of all testimony in general. That is, the affective bond surely still creates a simulacrum of truth when the speaker giving testimony believes his or her innocence outside the law, regardless of his or her guilt inside the law's confines. In Wilde's case, his testimony was an avowal of his innocence. To him, this was the only path to justice. His ability to stave off the brutal attacks of counsel revolved around his belief in the innocence of his actions, though he, again paradoxically, denied the actions outright. In this way, we see Wilde as creating a simulacrum of truth about his innocence. Indeed, from a reading of the trial accounts at all levels, Wilde was certainly convincing in his denials, and his testimony became a formidable persuasive force in the resultant hung jury. Wilde's personal morality challenged the morality of the law. He, in effect, was trying to assert a right that he thought natural, but that the law rejected. Yet the resolute strength of his testimony all but evaporated in *De Profundis*, his monographic letter to Alfred Lord Douglas.

De Profundis: Witness to the Mind's Eye

Wilde produced the manuscript of *De Profundis* during his last three months of imprisonment in Reading Gaol,[3] but the text was published only posthumously, in 1905, in an expurgated form.[4] According to Vyvyan Holland, "Wilde was allowed one sheet of this paper at a time; when it was filled it was removed and replaced by another. As will be seen, he never revised the finished document, and it is therefore remarkable that it should flow so smoothly; the original manuscript contains scarcely any alterations" (91). This is in rather stark contrast to Richard Ellmann's account of the writing, where he asserts: "[Major Nelson] appears to have encouraged him, and also to have relaxed the rules by allowing Wilde when necessary to see parts he had completed on earlier days. Because of this concession, the letter is revised almost throughout, and some pages appear to have been totally rewritten and substituted for an earlier version" (510). Ellmann's is the more plausible version, as Nelson, having replaced the tyrannical Isaacson (and his harsh practices) as prison warden, seemed to sympathize with Wilde's position. This is important because it is also part of the simulacrum of truth through confession that Brooks posits. In this environment, Wilde was encouraged to write and to confess his sins as a sort of therapy (Ellmann 510; Hyde 296). The resulting thirty thousand words were less an apologia and confession than a damnation of the trial process and the prison system.

Not unexpectedly, much of Wilde's letter to Douglas takes sharp aim at his companion. In many ways, Douglas had abandoned Wilde, most recently in his assurances that Queensberry's costs would be borne by Douglas and his other family members. As they were not, Queensberry was successful in further humiliating Wilde in bankruptcy court and causing his financial ruin. In the following passages, Wilde despairingly speaks about the influence he allowed Douglas in his life:

> I will begin by telling you that I blame myself terribly. As I sit here in this dark cell in convict clothes, a disgraced and ruined man, I blame myself. In the perturbed and fitful nights of anguish, in the long monotonous days of pain, it is myself I blame. I blame myself for allowing an unintellectual friendship, a friendship whose primary aim was not the creation and contemplation of beautiful things, entirely to dominate my life. From the very first there was a gap between us. You had been idle at your school, worse than idle at your university. You did not realize that an artist, and especially such an artist as I am, one, that is to say, the quality of whose work depends on the intensification of personality, requires for the development of his art the companionship of ideas, and intellectual atmosphere, quiet, peace, and solitude. (98–9)

Here Wilde's palilogia incorporates the refrain "I blame myself" and its permutations. That is, he uses this vehement refrain for emphasis, which works as the fulcrum on which he actually balances blame among himself and the other factors that resulted in his incarceration. Much like Brooks's explanation of "I confess," here, "I blame" stands in for the guilt associated with confession. Wilde has his audience, for three sentences, believing that the blameworthiness associated with his imprisonment was indeed of his own volition. Yet it is soon clear that this is but another rhetorical trope – his paradiegesis but a digression to introduce that which he really finds blameworthy. At this juncture Wilde begins to describe his outrage with Lord Alfred Douglas. Yet the refrain "I blame myself" still has some purchase, as it accentuates Wilde's internal disgust of having been so influenced by such a callow cad. To grasp the consequence of this, we need to return to the ways Brooks interprets Austin's ideas of the speech act.

After Austin establishes the constative and performative aspects of speech, he further delineates the locutionary, illocutionary, and perlocutionary components of an utterance.[5] Generally, the locutionary component carries meaning, the illocutionary carries force, and the perlocutionary carries consequence. None of these is independent of the other, but each is necessary in considering the "total speech act" (148). In Wilde's case, "I blame myself" is an illocutionary placement of moral blameworthiness; it is also a perlocutionary justification for the consequence of his imprisonment. But from the remainder of his statements, it is clear that this reading is too simple.

Judith Butler takes issue with Austin's "total speech act," and questions its self-professed totality: "If the temporality of linguistic convention, considered as ritual, exceeds the instance of its utterance, and that excess is not fully capturable or identifiable (the past and future of the utterance cannot be narrated with any certainty), then it seems that part of what constitutes the 'total speech situation' is a failure to achieve a totalized form in any of its given instances" (3). This kind of trouble with temporality is exactly what Wilde plays on in his self-professing blame. Although it has a component that, in an illocutionary way, attributes blame to himself, the self-professed blame is also self-reflexive. The real perlocutionary effect is more to project blame upon Douglas than to explain Wilde's consequences to the world. Wilde's turn from "I" to "you," to open his sentences, intensifies this distinction and shifts the importance of his utterance beyond the moment in which it exists. That is, it performs, as Butler argues, a speech act that assumes common familiarity or shared history. We can know the sheer acridity of Wilde's writing only if we consider the history of his trials and, further, the preceding events. In this sense, the "you" is both Douglas and the universal you of the reader, who is implicated in Wilde's trial and punishment as part of the social system that allows the persecution of homosexuals. "You," in essence, incriminates all who would turn their back on Wilde, or worse.

But if we read these utterances of blame in the way I suggest, we are left with little in the way of confession, and much in the way of deflection. This is, in fact, the tone of much, if not most, of *De Profundis*. Yet there is an instance where Wilde admits an ethical fall, and this, perhaps, is as close to a confession as we get from the man writing in Reading: "But most of all I blame myself for the entire ethical degradation I allowed you to bring on me. The basis of character is will power, and my will power became absolutely subject to yours. It sounds a grotesque thing to say, but it is none the less true" (103).

Wilde's contemporary readers might seize on his choice of the phrase "entire ethical degradation." Yet this is still another instance of Wilde's paradox. There seems little doubt that Wilde believed this ethical fall occurred, but, yet again, we see his inability to take the blame for that which he professes himself blameworthy. In this case, he sees Douglas as an irresistible force, and one that has brought havoc upon his artistic and emotional life. In keeping with his arguments developed in *The Soul of Man under Socialism*, where Socialism could spring only from Wilde's ideas of "Individualism," Wilde felt that his surrender to Douglas's will made him compromise his individuality, which for Wilde was the greatest ideological pursuit. His ethical degradation, then, has nothing to do with homosexuality, but with Douglas's having duped him.

I pause here to elucidate further Wilde's view of "Individuality" and how its paradoxical relationship – not confession, guilt, or moral blameworthiness – seems to undergird his comments in this section of the text. *The Soul of Man under Socialism* was published in the *Fortnightly Review* in 1891. One of its most eloquent yet paradoxical passages, which speaks to my ideas here, focuses on the relationships between art, individuality and crime:

> Art is the most intense mode of Individualism that the world has known. I am inclined to say that it is the only real mode of Individualism that the world has known. Crime, which, under certain conditions, may seem to have created Individualism, must take cognizance of other people and interfere with them. It belongs to the sphere of action. But alone, without any reference to his neighbours, without any interference, the artist can fashion a beautiful thing; and if he does not do this solely for his own pleasure, he is not an artist at all. (142)

Although the reference to criminal behaviour might seem rather an aside in the larger context of the paragraph, it is more prophetic in its import than Wilde could have known when he wrote it. What Wilde calls "Individualism" reflected his disdain for the society in which he sought to produce his literature. He was little concerned with what the law defined as normative sexual practices, but chose, instead, to live his life on the margins of the law and late Victorian culture. He was a dandy and an aesthete, yet he would not admit to sodomy. He challenged socially defined sexuality, but tried to stay clear of the law's definitive types. This, of course, all ended with his imprisonment, where, again paradoxically, the state found his interference with others to be exactly the risk to society that Wilde posed.

From this, we return to question whether Wilde's behaviour ever fit Brooks's model of confession at all. Wilde's testimony, his "confession" to Harris, and his thoughts in *De Profundis* all lack the kind of Brooksian confession we associate with trial. His testimony not only lacked confession; it failed to produce a speech act of guilt in his utterances, even under severe duress. Instead, the simulacrum of truth created was Wilde's steadfastness in his belief that his conduct was simply not for public censure. Regardless of the exact words he spoke to Frank Harris, Wilde still admitted guilt only for committing acts, but not the associated psychological shame that Brooks details. In *De Profundis*, too, we see Wilde shifting blame and bearing witness, not to the crimes for which he was convicted, but as a victim of a legal system that failed in its duty to protect citizens while allowing for their freedom:[6] "Reason does not help me. It tells me that the laws under which I am convicted are wrong and unjust laws, and the system under which I have suffered a wrong and unjust system" (155). Wilde's disgust for the legal machinery that stripped him bare was not confession at all, but, rather, a censure of the system itself. As the system challenged his autonomy, so Wilde challenged the rule of law on which the system functioned.[7]

But although these utterances fail in Brooks's model of trial confessions, they seem more akin to the psychological confessions he underlines in his discussion of the culture of confession, therapy, and the law (113–43). Here, Brooks differentiates between the emotional truths produced by psychoanalytic confession and the material truths the law exacts – the elusive "facts" the law persistently attempts to uncover. Returning to his idea of personal, honest, and authentic characteristics underpinning the modern confession, Brooks adds that "its honesty, its intimacy, its truth to the self don't necessarily always conform to the truth of the external world, the truth of fact" (141). This rift between psychological and material truths is exactly the difficulty we face when reading Wilde's testimony, his letters, and his literary works. As Brooks proposes, "[c]ertainly the confessional talk of psychoanalysis suggests that confession can be less a definition of the truth than a search for it, a posing of the question: who am I?" (141). Wilde arrived at the same conclusion when he spoke of the law and legal system as wrong and unjust: "But, somehow, I have got to make both of these things just and right to me. And exactly as in Art one is only concerned with what a particular thing is at a particular moment to oneself, so it is also in the ethical evolution of one's character (155). Wilde, though destitute, ill, and imprisoned, recognized that he could not simply ignore the law's insistence on the material truth, regardless of how much it was in conflict with his own emotional truth. Further, he recognized the ontological work his trials and imprisonment had done. The moral degradation and public humiliation he suffered under the justice system made him acutely aware of the law's invasive character; this, for Wilde, was something that challenged and changed his self-perception.

The law's invasion of subjectivity, autonomy, or, at least, the interiority of the civil subject, shook Wilde's belief in the justice system and in justice generally. Wilde expressed an approach to the law echoed in cultural and critical legal studies when he asserted: "To be entirely free, and at the same time entirely dominated by law, is the eternal paradox of human life that we realize at every moment" (123). In Wilde's estimation, the law, in its pursuit of rights, autonomy, and justice, fails when the morality of the majority guides the legal vision of the entire polis. Wilde's legal system inculcated his questioning and resistance to the laws he thought unjust, yet his incarceration and punishment of hard labour did much to shift his ontological framework. Autonomy – or at least a hyper-real version or simulacrum of autonomy – was simply not possible for an openly homosexual individual at the turn of the twentieth century. The failure of liberal democracy in this instance further illustrates Brooks's theory that both psychoanalysis and the religious tradition use confession as therapy, while the law's version of confession is more a pursuit of material fact. For Brooks, "the law takes literally what the other two domains express symbolically" (142).

Building on Brooks's comments, I argue that the law's search for material facts – or, as I call it, epistemological certainty – seeks the individual's emotional truth only when this emotional truth resembles the confession needed at law. That is to say, when the individual confesses, the confession bears the mark of authenticity only when the confession conforms to the *actus reus* and *mens rea* of the alleged offence. When it does so, it leads to conviction; when it does not, it leads either to acquittal or, more often, a finding that the confession was not credible. In Wilde's case, the lack of confession made the trial more scandalous; had Wilde confessed, the law would have been vindicated in its stripping bare this threat to the British citizenry. Because Wilde did not confess, his exposure as a criminal threat was not as complete as the law desired. Instead, in Wilde's second trial, the circumstantial evidence, en masse, became the foundation upon which the justice instructed the jury, and the jury found Wilde guilty.

Shoshana Felman, in *The Juridical Unconscious*, also focuses on the ways the law fails to find adequate means to deal with psychoanalytic problems, a position tied to both the ontological trauma I propose and the impossibility of the total speech act Butler envisions. Drawing on instances such as the O.J. Simpson and Eichmann trials, she argues that "the law – traditionally calling for consciousness and cognition to arbitrate between opposing views, both of which are in principle available to consciousness – finds itself either responding to or unwittingly involved with processes that are unavailable to consciousness or to which consciousness is purposely blind" (4). The law, in these instances, must respond not only to the uncovering of the material truths it needs for conviction, but also to the "traumatic historical experience" surrounding the circumstances of the trial (4). In much the same way that Butler critiques Austin's theory for its myopic view of a total speech act, Felman, here, critiques the liberal tradition of seeing, or at least pretending to see, only the parties involved in the lawsuit and only the facts relevant to the case.[8] The result, for Felman, is a wilful blindness towards issues – issues that undergird the very essence of what is actually on trial.

Although Felman's approach deals nicely with the trauma of trial, the problem with her analysis, however, is that, when the law puts both the individual and historical experience on trial, the individual, as in Wilde's case, can be overshadowed by the historical issue. In late nineteenth-century Britain, homosexuality was perceived as a traumatic historical threat; as a result, Wilde's trials were as much shows of intolerance as trials of material fact. Where the court failed to exact a confession, it used, among other things, circumstantial evidence to convict.[9] The driving narrative of the entire trial and of Wilde's post-trial writings was the treatment of an individual thought of as a threat to society based solely on sexual preference. In the end, some of Wilde's writings in *De Profudis* disclose his desire to make an ontological shift, to question his interiority, to become a "good civil subject." In this way, he conforms to Felman's demonstration of performing testimony as trauma. But just as "the trial, while it tries to put an end to trauma, inadvertently performs an acting out of it," so, too, do the *records* and *representations* of the trial constitute re-enactment. The court reports of Wilde's trials were never published in a legal reporting series, and the only remaining records are the stenographers' transcripts from firms involved in the proceedings.

In contrast, in *De Profundis*, Wilde seeks to re-perform the trauma of the event, and to make this performance available to the culture that perpetuated his downfall. Each time we read Wilde's accounts, we re-enact the trauma he felt as an individual, not as a type defined by his culture. Wilde and Felman, regardless of their historical separation, both write about the need for legal reform by elucidating the trauma of trial. In a sense, *they* both seek to re-evaluate the ways in which *we* seek the ever-elusive idea of justice. By juxtaposing these discussions with some further representations of trials and trauma by other British moderns, I hope to fill in some of the gaps in the framework of law and culture I investigate here.

Archiving Guilt: Conrad, Confession, and Violence in *Lord Jim*

The year Wilde died, Joseph Conrad published *Lord Jim* in *Blackwood's*. Nineteen hundred, the penultimate year of Victoria's reign, ushered in Conrad's rise to literary celebrity, as he had published *Heart of Darkness* the year before. Although these novels speak volumes about Conrad's interest in the interiority of his characters and the psychological violence that accompanies these representations, I first focus on the ways Conrad shifted and modified what Wilde undertook in *De Profundis*.

We see the precursor of the indirect interior monologue style in Wilde's prison work, not just because of the circumstances in which it was written, but also because of Wilde's use of the epistle as both a therapeutic and a censorial tool. Conrad's commentary on English legal procedure and practice continued the growth of self-reflexive writing about the law that Wilde began in his incarceration. I pause briefly to consider Wilde's style in *De Profundis* and to compare it to what Conrad does in *Lord Jim*. From this comparison, I return to a brief synopsis of Conrad's involvement with the legal system, and to the concepts of speech acts, violence, and trauma that punctuate the remainder of my discussion of the British moderns and their work.

It would be easy to discount much of Wilde's letter to Douglas as a protracted tirade of a jilted lover and to ignore the critical legal expression. Ellmann, for example, deals little with the ways Wilde's missive troubled *fin de siècle* notions of law and much more with the ways it affected Wilde's relationship with Douglas (513–6). In Ellmann's estimation, "*De Profundis* is a kind of dramatic monologue, which constantly questions and takes into account the silent recipient's supposed responses. Given the place where it was written, Wilde might have been expected to confess his guilt … More than half of *De Profundis* is taken up by his confession, not of his own sins, but of Bosie's" (513).

All of this is true,[10] but it is also true that this kind of monologue is what we associate most with a modernist poem such as T.S. Eliot's "The Love Song of J. Alfred Prufrock." In style and tone, these two works have much in common. Both address, in the second person, an audience we (the readers) have only clues to, both reveal the character of the speaker, and neither voice is, arguably, the poet's.

Although the first two comparisons are fairly obvious, my last claim arises from the argument I put forward above – namely, that Wilde, in his life before and after prison, was exceptionally fond and protective of Douglas, and it was only in *De Profundis* that we see such a marked shift in temperament towards his lover. This was, I think, a direct result not only of incarceration, but also of the trial process that made Wilde perjure himself to protect his friend and lover. All these factors contributed further to Wilde's ontological crisis. From these observations, we observe that *De Profundis* is a precursor to the indirect interior monologue, much as Prufrock is in Eliot's work. The speaker's voice in *De Profundis* is markedly different from everything we know of Wilde and his writing beforehand. The Wilde writing in prison is ontologically altered, and his prose poem to Douglas is arguably as much the voice of a character as is Prufrock's in Eliot's poem.[11]

It is unclear whether Wilde was really given only one sheet of paper per day and not allowed access to his previous work, as Vyvyan Holland claims, or whether he was allowed to revise sections of the work in progress, as Ellmann deduces. It seems clear, however, that Wilde never saw his entire monograph until his release from prison, when he immediately handed it over to Robert Ross (Ellman 510; Holland 91). This history further contributes to the fragmented nature of the work. Although there is an undoubted progression to the narrative, there is equally a visiting and revisiting of themes and events. There is a remembrance and a re-enactment. The transgressions of Douglas against Wilde are catalogued and re-performed, and *De Profundis* becomes a record of moral outrage, of trauma, and of the legal system as a vehicle for that trauma.

The last point I offer here follows this train of circumstance. Not only did the physical giving and taking of writing materials contribute to the content of *De Profundis*; Wilde's subjection to hard labour and prison conditions also added to the work's fragmented narrative. Oakum picking until his hands bled, unnutritious and sometimes inedible gruel, and long periods of solitary confinement were everyday factors that resulted in his eventual physical collapse (Hyde 274–94). These too made *De Profundis* a monologue that connected the prisoner to the prison system. Wilde's thoughts on his physical, mental, and social ruin arise over and over in his epistle written from cell C 33. These are the thoughts of a mind subjected to the torment of public humiliation at trial and further torment behind prison walls, the thoughts of a mind searching for self-recognition within a judicial system that had branded him a pervert and a danger to society. The therapeutic derivative of this labour allowed for what Ellmann calls the "regenerative" in Wilde's relationship with Douglas (515). Wilde never recanted the outrage and trauma so prevalent in *De Profundis*, as they were directed against the legal system, but upon his release he did recommence his relationship with Douglas. He could forgive his friend and lover, but he could not pardon the legal system that made him an object of public scorn.

I revisit Wilde in this particular section because I want to argue that there are striking similarities with the cultural production of Conrad's *Lord Jim*. If we provisionally accept my assertion that Wilde's style in *De Profundis* acted as a precursor to the interior monologue of many moderns, then Conrad's style in *Lord Jim* arguably advanced along this path. The narrative in that text exhibits many of the same characteristics we associate with both the dramatic monologue and interior monologue, but it also inhabits the space between these forms. That is, although it is fragmented in the sense that the events are narrated and re-narrated, and although the first-person and omniscient narrators attempt to declaim the mental states of Jim in his legal tribulations, we are never granted access to Jim's mind in the ways that later modernists such as Virginia Woolf or James Joyce made famous. In essence, *Lord Jim*, in my estimation, bridges works of early modernism (such as Wilde's *De Profundis*) and high modernism (such as Joyce's *Ulysses*), as it experiments with many of the stylistic characteristics of each. At the same time, we see that it connects Conrad both stylistically and culturally to the coterie of authors for whom the law played such an important part in their work.

Conrad's style in *Lord Jim* straddles the border of late Victorian colonial adventure and high modernist psychological interiority.[12] Driving this mixing is the shift in voice and focalization between Chapters 4 and 5. For the first four chapters Conrad uses an omniscient third-person narrator who sees and reports the inner workings of Jim's mind. In Chapter 5 we meet Marlow, who himself first sees Jim at the trial. Conrad's decision to introduce Marlow at the trial makes these courtroom events pivotal as an interstice between these points of view. It gives us access to the inner thoughts of Jim's mind, but shifts to the observations of Marlow, who also offers his estimation of the trial's effects upon Jim. Although this shift in focalization offers us a continuum between narrators, it is equally a space in which we lose some of the interiority of Jim's ontology. We no longer have direct contact with Jim's mental states. Instead, we must, first, question the reliability of Marlow's mediated story and, second, we must infer Jim's thoughts through that mediated narrative. This is particularly difficult, as the omniscient perspective of the first four chapters has offered very little in the way of resolving Jim's conflicted self-images. Marlow adds a further dimension of epistemological uncertainty surrounding the events, and at once fragments the telling of the tale while connecting it to both the discourses of law and literature: "Oh yes I attended the inquiry," opens Marlow, "and to this day I haven't left off wondering why I went." He goes further: "I am willing to believe each of us has a guardian angel, if you fellows will concede to me that each of us has a familiar devil as well. I want you to own up, because I don't like to feel exceptional in any way, and I know I have him – the devil, I mean. I haven't seen him, of course, but I go on circumstantial evidence" (26).

Here, circumstantial evidence suggests not only Marlow's mental states and associated reliability as a narrator, but also that he is integrated, somehow, into Jim's trial narrative, where no other form of evidence is present. In both cases, the narrative forms a variety of confession. Jim's confession sees him writhing on the stand while attempting to find some resolution between the ontological and epistemological demands on him; in Marlow's variety of confession to the reader, he is fighting to represent, as accurately as he can, the events as he sees them. This is still a long way away from Bloom's *flâneur*'s reporting, but the unanticipated and unexplained shift in perspective between chapters makes the storytelling that much more self-reflexive to us, that much more fragmented and diverse. This shift does, on the macro level of narration, what Bloom's musings do on the micro level: they question the hermeneutic of Western mimetic realism, and offer alternative perspectives that often conflict.[13]

Conrad's career as a sailor was so foundational to his work that it also influenced his thinking about confession and the British trial system. At the age of twenty, in 1878, he had arrived in England with only a cursory knowledge of the language. Regardless of, or perhaps despite, this disadvantage, he managed to pass his sailing examination for master within eight years. During his lifetime, he became known as one of the great writers of the sea, though the comparisons to his notable American contemporary Herman Melville often roused his sometimes rabid temper. Critics such as D.H. Lawrence rubbed sea salt in Conrad's oft-wounded ego, with comparisons to Melville that declared: "His vision is … far sounder than Joseph Conrad's, because Melville doesn't sentimentalize the ocean and the sea's unfortunates. Snivel in a wet hanky like Lord Jim" (Meyers 175). Aside from their comic value, these statements are useful for raising the issue of Jim's broken and fragmented character. Jim is a tragic hero not only because he falls from grace, but also, much like the speaker in *De Profundis*, because of the conflict raging between the speaker's truth and the legal system's insistence on what is true. The war between epistemological and ontological certainty is no less intense in *Lord Jim* than in *De Profundis*.

Conrad's sailorly melancholy and his fascination with both the maritime courts of justice and the seedy legal affairs of his friends and colleagues (most notably Ford Madox Ford) contributed greatly to what might be called his moral scepticism. The current scepticism with which many contemporary scholars approach traditional legal philosophy owes much to the kind of scepticism that foregrounds the violence of legal culture that Conrad began exploring. Kieran Dolin's study of *Lord Jim* ties the legal framework of colonial Britain to the sea as he notes: "Victoria ruled not only Britain but an Empire 'beyond the seas,' and British law provided one framework for both the colonies and the maritime service which connected them with 'home'" (145). In this way, Conrad comments not only on the justice system, but also on the ways the system's tendrils extend far outside its home jurisdiction.

Dolin also draws the important distinction that "[t]he hero of *Lord Jim* is not convicted of a crime in the technical sense of the word. He is not charged with an offence, tried by a jury or penalized by imprisonment or fine. Jim appears before a marine court composed of a magistrate and two nautical assessors, and his punishment relates to his profession (the cancellation of his certificate)" (148). Yet the search for justice, alongside the battles for epistemological and ontological certainty, is no less significant than in the work of Wilde. Necessarily, this springs from Conrad's understanding of the subject in both of these philosophical senses, which, in turn, turns on what Beth Sharon Ash terms "relationality" in regard to human agency. She explains: "the 'relational subject' is dialectical and dialogical: dialectical because it is defined by the continual interplay of relational matrices (the personal is bound to the interpersonal and the social, but cannot be reduced to them); and dialogical because the subject, in this selective reliance on assimilation and internalization, expresses itself by talking back, for example, in symptomatic conflicts with, and critical interpretations of, its world" (5–6).[14] This relationality is significant not only to creative nonfiction such as Wilde's *De Profundis*, but also to our understanding of the production of fictional subjectivity. This interpretation of history is more enriched than that offered by traditional New Historicist approaches, as it uses history as only one layer in the intricate construction. The "matricity" of the system demands nonlinear relationships to grasp the systemic complexity.

The legal framework that Dolin mentions ties Conrad's narrative securely to imperialism, just as Wilde's trials and his subsequent work were tied firmly to the culture of anti-homosexuality and its legal underpinnings. Many statutory instruments made explicit that, although the jurisdiction of the British courts did not extend to the colonies or the sea, the legal processes and procedures of these courts were still the models by which colonial or nautical courts of inquiry were to proceed. Using redundant and circumlocutory language, the drafters of the Admiralty Offences (Colonial) Act of 1849, for instance, gave admirals jurisdiction over certain offences in the colonies much as they already held on the sea. Section three, for example, dealt with trial procedure for the felonies of murder or manslaughter:

III. And be it enacted, That where any Person shall die in any Colony of any Stroke, Poisoning, or Hurt, such Person having been feloniously stricken, poisoned, or hurt upon the Sea, or in any Haven, River, Creek, or Place where the Admiral or Admirals have Power, Authority, or Jurisdiction, or at any Place out of such Colony, every Offence committed in respect of any such Case, whether the same shall amount to the Offence of Murder or of Manslaughter, or of being Accessory before the Fact to Murder, or after the Fact to Murder or Manslaughter, may be dealt with, inquired of, tried, determined, and punished in such Colony in the same Manner in all respects as if such Offence had been wholly committed in that Colony; and that if any Person in any Colony shall be charged with any such Offence as aforesaid in respect of the Death of any Person who having been feloniously stricken, poisoned, or otherwise hurt, shall have died of such Stroke, Poisoning, or Hurt upon the Sea, or in any Haven, River, Creek, or Place where the Admiral or Admirals have Power, Authority, or Jurisdiction, such Offence shall be held for the Purpose of this Act to have been wholly committed upon the Sea.

Through these types of rambling statutory mandates (note that the quotation above is one sentence), Britain expanded and diversified its colonial holdings while imposing common law systems of regulation and control and, simultaneously, equating many colonial and nautical jurisdictions. Conrad was aware of these legal nuances, as his depiction of the nautical court in *Lord Jim* makes clear. He was also clearly aware of the problems Britain was having maintaining the validity of its self-imposed dominion.

Apart from the obvious indications of nonacceptance of imposed laws by the colonized, in the form of demonstrations, uprisings, and revolts, there was an undercurrent of self-doubt even within the colonial judiciary. To quell such doubts, the British government enacted what was almost a comic self-reflexive statute, validating its own and other statutory instruments' validity. The Colonial Laws Validity Act of 1865, according to its preamble, strove "to remove doubts as to the validity of colonial laws." The echoes of Hart's rule of recognition should be particularly obvious here. The Act then went further to state: "Doubts have been entertained respecting the Validity of divers Laws enacted or purporting to have been enacted by the Legislatures of certain of Her Majesty's Colonies, and respecting the Powers of such Legislatures, and it is expedient that such Doubts should be removed." To effect the removal of such doubt, the Act – after defining what a colony was, whether a colonial law was or was not "void for repugnancy," and whether a law might be void for inconsistency – included a section giving colonial legislatures the power to establish courts of law:

> **5.** Every Colonial Legislature shall have, and be deemed at all Times to have had, full Power within its Jurisdiction to establish Courts of Judicature, and to abolish and reconstitute the same, and to alter the Constitution thereof, and to make Provision for the Administration of Justice therein; and every Representative Legislature shall, in respect to the Colony under its Jurisdiction, have, and be deemed at all Times to have had, full Power to make Laws respecting the Constitution, Powers, and Procedure of such Legislature.

This move towards establishing judicial machinery within colonies, however, did not alter the ability of the navy and merchant marine to set up courts of their own to try cases; not surprisingly, the procedures used at sea or in the colonies generally mirrored the British model quite closely.

This sort of nautical autonomy was fairly fictitious, however, as regulatory statutes existed to guide the ways nautical assessors were to hear trials, as well as the powers conferred on these persons. The Merchant Shipping (Colonial) Act of 1869, for instance, gave a wide definition of what it meant to be under "British possession" or control, while it defined, in an equally broad fashion, what constituted the legislature and the officials (s. 2). Again, this legislation seemed to give colonial and naval governing bodies more autonomy, but these kinds of validating statutes consistently tied the specific procedures of the legislating bodies to the practices of the British legal regime. Section 8 of the Act elucidated that it was the responsibility of the Board of Trade to report the "equal efficiency" of the qualifying examinations to the Crown regarding colonial certificates for master, mate, and engineer:

> **8.** Where the legislature of any British possession provides for the examination of, and grant of certificates of competency to persons intending to act as masters, mates, or engineers on board British ships, and the Board of Trade reports to Her Majesty that they are satisfied that the examinations are so conducted as to be equally efficient as the examinations for the same purpose in the United Kingdom under the Acts relating to Merchant Shipping, and that the certificates are granted on such principles as to show the like qualifications and competency as those granted under the said Acts, and are liable to be forfeited for the like reasons and in the like manner.

Further provisions in this section clarified the enforcement, application, and conditions to which the certificates were subject, and made equally clear that each of these colonial procedures should also model itself on the British template.

There is a liminal strangeness about the admiralty and colonial statutes of this period. At first they seem to grant autonomy, but closer examination reveals the underlying inability of the colonial and naval authorities to act at all independently. Conrad's sailing career in the merchant marine was subject to this legal framework, and his understanding of the examinations and procedures he underwent to pass from mate to master was equally inflected by this liminal strangeness. The conflict and instability of the legal structures of naval and colonial regulation became, for Conrad, fascinating topics for consideration, and they play out in most of his early novels. Yet postcolonial Conrad scholarship tends to largely ignore the legal aspects of identity politics. The historical inspiration for the narrative of *Lord Jim*, which accompanies this legal context, offers an interpretation of the narrative as a cultural document that voices each of these influences in a polyphony that makes any definitive interpretation of the law a most difficult endeavour.

The legal structures in *Lord Jim* frame the literary story of the fictitious vessel, the *Patna*. The literary framework, in turn, draws from Conrad's exposure to the legal machinery of nautical inquiry, and especially from the ship's real-life counterpart, the *Jeddah*. The historical record of the *Jeddah* affair within Conrad scholarship is not completely firm, though the facts seem to fall within a discernible interpretive range. Whether it was 950 or closer to 1,000 pilgrims aboard the vessel is of little consequence, and the material facts are these: the *Jeddah* was travelling with a human cargo from Singapore to the Arabian port of Jeddah on 8 August 1880; it encountered problems and the hull began to leak; the crew abandoned ship and left the passengers to fend for themselves; the crew was saved and taken to safety, reporting that the ship had sunk and all lives were lost; the *Jeddah*, however, did not sink, but was towed, the next day, to safety (Batchelor 61–8; Myers 196–7).

Some of the more pertinent disputed facts include whether or not the hull breach resulted from bad weather, running afoul upon a half-sunken vessel (referred to in the text as a "relic") or both, and whether the pilgrims had taken up arms to commandeer the lifeboats. Batchelor, for example, makes much of the crew's situation in relation to the pilgrims. He emphasizes that Captain Clark, his wife, and the young first mate, Augustine Podmore Williams, all feared for their lives (61). There was also the question of whether Williams abandoned the ship at all or was thrown overboard by the angry mob. All of these fissures in the facts make their way into *Lord Jim*, and the result is a mix of historical account and fictional fancy. This kind of play is much akin to what Linda Hutcheon describes as historiographic metafiction (122–3).

I am not suggesting that *Lord Jim* is the first postmodern novel, but I think it straddles the boundary between the nineteenth-century historical novel and the twentieth-century postmodern. It interpolates the old genre with the new, creating a space in which well-known historical events receive fictional literary attention. Yet this kind of attention does not seek historical certainty. Historiographic metafiction, at least as Bharati Banerjee interprets Hutcheon's terminology, does not create new master narratives (275). Rather, the irony and parody that stem from the intertextual use of narratives like that of the *Jeddah* within the framework of Conrad's work function to make the reader rethink, or revision, accepted master narratives of history.

Drawing on György Lukács, Hutcheon argues that the protagonist in a historical novel is usually a "world historical" type, and that "it is clear that the protagonists of historiographic metafiction are anything but proper types: they are the ex-centrics, the marginalized, the peripheral figures of fictional history" (113–4). Edward Said makes a related point: "Conrad's writing therefore has a critical place in the history of the duplicity of language, which since Nietzsche, Marx and Freud has made the study of the orders of language so focal for contemporary understanding" (29). For Said, this "duplicity" comes from the problem of representing in words the meanings of events: "For what Conrad discovered was that the chasm between words saying and words meaning was *widened*, not lessened, by his talent for words written" (29). From these various observations I emphasize that Conrad's novel is a dialogic document. Although it lacks the self-reflexivity of a postmodern novel, it nevertheless possesses many of the genre's traits. Although it seeks to accentuate the problems of articulating epistemological or ontological truth, it recognizes that it is the progeny of a literary tradition that endows the novel with a "special kind of authenticity." The historical references in Conrad's novel create authenticity in the minds of his modern readers, much as Brooks argues the contemporary confession does in ours. As he plays in these spaces, Conrad not only constructs a narrative that lays bare the trauma of legal procedure; he also maps this trauma onto Jim's psychological framework. The particulars of this cartography figure Conrad's work in the emergence of the new modern novel, connecting the *fin de siècle* to the high modernist canon.

The narration in *Lord Jim* describes Jim's dealings with the court of inquiry convened to try the crew of the *Patna*. The ship, travelling with a crew and approximately eight hundred Muslims to Jeddah, runs afoul upon a half-sunken relic, and the crew abandons its human cargo. Jim cannot recall whether he jumped from the sinking vessel or fell in the water by another means. Marlow relates his uncertainty about the event: "[Jim] didn't know. It had happened somehow" (82). Jim willingly stands trial, although the other officers flee. Both the omniscient third person and Marlow's narration of the ensuing trial underline the confusion and stress Jim undergoes while trying to uncover the so-called facts. Through its search for truth beyond a reasonable doubt, or even on the balance of probabilities, the common law tradition of precedent creates an archive that both delineates and justifies violence against individuals at the hands of the law.

Using the courtroom as a venue to establish guilt, the law records and catalogues each confession, first, in trial transcripts, as evidence of the accused's wrongdoings and, second, as legal precedent, by which to try forthcoming similar cases. By claiming to establish the defendant's *actus reus* and *mens rea*, the court both challenges and reworks Jim's ontological status. In effect, the court claims the privileged knowledge of Jim's "true" identity and then labels this identity criminal. This indelible mark allows continued brutality against the convicted, in the form of public humiliation. Marlow's account of the problems Jim faces once convicted of his crime details the violence associated with this archival classification, among other kinds of violence. These archival acts in the court of law are competing narratives to those representations of the legal system made by the moderns, and each vies to embody as accurate a picture of legal procedure as is possible in legal and literary writing. Yet neither the critical approach of fiction nor the justificatory approach of judicial decision writing can fully capture the polyphony of voices engaged in a single legal issue.

Legal argument is obsessed with "the facts," as is much of the first few sections of *Lord Jim*. Conrad's omniscient, third-person narrator of the first four chapters, before we meet Marlow, introduces us to Jim and the crew of the *Patna*, and then moves to the incident upon which the rest of the novel turns: the compromise of the ship's hull in the dark, foreboding sea. The fourth chapter commences with a description of the trial in which Jim finds himself embroiled. The narrator relates the *mise en scène*:

A month or so afterwards, when Jim, in answer to pointed questions, tried to tell honestly the truth of this experience, he said, speaking of the ship: "She went over whatever it was as easy as a snake crawling over a stick." The illustration was good: the questions were aiming at facts, and the official Inquiry was being held in the police courts of an Eastern port. He stood elevated in the witness box, with burning cheeks in a cool lofty room: the big framework of punkahs moved gently to and fro high above his head, and from below many eyes were looking at him out of dark faces, out of white faces, out of red faces, out of faces attentive, spellbound, as if all these people sitting in orderly rows upon narrow benches had been enslaved by the fascination of his voice. It was very loud, it rang startling in his own ears, it was the only sound audible in the world, for the terribly distinct questions that extorted his answers seemed to shape themselves in anguish and pain within his breast – came to him poignant and silent

like the terrible questioning of one's conscience. Outside the court the sun
blazed – within was the wind of great punkahs that made you shiver, the
shame that made you burn, the attentive eyes whose glance stabbed. The
face of the presiding magistrate, clean shaved and impassable, looked at
him deadly pale between the red faces of the two nautical assessors …
They wanted facts. Facts! They demanded facts from him, as if facts could
explain anything! (23)

From this point, the narration details the oleaginous behaviour of the
nautical assessors, the stand-ins, in nautical police court, for the barristers more commonly associated with the English legal tradition. This
description reveals much about Conrad's temperament in relation to
the law and its structures. Conrad notes that the trial begins a month
after the events. Though not made much of, this scene begins a long
line of circumstances that put into question the accessibility of accurate
perception. Jim's trauma has percolated for an entire month; his guilt
festers, and he wallows in self-doubt before he is put on the stand to testify. By the time he gives evidence, his conscious and subconscious recollections of the events are already compromised. Yet the narrator also
notes Jim's earnest attempt at honesty, at somehow striving to access
the truth of the events. At this juncture, there still seems hope that Jim
might somehow gain that kind of Brooksian authenticity through his
confession. But this internal conflict between Jim's desire and his ability to access the truth of the month-old events is already brewing. Jim
becomes a paradigm of inauthenticity, in fact, as he refuses either to
admit to his actions fully or to offer another version of the events that
might vitiate the accusations against him.

The narrator's Orientalist description of Eastern police courts further
fuels the strangeness of the situation. Although Jim's career as a merchant sailor has exposed him to much cultural diversity, the faces that
stare back at him are nonetheless noticeably different from his own. His
position in the elevated witness box is an inversion of power here, as it
makes him a spectacle at the mercy of the assessors, under the surveil-
lance of all. Jim's cheeks burn, though the courtroom is cool; the narrator, to emphasize this point, later also mentions that it is shame that so
colours them. Even Conrad's choice of the word "enslaved" to describe
the audience seems self-reflexive here, as it is Jim who is enslaved by
the necessity of giving testimony, and it is Jim who also finds himself
listening to the echoes of his voice as though they came from another.
The questions "extort"; the eyes "stab." The questions posed become

Jim's psychomachia, and his psychological position is most markedly one of ignominy. In the end, Jim's thoughts, through the omniscient narrator's description, dwell on the incongruity of facts and meaning: how can facts, and especially facts given under the strict protocols of cross-examination, approach some kind of certainty?

The narrative deals with Jim's intense efforts to recognize what is to him the importance of being earnest. The narrator describes Jim's recollection:

> He wanted to go on talking for truth's sake, perhaps for his own sake also; and while his utterance was deliberate, his mind positively flew round and round the serried circle of facts that had surged up all about him to cut him off from the rest of his kind: it was like a creature that, finding itself imprisoned within an enclosure of high stakes, dashes round and round, distracted in the night, trying to find a weak spot, a crevice, a place to scale, some opening through which it may squeeze itself and escape. This awful activity of mind made him hesitate at times in his speech. (23)

Here the narrator describes Jim's earnest attempt to tell the "whole truth" while finding himself increasingly threatened by the very facts he attempts to utter. That Jim wanted to talk for "truth's sake" and for "his own sake also" seems to distinguish the two; it seems to point, again, to the Brooksian notion of authenticity through confession, but forestalls the possibility of authenticity for Jim. The "serried circle of facts," in contrast, begins to weigh upon Jim, and his answers to the questions posed to him sound hesitant and suspect. While Jim willingly admits what he did, he is vilified by the common law's insistence that there is, in fact, a discernible and *complete* truth, and that this truth is *always* plain and *always* simple. The narrator's description of Jim's physical features as reddening and his performance in the "elevated witness box" as a creature trying to find escape clearly signifies the traumatic experience of giving testimony.

A short time later, even the act of truthful confession becomes interpolated by courtroom practice. The narrator relates Jim's rambling testimony, truncated by the assessor: "He was becoming irrelevant, a question to the point cut short his speech, like a pang of pain, and he felt extremely discouraged and weary. He was coming to that, he was coming to that – and now, checked brutally, he had to answer by yes or no. He answered truthfully by a curt 'Yes, I did … '" (23). In his efforts to access the inaccessible truth, Jim flounders as he comes under further attack through cross-examination. He is never allowed to express what he wants to say; instead, he is forced to answer either "yes" or "no." We are never told the question to which Jim responds, only that, at the hands of counsel, he admits, he acknowledges, he confesses. The effects of the trial on Jim are permanent, and as the point of view in narration shifts in Chapter 5, Marlow continues to familiarize us with Jim's injured subjectivity.

Movement in Modernist Style: Turning Inward

Marlow picks up where the third-person narration leaves off, and relates his first seeing Jim at the court of inquiry. He describes Jim's actions in the witness box as "overwhelmed, confounded, pierced through and through, squirming like an impaled beetle" (32). He then relates: "Nothing more awful than to watch a man who has been found out, not in a crime but in a more than criminal weakness. The commonest sort of fortitude prevents us from becoming criminals in a legal sense; it is from weakness unknown, but perhaps suspected, as in some parts of the world you suspect a deadly snake in every bush – from weakness that may lie hidden, watched or unwatched, prayed against or manfully scorned, repressed or maybe ignored more than half a lifetime, not one of us is safe" (32). For Marlow, then, criminality is begotten not from inherent criminal genealogy or an innate penchant for criminal endeavours; it is, instead, a child of circumstance, and none of us is safe. The weaknesses to which we are all susceptible become more than criminal in the act of their being "found out," as Marlow puts it; the publicity surrounding crime, in other words, makes monsters of criminals. This finding out, in turn, is the result of the individual's internalized weakness rising to external behaviour. The *mens rea*, here, is inextricably tied to the *actus reus*. Jim's confession, in this instance, becomes a brand of criminality, both as it marks him as authentically criminal and as it becomes part of the legal archive. But his act of confessing – that is, the act of publicly admitting his weakness, his guilt, his humiliation – becomes Jim's truly frightening and recurring nightmare.

Marlow, later in the text, describes Jim's attempts to regain his self-esteem, his previous belief that he is, in fact, a "good" person. Yet the trial haunts Jim, and Marlow details Jim's inability to hold down work after being stripped of his first mate certificate. (The cancellation of the certificate is narrated in yet another section of the novel.) Denver's rice mill, Egström and Becker, and the Yucker brothers are all employers for whom Jim works. Yet at each job, Jim's past is revisited, and as the characters in each situation come to an awareness of his past, feelings of shame and guilt make it impossible for him to assert himself in the new subjectivity he attempts to solidify. In essence the trial's effect of creating a denigrated subjectivity for Jim blocks his ability to assert any identity other than that of the guilty, broken criminal, to which the archival record attests. The fragmented, alienated feelings of the character mirror the method Marlow uses to tell us his tale.

The pursuit of knowledge and its unavailability, again, underline the epistemological trauma in the text. That is, how can Marlow, as narrator, or we, as readers, have any certainty as to either the acts or the mental state of the actors? Even in the case of the omniscient narrator, we are always sceptical of his reliability, and even when we trust the narrative strands, how can we trust that we are given *all* the relevant details? To pursue these questions, we must also inquire into the *ontological trauma* in the novel: in which ways are the very existence and identity of the actors formulated within the context of the narrative's events?

In these sections of the text dealing with Jim's trial, Conrad, like Wilde in *De Profundis*, explores the relationship between the law's insistence on epistemological certainty and the competing challenges to the identity of the subject giving testimony. Although the law insists on the "truth" from individuals, the juridical framework also allows legal counsel to suggest alternative versions of events, which often challenge that of the person on trial. A testifying witness can be invalidated either because he or she is truthfully unaware of the events or because he or she has lied and thereby committed perjury. There are, of course, cases where the witness tells the truth, yet seems incredible. In these cases, where counsel calls the credibility of the "truthful witness" into question, the witness's identity as a "good civil subject" is challenged as he or she is accused of being a liar or worse. In effect the law allows for no exception in its epistemological quest for truth, while allowing for multiple and often rather violent challenges to the ontological status of the accused or the witness giving testimony. There is, in essence, a significant gap between the authority with which the law insists on truth and the ability of the subject to access this knowledge.

This puts the testifying subject in an exceptional and precarious position. In Jim's case, although he goes to trial believing, for the most part, in his innocent weakness, counsel's constant accusations of cowardice lead to his ontologically traumatic crisis, which, in turn, leads to his decision that he is, in fact, an immoral and despicable person.

This, narrates Marlow, is the point from which Jim's psyche begins to devolve into a broken, self-effacing identity. Of crucial importance are the ways this literary narrative uncovers these sorts of gaps in legal procedure – the ways, if you will, representations of epistemological and ontological trauma in the novel foreground the law's inability to deal with the testifying individual in a manner that simultaneously pursues justice and protects the subject.

This ontological trauma is a variation of what I see as Brooks's theory of the testifying subject's exceptional position. Recall that, when the state requires an individual's testimony, according to Brooks, the forced act of testifying on the stand does violence to the accused, because it requires public performance, and thereby intensifies feelings of guilt in guilty and innocent alike (21–2). The accused is in the exceptional circumstance of having only limited knowledge of the facts, yet still required to discover the truth. This circumstance leads to a challenge to the ontological position of the testifying subject. Moreover, it allows for a situation where, because the facts are sufficiently fluid, a confession on the stand is always a possible outcome.

This problem, again, challenges the position of authenticity that is supposed to result from the act of truthful confession. Put more crudely, the truth should, at least for authenticity's sake, set you free. In Jim's case, in contrast, though he tells what is as near to the truth as he believes possible, he becomes convinced that he is neither sincere nor authentic. He becomes convinced that the act he committed without malice was, in fact, what the accusers said it was. He becomes convinced of the *mens rea* of his offence. His performance on the stand under cross-examination makes Jim trace and retrace the incident again and again, and he comes to believe that he is, indeed, a criminal. This becomes the turning point in his ontological trauma, which, in turn, prompts his devaluation as a civil subject. In an ironic twist resulting from his confession, Jim assumes the devalued identity suggested to him by legal counsel. Again, the alienation of Jim from his position as a "good civil subject" to that of a broken man immersed in shame all stems, Jim is convinced, from this fundamental trauma suffered by performing his testimony.

Through telling and retelling the story, Marlow's fragmented narration again mirrors the fragmented and broken consciousness of the civil subject giving testimony. The actual testimony Jim gives on the stand informs the metaphoric testimony Marlow relates to readers of his story. Readers, in this chain, then experience the epistemological trauma of being unable to ascertain the facts involved in the case in any reliable manner, while understanding the ontological trauma involved when the law challenges the subject position of the testifying individual. This, once more, draws on Felman's idea that "the trial, while it tries to put an end to trauma, inadvertently performs an acting out of it. Unknowingly, the trial thus repeats the trauma, re-enacts its structures" (5).

These structures, in turn, are catalogued in the legal archive. Jim's status as a man stripped of his sailing certificates is recorded. Although court transcripts *are* official records of this violence, they are archived deep within the confines of the legal bureaucracy, and are both difficult and costly to acquire. Judicial decisions, in contrast, are somewhat less inaccessible, although they choose to draw, or not to draw, from transcripts when they become part of the more obvious public record in a reporting series. In effect, both of these archival acts amount to devaluations through distancing of the violence associated with trial. In contrast, the polyphony of narrative that follows high-profile cases intensifies the significance of violence in these circumstances.

Wilde's *De Profundis* and Conrad's *Lord Jim* both took experiences with which the authors were intimately familiar, and narrated a version of judicial events that questioned the ways individuals give testimony. Although the circumstances are quite different in many respects, and although the most pertinent of these is Wilde's knowledge of his "criminality" versus Jim's struggle at defining his innocence, his lack of *mens rea*, there is still clear evidence of the inherent trauma in testimony that Brooks and Felman define. Wilde thinks himself morally above the legal morality that convicted him, although he knows that he falls within the *actus reus* and *mens rea* of the defined offence. Jim is not certain of any of these positions, and the extorted answers he gives end up both convicting him and convincing him of his moral and legal guilt. Aside from these differences, however, there is also the definite suspension of rights of the individual; the rule of law carries the day and justice is done, at least from the perspective of the culture that drives the legal proceedings.

Inasmuch as this is the case, it is also true that any kind of state-sponsored autonomy in these situations is equally fallacious. The accused is autonomous only as far as he, in Wilde's and Jim's cases, must answer to the morality of the culture that convicts him. The "facts" in each of these situations, although they are relied upon by the judiciary as the basis for justice and although they are never clear in either circumstance, are more malleable tools to convict than they are markers of authenticity or established truth. All these conflicts are painfully related, not so much in the transcripts or the decisions from which the literary narratives stem, but within the literary narratives themselves. As the literary subject grows more complex with the moderns' treatment of the interiority of subjectivity, so, too, does this practice critique the legal framework that asserts so adamantly its privileged position vis-à-vis the truthfulness of this literary interiority. The annals of fiction, in effect, provide a body of criticism about the legal archives, and especially the practice of archiving, which always, through simplification, diminishes the significance of the violence associated with forced sworn testimony.

Chapter Three

High Modernist Challenges to Legal Authority in Ford and Joyce

This chapter begins by comparing Oscar Wilde's and Joseph Conrad's stylistic markers to the style Ford Madox Ford uses in *The Good Soldier*. Building on his style of telling and retelling, I situate Ford's writing within his legal experience and within the work of Wai Chee Dimock, Peter Brooks, and Maria Aristodemou. I link Ford's court experiences to both the law and the media, and argue that the dialogues among these discourses inspired Ford's depiction of Edward Ashburnham. The traumas of ontology and epistemology drive Ford's work, while they reveal the ways the law manufactures *mens rea*. James Joyce figures in the second part of the chapter and in the culture of jurisprudence, legislation, literature, and the press. Defining the unique style of the "Circe" episode, we see that Joyce's legal experiences formed his understanding of its polyphony. Joyce emphasizes the law's double character as both an indigenous and colonial presence, and creates a parodic *roman à clef*, parodying colonial authority. In the context of Ann Ardis's theories of sexuality and Linda Hutcheon's theories of parody, I discuss Joyce's use of the law to revision Jewishness, nationalism, and sexuality. The polyphony in "Circe" undercuts the law's insistence on epistemological certainty and brings us further into the interiority of Bloom's mind, and, by default, his *mens rea*.

Ford Madox Ford and the Dialogue of Contempt: Challenges to Legal Authority

To begin my discussion of the connections between Wilde's and Conrad's legal writings and Ford's fictional representation of the English legal system, I look at the ways Ford's style both draws from and pushes forward some of the interiority we see in Wilde and Conrad. From this, I want to contextualize Ford's style within the applicable legal framework in which Ford found himself embroiled, and, finally, I want to take up his literary narrative in *The Good Soldier* to discuss the cultural dialogue between the law and literary production in Ford's work. Although the circumstances are decidedly different than Wilde's trial for gross indecency or Conrad's depiction of the proceedings of the colonial nautical assessors, Ford's experiences in civil court still underscore the relationship between trial and trauma. Ford's practice, from an early age, of seeking the love of underage women and then abandoning them exposed him to the inner workings of the English judicial system on more than one occasion. The effects stayed with him and contributed not only to the literary style he adopted, but also to his critique of English trial procedure, which provides yet another nexus between state-authorized trial and punishment and the inner confusion and distress associated with the act of giving oral testimony.

Many critics have likened Ford's style to cubist painting in that his work combines multiple, simultaneous, and sometimes competing perspectives. Although John Dowell, one of four main participants in *The Good Soldier*, narrates what he says is "the saddest story [he] has ever heard" (7), the reader struggles to figure out what has gone on among the characters. Dowell narrates the story repeatedly, with the goal of epistemological certainty in mind. He realizes, after his first writing, that he has much of it wrong, and goes through it all again, still looking for "knowledge of the facts."

In effect Dowell and the reader struggle side by side. Dowell's disconcerted effort to recollect the events in question privilege his quest for knowledge, for knowing not just *what* happened, but for discovering the psychological reasons behind the events. Thomas Moser notes: "[F]orms of the verb 'to know' occur seven times in the first paragraph alone of *The Good Soldier*. Indeed, as its *Concordance* reveals, forms of 'to know' occur 289 times in the text, far more frequently than any other verb, except, of course, for linking and auxiliary verbs; more frequently even than that work-horse of narrative, 'to say.' Moreover, the telling phrase, 'I don't know,' itself appears about fifty times, and other negations of 'know' some forty times more" (xx–xxi). Knowledge and its inaccessibility drive the text thematically, but it is the style of telling and retelling that is most pertinent to my discussion here. This style reflects the model of the proceedings of a trial, where each witness gives testimony and the judge or judge and jury make findings of fact.

In Dowell's narration he is both actor and judge. *The Good Soldier*, moreover, goes further into subject interiority, as Dowell tries to capture the inner workings not just of his mind, but of the minds of all the actors involved. In this role he acts as a narrator akin to both Marlow and Wilde. Marlow struggles to piece together the events that surround Jim and Jim's subjectivity, while Wilde searches to piece together his own subjectivity and make sense of the legal proceedings that have incarcerated him. Dowell, in effect, does both: he struggles with his own interiority, but also scrutinizes the other characters in the narrative. In the liberal legal tradition, this parallels ideas of the individual's *mens rea* once again, as we are drawn closer to both the character's intention and his position as a conscious violator of the law.

The very manner in which he addresses his audience reveals the self-reflexivity of a subject struggling to make sense of events while psychologically doubting his ability to do so. Dowell relates his angst at even attempting accuracy in his narration: "I don't know how it is best to put this thing down – whether it would be better to try and tell the story from the beginning, as if it were a story; or whether to tell it from this distance of time, as it reached me from the lips of Leonora or from those of Edward himself" (17). Aside from his troubled musings, Dowell's comments here also reveal the mediated nature of the story. He is, in a legal sense, reproducing hearsay for much of his narrative. That is, Dowell cannot corroborate much of what has been told to him, but he nonetheless tries his best to piece together the cogent strands of events as they are reported. Even his own recollections of the events come filtered through his broken psyche and his own admissions of the impenetrability of other's minds: "I know nothing – nothing in the world – of the hearts of men. I only know that I am alone – horribly alone. No hearthstone will ever again witness, for me, friendly intercourse. No smoking-room will ever be other than peopled with incalculable simulacra amidst smoke wreathes. Yet, in the name of God, what should I know if I don't know the life of the hearth and of the smoking-room, since my whole life has been passed in those places?" (11–12). This kind of self-doubt pervades Dowell's narration; it at once connects him to his audience and accentuates his unreliability. It also throws doubt on his intention as a potential criminal. He does not assert his authority over the narrated events; instead, he warns the reader of his inability to access truth. Perhaps it is no surprise, then, when Dowell first parenthetically mentions the legal proceedings that appear and reappear in the text, that he admits his ignorance of them, but for their second-hand reporting. The proceedings deal with Edward Ashburnham's sexual advances towards a stranger on a train, and although they are never fully explained in the text, they are foundational to the Fordian use of fragmentation and repetition in the narrative. "Of course, at that date, I had never heard of the Kilsyte case," discloses Dowell (59). This not having heard, of course, assumes his not having known. Again the lack of knowledge is the constant and commanding force behind Ford's fragmented style. It at once recalls the second-person epistolary style Wilde uses in *De Profudis* and the perspective of the outside observer, so prevalent in Marlow's narration and so essential to Conrad's formulation of the fragmented civil subject.

For Ford the legal system was a constant check on the morality of his sexual practices, his rights, and his individuality. Like Wilde, he found the legal system a constraint on what he thought should be his unfettered sexual liberty. Ford found himself the subject of court proceedings on five separate occasions, four stemming from his marriage to and abandonment of Elsie Martindale and the fifth declaring his bankruptcy.[1] There is a strange parallelism between Wilde's and Ford's legal entanglements, especially as it was the father of each of their lovers who undertook to protect the children to whom Wilde and Ford made their respective advances. I look closely at the first of these proceedings, not only because of its pertinence to the legal culture of the time, but also as it shows a striking similarity between the experiences of two of the most notable moderns of the age. Moreover, it further accentuates the law's focus on intention and autonomy, not just in criminal matters such as Wilde's, but also in civil procedures such as Ford's. First, however, I want to emphasize the importance of Ford's initial dealings with the court, specifically because this resulted in the only fully reported court record of any of the moderns I discuss.[2] By "reported" I mean judicial opinions sent to press, not media reporting. This distinction is crucial to understanding the importance that legal bodies attach to the various cases they decide. It is rare that everyday, run-of-the-mill cases see their way into a reporting series, as they neither change the law in any notable way nor set a precedent by which other cases are to be decided.[3] Ford, at age twenty, created a disturbance in legal precedent that warranted a full court report.[4] Justice North, who presided over the action, cited no statutory authority in his reasoning, instead relying on the common law tradition of precedent. His reasoning was inherently analogical, drawing from similar cases and forging new space to discuss the legal issues of wardship and contempt of court.

In re Martindale and *The Queen Who Flew*:
Conversations between the Law and the Press

The Chancery Division of the English courts tried the case and delivered its written judgment on 9 August 1894. The "facts," as they appear in that decision, are as follows. On 11 April 1894 Elsie Martindale, on her father's petition, was made a ward of the Court to protect her from Ford. On 1 June Elsie's father applied before Mr Justice North, in the Chancery Division, who made an order restraining all communication between the young lady and Ford. Five days later Ford was summoned before the court, where his case is heard *in camera* before Justice North. Ford produced an affidavit swearing that "he did not know, and had no reason to believe, that the young lady was a ward of the Court." The justice found this false, as Ford wrote a letter in reply to Martindale's letter of 18 March saying that Elsie had been made a ward of the Court. Martindale's claim, of course, was equally false, as this proceeding was not undertaken until 11 April. Ford's lawyer then made the surprise announcement that the couple was married on 17 May, in response to the impending restraining order. Justice North ordered an adjournment until the marriage certificate was produced. Ford looked "pink & white & limp" through these carnivalesque proceedings, having taken brandy beforehand (Saunders 1:82).

Justice North received the certificate, and was furious because the couple lied about their ages to the registrar: Ford was twenty and Elsie seventeen, although they claimed to be twenty-four and twenty-one, respectively. Nonetheless, the justice somehow recognized the marriage as legally valid. Ford left the court and published "A Poet's Love Affair" in the *Star*, a London evening newspaper, which treated the hearing as a farce. On 9 June Justice North opened the continuation of the hearing by saying the newspaper reports of his previous hearing were in contempt of court and that, if Ford divulged the *in camera* proceedings again, he would prosecute. He quashed the restraining order. He warned Ford that he could be prosecuted criminally for multiple malfeasances and that he was also open to prosecution for perjury, although, in the justice's opinion, the whole matter was better dropped. On 22 June Mr Martindale, refusing to admit defeat, tried to have Ford and the four papers that carried the story prosecuted for contempt. On 9 August Justice North delivered his judgment, stating that there was not an intentional contempt of court, but rather "vulgarity and bad taste" in reporting to the papers that which he had decided to hear in private.

Both the striking similarities and the serious differences between this and Wilde's case are worth elucidation. In both instances the court sided with the father of the child thought to be under attack by an immoral force – in both cases an author and poet. Where the child's father failed, in either case, to constrain the relations between his child and the suspect person, the court stood *in loco parentis* to impose a legally sanctioned paternalism over the moral paternalism already imposed by the father. This paternal relationship, again, raises the question of morality, autonomy, and the law. It emphasizes the historical links between cultural moralism and the rule of law, and shows again the state's willingness to suspend the rights of individuals when it sees fit. In both instances the result was literally paternal.

The differences between their trials, perhaps, speak even more particularly to the cultural morality driving the decisions. In Wilde's case, the court immediately, upon settling the libel suit, arrested and imprisoned him. He was treated as a serious threat to English society, as reflected by his sentence and punishment. In Ford's case, Justice North noted: "[T]the false statements made by [Ford] to the registrar did not affect the validity of the marriage, although [Ford] had laid himself open to criminal proceedings under more than one head, I stayed the operation of the [restraining] order. At the same time I declined to entertain any application to commit him for contempt, considering that if he was to suffer imprisonment it had better be by the sentence of a criminal Court in the proceedings to which he had exposed himself" (199). The criminal court never saw Ford's face. The state did not initiate proceedings into any of the possible causes of action, regardless of Ford's clear disrespect for the court, his fraudulent misrepresentations, and his failure to follow court directions. In Wilde's circumstances, he refused, counter to the suggestions of many of his friends and advisors, to hide on the Continent. His conciliatory behaviour reflected his acknowledgment of the rule of law, and his punishment reflected his position as a perceived threat to that rule. That is to say, the culture that passed the Act that made "gross indecency" such a serious offence created and archived a legal precedent of inherent homophobia, which, in turn, ruined Wilde's career, reputation, and health. Ford, in contrast, was never subjected to any criminal proceedings, even by Justice North, who had full authority to find him in contempt of court not only for releasing the *in camera* proceedings to the papers, but also for treating the entire affair with mockery.

Justice North's reasoning for not making Ford liable for contempt occupied the remainder of the judgment, and it is this reasoning that made *In re Martindale* an important legal precedent. The justice catalogued the instances in which court proceedings historically were kept private – cases that went against the general rule of ensuring public hearings. Restraining the publication of private letters,[5] the disclosure of matters communicated to a solicitor,[6] and the infringement of a patent[7] were all cited as instances where *in camera* proceedings were warranted. To this he added the protection of wards and lunatics to ensure "that the lunatic or ward may not be prejudiced," and then stated: "I cannot conceive a clearer contempt of Court than that a party concerned, or any person, should proceed forthwith to make known to the world the very matter which the Court had deliberately, in the exercise of its discretion, decided ought not to be published" (201). Here Justice North made an analogical remark, and the logical conclusion we might have expected him to draw was that Ford, like the justice's example, fell into this hypothetical situation. Instead he took a rhetorical turn, differentiating the case at bar, and remarking: "In the present case I do not believe that any contempt of Court was *intended*, though this in itself would be no excuse for contempt actually committed. The paragraph inserted in the *Star* was so inserted without premeditation, having been concocted and handed in by [Ford] and his friend *Perris* merely as an advertisement for the former" (201, emphasis added). Justice North's reasoning unconvincingly eviscerated, then emphasized, the importance of individual intention within the action of contempt. While finding that intention need not be shown in a contempt proceeding, he nonetheless decided to speak about the details of how the paragraph was published and the intentions behind those actions.

The logical inconsistency was only made worse when he continued: "[The paragraph's] vulgarity and bad taste are enhanced by the references to the Court of Chancery, and the sitting being in private – references obviously made, without any regard to the credit of the lady, for the purpose of attracting the attention of readers to a puff which, if not thus embellished, would have been passed by unnoticed" (201). Again it seems clear that there was contempt of court, at least in the mind of Justice North, although he continued to negotiate what the intention of the paragraph might have been, if it were not to defy the court's decision to proceed *in camera*. A further comment makes this even clearer: "The paragraph, so far as I have quoted it above, was intended to appear to be and would be understood as a concise statement of what took place in my private room; and the disclosure is held out as an inducement to the public to read the whole paragraph" (201). Here Justice North showed that, although the paragraph was clearly contempt, it was intended more as an advertising puff to introduce Ford's literary publications. The sensationalism of the first sentences detailing the court proceedings was meant, for North, only to hook the reader, not to debase the proceedings themselves.

I have suspended my revealing of the paragraph's exact phrasing until now, as I wanted to underscore the issue of intention and to flesh out the strange ways in which Justice North drew his conclusions first. From his comments, it seems terribly clear that he relied greatly on intention, although he largely ignored this line of reasoning. The decision of *In re Martindale* reproduces the paragraph in question from the *Star*, which came under the headline, "A poet's love affair":

A Chancery Court Chapter of "The Queen who Flew."

In Chancery Court Nr. 2 to-day a rarely romantic story was unrolled before Mr. Justice *North*, who sat in private to hear the action innocently set down as "*In re* Martindale." The action was one to forbid a Miss *Martindale*, said to be a ward in Chancery, from perpetrating matrimony, the danger arising in connexion with the attentions of a young poet and novelist who has already achieved a certain measure of distinction by "The Shifting of the Fire" and other of his books – to wit, Mr. Ford H. Madox *Hueffer*, of *Brook Green W.* Mr. *Hueffer* is well known as son of the late Dr. Hueffer, the once champion of *Wagner* in *England* and musical critic of the *Times*, and as grandson of Mr. *Ford Madox Brown*. His intimate connection with the Pre-Raphaelite Brotherhood is also marked by the fact that his just-published novel, "The Queen who Flew" (significant title) is illustrated by Sir *Edward Burne-Jones*. The proceedings to-day might have been comparatively tame but for the fact that it turned out that there no longer was any Miss *Martindale* to protect. That lady became Mrs. *Madox Hueffer* some three weeks ago. The case stands adjourned for the present. (195)[8]

Max Saunders's biography of Ford includes most of this paragraph, with the introduction: "[Ford] persuaded Perris to let him write a paragraph for the *Star* about the hearing which he hoped would puff *The Queen who Flew*, published about a week before the wedding" (1:82–3). His comments do not deal with the particulars of the court proceedings and make no critical claims as to Ford's behaviour. He only summarizes that "[Justice North] said that the newspaper reports of his previous hearing were contempt of court, and that if it happened again he would prosecute" (1:83). Yet from the text of the judgment the outcome seems, until the final paragraphs, that Ford will be held in contempt and punished. Saunders's historical gloss on the proceedings makes them more anecdotal and quaint, rather than emphasizing Ford's serious flirtation with judicial censure. But perhaps this gloss reflects the very conclusions the justice made after writing for paragraphs about the seriousness of the offence of contempt of court, and how Ford's actions fell squarely within these common law circumstances.

In the end Justice North found: "I have already said, there was no contempt in announcing the fact that the ward had become the wife of [Ford]; the contempt was in purporting to give the public information, though meagre, of what the Judge had decided ought not to be disclosed, by determining to hear the case in private and excluding the public" (202). Justice North ensured that the issue here, not to be confused with the truth of the statements, was that the statements were made at all, in direct opposition to the direction the court took to hear the proceedings. After all this, it seems that Justice North had decided firmly in favour of finding contempt, but again he took a strange rhetorical turn, stating: "I do not regard the contempt as a serious one; at the same time, it was not mitigated by the line of defence which counsel adopted, the boldness of which cannot be appreciated by any one who did not hear it" (202).[9] He then commended Ford for having his counsel offer an apology if Ford did in fact commit contempt, as, according to counsel, this was completely unintentional (198, 202). Again, intentionality seems to have driven the justice's findings, although he still made no admission as to this possibility. Instead, he found that both the *Star* and Ford should pay the costs of the actions brought against them, and that "justice will be met" by this course of action.

The difficulty of accepting the "justice" of the situation does not lie with the commensurability of crime and punishment, but with Justice North's reasoning. In each instance of the discussion about contempt, the justice found that Ford was, in fact, guilty, though he did not intend to commit the act. Even his barrister's apology rested upon Ford's "unintentional" act. The justice recognized this apology, although he was under no obligation to do so, and this, too, speaks to his perhaps subconscious recognition of the underlying intentionality of the apology. Justice North fashioned his judgment to slap the wrists of Ford and his accomplices, and although the tone of his condemnation was stern, it nonetheless confirmed, rather than reproached, the newspaper headlines. The "poet's love affair," as the *Star* put it in this case, seems to have transcended the power of the court. The justice's paternalism collapsed not just in validating Ford's marriage, but also in finding his act of contempt a fanciful flight of heterosexual youth.

All of this reasoning accentuates the need for courts to base justice on commensurability – on some softer formulation of *lex talionis*. Wai Chee Dimock's theory states that commensurability is only one of many competing values active in a judge's reasons, but, because of the epistemological violence inherent in "fact finding" and "truth determination," this produces the illusion that it is the *only* one.[10] If we consider this proposition, Justice North's decision makes more sense. Intentionality drove the reasons for his judgment, but that was one of the competing values not recognized by the rigidity of the law. The justice, instead of attempting to change the law of contempt by including intention as a prerequisite, used vague and terse language that vitiated what might otherwise have been a rhadamanthine decision. Finding the need to adhere to commensurability, the justice instead created confusion in his reasons and in the law of contempt. Denying intention in this case was bizarre, especially as this was the only mitigating factor in the justice's punishment of Ford. Yet it is the metanarrative of justice and its innate commensurability that made this the only available judicial measure.

The result of these much-publicized proceedings was that Ford paid nominal court fees and was never tried criminally. His reputation, far from being injured, instead flourished under this rigorous treatment by the tabloids. The puffs, which served as copy for four English newspapers, connected Ford's matrimonial legal dealings with his literary endeavours, and the resulting contempt action wrote back. Justice North produced a judgment that both archived the matter and set a precedent regarding contempt applications, thus connecting newspaper publications and *in camera* proceedings at the locus of the law.

This dialogue continued, as, fifteen years later, Ford became embroiled in legal proceedings again. Although this was not a reported judgment, it still merits comment, especially as it marked the start of over three years of legal proceedings that – at least chronologically, if not causally – led to the publication of *The Good Soldier*. In 1909, after fifteen years of marriage to Elsie Martindale, Ford left her for Violet Hunt. Ironically, Elsie, the woman he had fought so hard to wed in 1894, became the very person who brought him back under the authority of the English civil courts in 1910.

Humiliated by her husband's desertion, Elsie sued Ford in divorce court for a decree of restitution of conjugal rights and for spousal maintenance in the amount of £3 per week. (Saunders 1:305). The order granted stipulated that Ford was to return to Elsie within fourteen days. Ford was appalled, not merely because of the order, but because of the implication that he had not been paying Elsie support previously, when, in fact, he had. The matter, this time public, found audiences in the *Star*, the *Globe*, the *Evening News*, the *Standard*, and the *Daily News* (Saunders 1:566). Incensed by the publicity and his paternalistic treatment by the courts, Ford simply refused to obey both parts of the order, opting to pay the money not through the court but through an intermediary. This time the court was not so lenient. Ford's hubris, coupled with his thrasonical disdain for the law, landed him in Brixton Gaol for ten days for this particular contemptuous action. According to Saunders, Violet Hunt reported that Ford, with an author's thirst for empirical background, "longed for the experience" of prison; if true, this again confirms Ford's predilection for refusing to take seriously the law he so disparaged.

Only a year later, on 5 September 1911, Ford, now residing in Germany, married Violet Hunt, according to a letter he sent to his friend Pinker (Saunders 1:348). When the *Daily Mirror* published the story, Elsie Martindale sued the paper and won damages and a printed apology, as Ford was never legally divorced from her (Mizener 218–20). Ford, in his usual pusillanimous fashion, avoided confronting the subject, and instead continued to pretend his previous marriage would simply go away. But the persistence of both Ford and Hunt in asserting that they were indeed married had even greater consequences the following year. Hunt, enmeshed in her own legal battles with her sisters concerning what was purported to be Hunt's mismanaging of their mother's affairs, finished the mother's novel, *The Governess*, and had it published. Ford aided in this endeavour, and he also wrote the introduction. The *Throne* published a publicity piece about the book, and borrowed the following from Ford's introduction: "The forthcoming book is a romance ... by Mrs. Alfred Hunt, one of the popular novelists of the old days and her daughter, Miss Violet Hunt (now Mrs. Ford Madox Hueffer), one of the successful of the modern school" (Mizener 220).

To this report Elsie took great offence and, some months later, on 7 February 1913, she sued Illustrated Journals Ltd., owners of the *Throne*, in the King's Bench Division before Mr Justice Avory. Saunders, taking his information from the *Times*, outlines Elsie's cause of action: "The nub of Elsie's case was that she had been exposed to 'ridicule, hatred and contempt' by Violet's use of the name 'Hueffer,' which either implied that Elsie 'was not his wife at all or that she was divorced' – this in the days when divorce was still considered scandalous" (1:373). Both Ford and Hunt were clearly upset and confounded by the verdict in Elsie's favour, which assessed damages at £300 and costs of the action of approximately £700. The sum of these awards was enough to financially ruin the *Throne*.

According to newspaper accounts in the *Daily Herald* and the *Daily Mirror*, Hunt's lawyer, Mr Storry Deans, after hearing the verdict, began the following dialogue with Justice Avory:

> I am instructed by a lady whose name has been mentioned with great frequency – Miss Violet Hunt – to state that she wishes it to be known that she believes herself to be Mrs Ford Maddox [*sic*] Hueffer, and intends so to call herself.
>
> Justice Avory: I have nothing to do with this belief or any of her beliefs.
>
> Storry Deans: Statements have been directed against –
>
> Justice Avory: I cannot hear you any further ... I decline to allow this Court to be made a medium of advertisement. (Saunders 1:373)

The bitter irony here, of course, is that these words were transcribed into the dailies and served not only as advertisement but as fuel for scandal. Ford, who longed for social acceptance and, more, for literary prestige, loathed the smears these proceedings placed on his reputation. Even Hunt, who displayed far more pluck throughout the affair than he, shortly after the trial gave up any possibility of using Ford's previous patronymic handle. René Byles, friend to both Hunt and Ford and owner of the *Throne*, also acted on the assumption that both Hunt and Ford would testify to the validity of their marriage. This absence sealed the *Throne*'s fate and cemented Ford's reputation as an outsider in British society.

The reasons for, and results of, Hunt's and Ford's absences are integrally connected to Ford's work immediately following these events. Arthur Mizener speculates that it was Ford's cowardice that prevented his testimony: "With his passionate hatred of scenes, Ford probably could not have stood the experience of testifying in the *Throne* suit. Even on social occasions he would go badly to pieces under determined cross-examination; one vigorous old lady who cornered him about Violet Hunt reported that 'He behaved like a jelly at bay'" (230). The anecdote further underscores Ford's inability to understand the trial process as anything but an ordeal. But although he was still sensitive to the ordeal of 1894 and all its scandal, his absence at court did not forestall the media from portraying him as lacking decorum and social fibre, on which Ford so prided himself.

Saunders speaks about the affair as a "considerable scandal," and summarizes the equally considerable effects it had, not just upon the participants, but also upon the culture of the time:

> Both Ford and Hunt were well-known literary figures, at a time when intellectuals were pressing for divorce reform. Hunt was also a society suffragette. The *Throne* case put them at the centre of the Edwardian debates about sexuality, divorce, morality, and censorship, debates which the *English Review* had helped to air, and which were sharpened by other high-profile cases, such as that of Arthur Balfour, who lived with a woman he wasn't married to, and Edward VII himself, who not only had mistresses, but was involved in scandals and testified in divorce cases. Hunt evidently saw their case as a *cause célèbre* comparable to what she called "the Holman Hunt imbroglio," or Lord Russell's trial for bigamy. (1:374)

Here, Saunders emphasizes that this kind of scandal was neither unique nor limited by the English class structure. At the same time, the indignity of the situation was not alleviated for Hunt and Ford, either by the copious press coverage or by the growing rancour directed at them in society circles. The result was a more bohemian lifestyle for both, as their social circles reflected only that cross-section of English society interested in – or, at least, not disgusted by – their matrimonial fiasco.

But the effects of the scandal reached beyond the personal lives of the authors and into their literary production. Saunders notes the general change in Ford's methods of characterization, and posits a causal connection between this effect and the *Throne* debacle:

> Before the *Throne* case Ford's protagonists are misunderstood and betrayed idealists; the motives of their idealism is [*sic*] questioned, and they undergo their neurasthenic episodes, but they are fundamentally sound. Afterwards the soundness is itself called into question; Ashburnham, Dowell, Tietjens, Henry Marin, are all more problematic figures, living a lie, deceiving their friends, and often deceiving themselves. Ford spent the rest of his life grappling with the doubts raised by the *Throne* case. (1:375–6)

The doubts raised by the *Throne* case are just as much about the justice system as about human infallibility. The turn in the soundness of the minds of the characters that Saunders notes turns, itself, on Ford's inability to see a just result from the judicial system he so scorned and avoided. In 1894, when he was found in contempt of court, his soft punishment clearly indicated to him a judicial system he could challenge. Even his ten-day sentence for his second action of contempt, when refusing to return to his wife, did little to transform Ford's opinions of judicial thinking, as he immediately proceeded to act as he had before his incarceration, identifying Hunt as his wife and ignoring Elsie's entitlements. Ironically, however, it was the *Throne* case, in which Ford took no direct part, that gave him the most anxiety. It caused the collapse of the small publication and damaged his friend Byles financially; it created ripples in literary circles that hurt his reputation, sales, and financial security.[11] These repeated altercations with the law shaped not only the trial descriptions in *The Good Soldier* (the novel he started the month following the case), but also the fragmented narrative that undermines any attempts at epistemological certainty in the text.

The four main protagonists in *The Good Soldier* are Edward and Leonora Ashburnham, Florence Dowell, and the narrator himself, John Dowell. The text immediately presents a problem with identification, as Ford's narrator shifts between first and last names with colloquial familiarity. We have to assume that "Mrs Dowell" is, in fact, the same "Florence" referred to a page earlier, that "Leonora" is also an "Ashburnham," and that "Edward" and "John" are not brothers but only acquaintances. These confusions stem also, at least partially, from Ford's euphonic choice of names, the lilting minuet-like propriety inherent in the syllables – balanced, yet syncopated. The names seem to flow into one another, yet they contain as much British *politesse* as each character deserves, given their upper-class constructions. Although I believe Ford's patronymic confusions were intentional, as much of the book concerns itself with making some sense of the muddle these four participants weave, they are just as much an indicator of the narrator's own challenge in telling the story with some accuracy – in making the confusing situation lucid through intractable, repetitive narration.

The obsession here with knowledge and its unavailability is yet another instance of epistemological trauma in a British modern text. Again the question of certainty in John Dowell, as narrator, or in ourselves, as interpreters, that results from the perseverating narration leaves us hanging, experiencing ambiguity as to the acts and the mental states of the actors. As in the discussions of Wilde and Conrad, the epistemological problem is linked inextricably to the ontological trauma depicted in the writing. By examining the ways that the very existence and identity of the actors become formulated within the context of the narrative's legal events, one can tie Ford's literary work to the legal culture of the age that he, in some small ways, helped shape.

My presentation of some inroads into these questions focuses on a trial in the novel that is, as far as I can tell, wholly neglected in scholarly writing about the book. Less prominent than the main narrative line, but of crucial importance to the representation of epistemological and ontological trauma in the novel, Edward's sexual assault trial, which occurred many years before the two couples met, is described by John Dowell through multiple analeptic shifts in narration. In these sections of the text, Ford explores, in ways similar to both Wilde and Conrad, the relationship between the law's insistence on epistemological certainty and the competing challenges to the identity of the subject who is giving testimony. That is to say, although the representation of the law in the text insists on the so-called truth from Edward Ashburnham, the juridical framework again allows legal counsel to suggest alternative versions of events and of character that challenge the subject position of Edward on trial. Again we must recall that a testifying witness can be invalidated either as truthfully unaware of the events or because of incredible or simply false testimony. Just as in Jim's fictional case in *Lord Jim* or Ford's real-life trial in *In re Martindale*, there exists, in *The Good Soldier*, the situation where the witness tells the truth, yet seems incredible. In all three cases, counsel vitiates the credibility of the "truthful witness" and challenges her or his identity as a "good civil subject." Again in Edward's case, the law allows for no exception in its epistemological quest for truth, while allowing for multiple and often rather violent challenges to Edward's ontological status. Recall the significant gap between the authority with which the law insists on epistemological certainty and the ability of the subject to uncover this knowledge as we search for truth alongside the narrator, John Dowell. This puts the testifying subject in an exceptional and precarious position. In Edward's case, although Dowell tells us that he goes to trial believing his innocence, counsel's constant accusations of lechery lead to an ontologically traumatic crisis that, in turn, persuades him that he is, in fact, an immoral and despicable person. This, narrates Dowell, is the point from which Edward's marriage devolves.

The remainder of my discussion of *The Good Soldier* focuses on the ways this literary narrative uncovers these sorts of gaps in legal procedure – the ways, if you will, representations of epistemological and ontological trauma in the novel highlight the law's inability to deal with the testifying individual in a manner that both pursues justice and protects the testifying subject.

The Kilsyte Case: Fiction Feeding on the Law

In the first telling of Edward's trial, John Dowell only alludes to Edward's having been mixed up in "the Kilsyte case" long before the narrative's main events. We are told, about one-third through the main narrative, that Edward had committed an act of impropriety with a girl, although we are never given sufficient details to discern exactly what happened. Instead, Dowell recounts: "Of course, at that date, I had never heard of the Kilsyte case. Edward had, you know, kissed a servant girl in a railway train and it was only the grace of God, the prompt functioning of the communication cord and the ready sympathy of what I believe you call the Hampshire bench, that kept the poor devil out of Winchester Gaol for years and years. I never heard of that case until the final stages of Leonora's revelations" (59). Dowell's knowledge of the case, he reports, comes second-hand from Leonora. Not only that, but his musings about it point to some disruption between law and justice. From Dowell's perspective, intermediaries such as the grace of God and a sympathetic judiciary led to Edward's evading a penal term. His tone is sympathetic, yet there is also a hint that Edward has committed some odious act. The narrator's ellipses, however, leave unrevealed until later the gravity of Edward's crime.

Dowell continues his musings: "Supposing he had spent his seven years in Winchester Gaol or whatever it is that inscrutable and blind justice allots to you for following your natural but ill-timed inclinations – there would have arrived a stage when nodding gossips on the Kursaal terrace would have said 'Poor fellow,' thinking of his ruined career" (60). Here, Dowell restates more powerfully his belief that justice was biased in Edward's favour, and, just as significantly, that the publicity he suffered as a result of the trial was nowhere near as damaging as it could have been. "Justice," in this case, is neither blind nor inscrutable; the common image of justice blindfolded, weighing the facts of the case without prejudice or partiality, is not working here, as Dowell relates clearly that Edward received some form of preferential treatment. Recalling Wilde's ruin at his public trials and Ford's humiliation at the hands of the press, this element of the plot is crucial to interpreting Edward's interiority and the battle of conscience that rages within him. Edward was not "damaged" as badly as he could have been by the press, according to Dowell, but the latter instances of this reminiscence accelerate, at each telling, the associated guilt Edward feels because of his actions.

The law and its ability to censure the reputation of an individual convicted, or even accused, of a crime become another point of intersection between the literary narrative Ford weaves and the judicial framework of the modernist period, although his examination of legal proceedings points equally to the effects of these ontological challenges on the interiority of the civil subject. Public humiliation becomes the vehicle by which the law exacerbates the psychological violence imposed upon the subject at trial, but it is not just the re-enacting of the facts at trial that scar; it is equally the remembrances of this public spectacle that continue to re-enact, continue to scar, continue to punish.

While Dowell's remembrances alert the reader to the potential harm Edward faced and the harm he might have committed, Dowell also, at this point in his tale, emphasizes Edward's having escaped the procedure relatively unscathed. It is not until two-thirds through the narrative that Dowell returns to Edward's trial and details that the "girl" was nineteen, pretty, a nursemaid, and crying. Edward, also unhappy at that time in his life, thought it "natural" to comfort her, as "that was his job in life," and equally "natural" to "pool their sorrows" (175). He talked to her, found that her love interest had been seen walking about with another, moved to her side of the carriage, put his arm around her waist, and kissed her (175). Dowell, assuming omniscience while recounting her reaction, offers yet another appraisal of the effects on Edward:

> All her life, by her mother, by other girls, by school-teachers, by the whole tradition of her class she had been warned against gentlemen. She was being kissed by a gentleman. She screamed, tore herself away; sprang up and pulled a communication cord.
>
> Edward came fairly well out of the affair in the public estimation; but it did him, mentally, a good deal of harm. (175–6)

Part of the strangeness in this passage comes from Dowell's light treatment of the sexual assault. He tells it with a rather comic flourish, thereby attempting to diminish the seriousness of the action and to persuade the reader of Edward's virtuousness. In the first quoted paragraph, he relates the details of class and gender that make a female servant suspicious of the sexual advances of an upper-class male. Rather than accentuating any fiduciary obligation Edward should feel towards the young woman, Dowell, instead, makes a joke of it. He relates the comic pause as a temporal one, in which she, while being kissed, realizes she is being kissed. Surely, at nineteen, and regardless of her sexual experience, it would not take so long to process this act of sexual aggression or to consider the class of the individual perpetrating the action. Clearly the joke centres on the inversion of class character-istics, on a kind of Wildean satire of the upper classes. Yet this kind of light treatment of the situation also speaks to a kind of myth propaga-tion and to the law as a vehicle for its dispersion. That is to say, the language defining what is "natural" is seeded within the story of the sexual assault, and it is this myth the court played to when it refused to censure Edward's conduct.

The myth that Edward was only doing what a man naturally does when he sees a distraught, young, lower-class girl is something that Maria Aristodemou, in *Law and Literature: Journeys from Her to Eternity*, would view as propagated from within the law. Aristodemou stresses the inherent paternalism in legal representations and, especially, repre-sentations of sexuality. The central ideological framework of *Law and Literature* compares the mythic origins of the law to similar mythic ori-gins in literature. In Ford's narrative, there is a double character to Dow-ell's description of Edward's behaviour, which at once plays into the pre-established myths of female wantonness and the sexual availability of the lower class, while also challenging us by inflecting the comic with a lecherous morbidity that makes Edward suspect. It is Dowell's feigned friendship with Edward that drives the depictions, and it is this drawing attention to the motivation of Edward's actions that leaves space for challenges to these female and class myths. In essence, this creates space for new myths – narratives that not only challenge exist-ing ideologies of law, but also empower individuals to challenge their treatment under the law.

Another issue arises at this point in Dowell's narration, one more central to my argument about testimony and trauma. Dowell reiterates the two key points of public humiliation and mental harm. He under-plays the former and revalues the latter. That is, in his original musings, he thought Edward had escaped any lasting punitive measures. Now, he admits, the legal proceedings did Edward "mentally, a good deal of harm." He still thinks, however, that, in public circles, Edward was lit-tle beleaguered. This progression, from a position of relatively little to a great deal of harm, marks one of the many problems with Dowell's narration, conducted as it is in a style that asserts, questions, and reasserts. Although I have already mentioned the self-reflexive style Dowell incorporates into his narration, I want to emphasize the connection between this kind of telling and the mental harm Dowell suggests. It is true that Edward's trauma is not Dowell's, but it is equally true that Dowell's narration mimics Edward's reported statements of confusion about coming to grips with both the Kilsyte case and his own failed marriage and friendships. For Edward, the mental strain of trial was as much a catalyst for his ontological downfall as his reliance on cultural myth – his confidence in his position in the modern culture in which he holds a position of privilege. In this way, Ford presents a character torn by his conscience, although not much maligned by the law or the press. But the progression continues, and Dowell narrates once more.

When the fragmented narrative returns to this incident for the final time, Dowell changes his emphasis again and considers that the trial did, in fact, do Edward "a great deal of harm" (183). Dowell's legal soliloquy begins as follows:

> I have said that the Kilsyte case eased the immediate tension for [Edward] and Leonora. It let him see that she was capable of loyalty to him; it gave her her chance to show that she believed in him. She accepted without question, his statement that, in kissing the girl he wasn't trying to do more than administer fatherly comfort to a weeping child. And, indeed, his own world – including the magistrates – took that view of the case. Whatever people say, one's world can be perfectly charitable at times … But, again, as I have said, it did Edward a great deal of harm. (182–3)

Two-thirds into the narrative, Dowell begins by connecting Edward and Leonora. As Ford devotes almost the entire book to having Dowell explain the dissolution of this marriage alongside Dowell's own, this connection is somewhat strange. Yet these descriptions go more to establishing Edward's place in the community, his privilege, his exception from moral reproach. Dowell underlines Leonora's support, and mentions that the magistrates took a similar opinion in the case. The reference to both his wife and the magistrates as being of "his own world" solidifies Edward's social position, and creates an association of family among these participants in Edward's life. Further, it underlines the hypocrisy of keeping up appearances for the sake of appearing as a member of the upper class.

Returning to the idea of the rule of law, it seems difficult to conceptualize a theory that might circumscribe these particular facts. It surely would be a perverse reading of the case to predict Edward's absolution due to his social standing, although this was clearly the outcome. Again, if we attempt to understand the law in its liberal ideological framework, the rule of law fails in this instance. Ford's depictions further enrich the ideas of rights and autonomy, as Edward's standing trumps the rights of the assaulted woman. As Dowell reports the details, we cannot be certain of the exact rhetorical outcome of the judicial decision – that is, we have access neither to the written judgment nor to the justice's oral reasoning. Yet it seems telling that Dowell chooses the word "charitable" to describe both Leonora's and the magistrates' treatment of the criminal action.

Compounding this representation of injustice is Dowell's omission of the young woman's voice. Although there was surely occasion for her testimony, there is absolutely no mention of her even appearing at the courts. Her silencing again focuses attention on Edward, leaving only speculation as to any dialogue that might have occurred between the complainant and the other actors on the legal stage, including the lawyers, the magistrates, and the press. Dowell explains, over and over, the significance of the case to Edward and its effects on his personal life as well as his reputation, but he never canvasses the complainant's aftermath. We can assume that the young woman's surname was Kilsyte, as Dowell refers to the case by that name, but we are never even given her first name. Further, although she is repeatedly called a "girl" in the narrative, we are afforded her age: nineteen. Although the suffrage movement was well under way in England when Ford wrote *The Good Soldier*, it was not until 1918 that British women over age thirty gained the right to vote. It is arguable whether Dowell's paternalism therefore speaks more to his own bias or to that of the age, but in either case, there seems no doubt that the unnamed girl is treated as an autonomous citizen with equal rights.[12] In one sense, this might mean that she could have been given even stronger protection under the law, as she could have been made a ward of the court, in much the same manner as Elsie Martindale. In effect, the inherent cultural paternalism of the time might have influenced the court to act *in loco parentis*. Yet the outcome of the case, just as in the Martindale affair, seems to have favoured the rights of the accused man over the unprotected woman, at least as Dowell represents her. The legal reasoning protects the established social and class positions of the accused, rather than the rights of bodily security of the complainant.

Sadly, the narrative is shocking not for its novelty, but because these representations of sexual assault are insidious components of legal precedent in England and, more so, because they undermine the very basis of the liberal legal structure on which the system is based. In this situation, the harm principle is subject to class and social standing: some individuals are simply "more equal" under the law. Again this might not vitiate the common conception of justice of the time, as it is entirely possible that the prevailing attitudes of the day would not have thought it worth ruining the reputation of a lecherous, yet well-established, gentleman. Oxymoron aside, it seems the most plausible reading of the text, as there is little evidence of another interpretation. Edward did not deserve light treatment under the letter of the law, but he received it anyway. If justice was served, it was not a liberal democratic justice, but a conception of justice not related to equality of individuals.

Arguably the most interesting turn in the narrative comes in its next paragraph. Dowell reports Edward's mental processes as he testifies, and engages an ideological framework very similar to ideas put forth by Felman and Brooks about testimony, performance, and trauma on the stand:

> That, at least, was his view of it. He assured me that, before that case came on and was wrangled about by counsel with all the sorts of dirty-mindedness that counsel in that sort of case can impute, he had not had the least idea that he was capable of being unfaithful to Leonora. But, in the midst of that tumult – he says that it came suddenly into his head whilst he was in the witness box – in the midst of those august ceremonies of the law there came suddenly into his mind the recollection of the softness of the girl's body as he had pressed her to him. And, from that moment, that girl appeared desirable to him – and Leonora completely unattractive. (183)

Here Dowell turns from Leonora's affirmed loyalty to Edward's unfaithfulness. The previous paragraph confirms that the trauma of Edward's trial allowed Leonora to show her support for her spouse, at least on the surface. In this narrative excerpt, we see Edward's ontological change occurring exactly at the moment of his cross-examination. Although we are conditioned to be somewhat sceptical of Dowell's accuracy, as this is now the third time in the text that he has revisited the trial, we see that, each time, he is taking a more detailed and self-reflexive look at the events and the participants. Each time, the tone of the narration becomes graver, starting as a harmless frolic and terminating as a serious psychological trauma for all involved.

Edward's pronounced change in perspective comes at the hands of counsel, who searches for epistemological certainty – for the underlying and undeniable "facts" of the case. These facts, while they must prove Edward's actions and while he does not deny them, must also prove his mental state to make the action criminal. In Dowell's final telling of the trial, his narration shifts focus from Edward's actions to Edward's mental state. Again the elements of a criminal offence, the *actus reus* and the *mens rea*, are crucial here, and they drive Dowell's narrative. Dowell claims that Edward's actions were indeed without malice – although, again, we might question this, as Dowell's position as an unreliable narrator complicates things, especially as we are aware of Dowell's knowledge that Edward was involved in a protracted affair with Dowell's spouse, Florence. But we are presented only with Dowell's recollection of the trial, and it is this that underlines the fragmentation of Edward's subject position. Dowell reports that it was being "wrangled about" by the legal counsel for the plaintiff that caused an alteration in Edward's understanding of his identity. The "dirty-minded suggestions" of the lawyers, though not described in detail, notes Dowell, are traumatic affronts to Edward's conception of "self." In essence, counsel's barrage of accusatory questions does Edward "a great deal of harm" and causes him ontological trauma.

Although we might have manufactured some sympathy for Edward through Dowell's seemingly compassionate "saddest story," and although it is not impossible to feel that Edward was terribly unhappy in his marriage and its deceptions, it is still difficult, if not impossible, to understand his actions on the train as a desperate man's sad longing for love. The lecherousness of it all still undergirds the structure of Edward's motivations in our eyes and, at this point in the narrative, he, too, begins to come to this understanding. He is self-deceived or, at the very least, wilfully blind to his mental state until this time in his trial, but the suggestions of counsel bring home the gravity of his offence, and he is at once thrown into introspective awakening.

This epiphany comes during "those august ceremonies of the law," a description that, through its somewhat sardonic depiction of the legal process, puts the legal setting in ironized low relief, diminishes its authority in the situation, and draws the reader into the internal state of Edward's being. The effect makes us question the authenticity of Edward's thoughts, however, in a much different way than Brooks describes the authenticity of confession. Unlike Wilde, who refused to confess to either the *actus reus* or *mens rea* of his offences, but similar to Jim, Edward admits his actions but not the *mens rea*; the operable and necessary verbal confession in law never comes. Edward allows the court to take the view of the events as "innocent" in as much as he is ashamed to admit his desire or denies this mental state out of cowardly self-preservation.

Regardless of the motivation behind his denial, however, we, unlike the court, know his desire but can still only speculate as to his *mens rea*. The image of Edward's "pressing" the "softness of the girl's body" to him emphasizes not only the force he used to procure his kiss, but also the visceral recollection of the physical act. In this way, Edward begins to eroticize the act – to concentrate on its libidinous aspects. In Dowell's last words on the subject, he delves further into Edward's paternalistic sexual predation:

> He began to indulge in day-dreams in which he approached the nurse-maid more tactfully and carried the matter much further. Occasionally he thought of other women in terms of wary courtship – or, perhaps, it would be more exact to say that he thought of them in terms of tactful comforting, ending in absorption. That was his own view of the case. He saw himself as the victim of the law. I don't mean to say that he saw himself as a kind of Dreyfus. The law, practically, was quite kind to him. It stated that in its view Captain Ashburnham had been misled by an ill-placed desire to comfort a member of the opposite sex and it fined him five shillings for his want of tact, or of knowledge of the world. But Edward maintained that it had put ideas into his head. (183–4)

From these latest recollections, if not before, it appears clear that Edward now considers his actions on the train a discovery of a part of his character that changes his self-image. It also marks the precipitous swing towards a more highly sexualized and rapacious being, a character who now dreams of seducing women in vulnerable situations. The tactic of "tactful comforting," followed by "absorption," reveals Edward's willingness to deceive, to take advantage, and to engage in adulterous behaviour. The passive construction of the sentence that details Edward's having been misled separates his "desire" from his mental processes. It works to externalize desire, to make it almost an unnatural force directing Edward, rather than an internal impulse. The penultimate sentence in the paragraph also makes it clear that he was fined for "his want of tact, or of knowledge of the world," not for sexual assault.

Yet there is, again, a strange and surprising mid-paragraph-turn in this piece of Dowell's narration. If we are to believe his account, after all of these revelations, epiphanies, dreams, and passions, Edward believes it was he who was the victim at the hands of the law. Although Dowell distinguishes Edward's case from the Dreyfus affair, and acknowledges that, at least in its formal punitive treatment of him, the law was indeed charitable,[13] he still recounts that it was the legal proceedings that caused this change in his ontological status.

This ontological trauma again evokes Brooks's idea of the violence in public testimony, although it troubles the theory's authenticity constituent. Brooks's theory, again, is that the forced act of testifying on the stand does violence to the accused because it requires public performance, and thereby manufactures guilt in the guilty and the innocent alike (21–2). Recalling also the descriptions of legal testimony and its effects in *De Profundis* and *Lord Jim*, the situation in *The Good Soldier* is markedly different. Wilde knew his guilt, but did not confess. In *De Profundis* he wrote about his need to conform, and the lasting effects of trial included his doubting his previous conviction in the blamelessness of his homosexuality. He was pushed towards perspectives of moral conformity. In Conrad's work, Jim goes to trial confused, and his experience on the stand only heightens this confusion, ending with the lasting scars of shame that haunt him through his career and personal life. In both instances the violence happens in the courtroom, but the ontological shifts come only later.

In *The Good Soldier*, however, the effects of testimony appear to be immediate. Although one might argue, quite convincingly, that the shift merely uncovers the repressed sexual lechery that Edward harbours, it is nonetheless also possible that Edward's change is a direct effect of being "wrangled about by counsel with all the sorts of dirty-mindedness that counsel in that sort of case can impute" (183). If we take Dowell's storytelling at face value, Edward is, in fact, a victim. Yet, because we have a fairly accurate description of the actions of the parties in the lawsuit, this conclusion is simply implausible. Add to this Dowell's detached and suspect narrative style, and we are left believing that Edward did suffer trauma on the stand, that he did undergo an ontological crisis, but that neither of these results was in any manner unwarranted.

When Brooks argues, "Western literature has made the confessional mode a crucial kind of self-expression that is supposed to bear a special stamp of sincerity and authenticity and to bear special witness to the truth of the individual personality" (18), we recognize the problems of cases such as Edward's. Edward becomes convinced that he is neither sincere nor authentic, that the act he originally thought he committed without malice was, in fact, what the "dirty-minded" accusers said it was. He becomes convinced of the *mens rea* of his offence. His performance on the stand under cross-examination makes Edward retrace the incident again and again, and he comes to believe that the sensation of the nineteen-year-old girl's body pressed against him was the turning point in his ontological trauma, which, in turn, prompted his devaluation as a civil subject, although this happens only during the trial. In an ironic twist, Edward assumes the identity suggested to him by legal counsel. Again the alienation of Edward from his position as a "good civil subject" to his becoming a man broken and immersed in infidelity stems, Edward is convinced, from this fundamental trauma suffered by performing his testimony.

Through writing and rewriting the story, Dowell's fragmented and multilevelled consciousness again mirrors the fragmented and broken consciousness of the civil subject giving testimony. The actual testimony Edward gives on the stand informs the metaphoric testimony Dowell relates to the reader. The reader, in this chain, then experiences the epistemological trauma of being unable to ascertain the facts surrounding the case with perfect certainty, while also understanding the ontological trauma involved when the law challenges the subject position of the testifying individual. Felman's comment that the pattern of a trial, "while it tries to put an end to trauma, inadvertently performs an acting out of it," again rings true (5). Since the trial becomes a repetition of trauma and a re-enactment of structures, we understand that Dowell's is just another re-enactment of this trauma, and that we, as readers, participate in this re-enactment each time we read the book.

Testimony, as one of the ligatures between law and literature, is troubled by the possibility that it lacks authenticity. Again, although Brooks's comments deal with confession as a subset of testimony, I believe that what he says of confession is equally true of testimony in general. The words "I confess" might be absent orally, but they are implicit in swearing that the testimony given is "the whole truth and nothing but the truth." In so doing, testifying subjects encounter a situation where they confess what they believe is the truth, although they might or might not believe they have access to that truth. The legal imperative of truth telling and the trauma of having only a limited understanding of the facts thus become a problem in law; simultaneously, they become a fertile point of inquiry for literary study. The failure of the law to provide a means to its ultimate end of justice rests, at least in part, upon its inability to abandon the notion of the truth as always plain, if not always simple. The inaccessibility of the notion of truth in novels such as *The Good Soldier* demonstrates the possibility for a reworking of liberal ideas of legal procedure.

Bloom in Nighttown: The Legal Face of Violence in *Ulysses*

To state that Joyce's *Ulysses* is stylistically complex is rather obvious, but to link this style to the historical context of the time and especially to the legal processes at play provides insight, I think, into both trial and trauma. Wilde, Conrad, and Ford all employ stylistic rhetorical strategies that move further and further along the path connecting literary narrative to internal ontological questions. Yet we see an exponentially large gap between the kinds of interiority that even Ford uses in his telling and retelling and what we find once we delve into the depths of *Ulysses*, a work so utterly large that it contains worlds. Nevertheless, there is value in laying down some basic, yet crucial, premises about the ways that style works in *Ulysses*, even if these premises are doomed to incompleteness.

Joyce opted to remove the Odyssean section titles from Shakespeare and Company's book-length publication of *Ulysses* in 1922, although his correspondence on the original serial publication of the first few chapters in the *Little Review* in 1918 carried the Homeric titles. These parallels, much to Joyce's delight, proved irresistible to scholars, and the practice of such reference is, and has always been, commonplace in Joyce studies. The convention of following the Homeric text, which labels the first three sections the Telemachiad, the middle twelve as the Odyssey proper, and the final three as the Nostos, is also commonplace. These are, perhaps, the most obvious intertexts, but they also function as a structuring mechanism for the narrative. By adhering to the Homeric conventions, Joyce creates a palimpsest that layers classical narrative under the pedestrian modern Irish epic.

These choices in structuring the text do little, however, to curtail the narrative polyphony of voices. One such voice is the law. This, in turn, is intrinsically tied to imperialist and nationalist narratives; in effect, the politics surrounding Ireland and, for that matter, Irish exiles serves as a springboard to conversations about law. For Joyce the rule of law was a troubling subject, especially as he perceived this legal authoritative voice as so distinctly English. The styles of *Ulysses* challenge that authoritative voice, moving away from singularity to polyphony. While this polyphony pervades most of the text of *Ulysses*, many critics rightly call attention to the division between the first fourteen episodes and the style in "Circe." Wolfgang Streit, for example, argues that "Circe" is polyphonic, but not in the manner of the parade of styles in "Oxen of the Sun": "After fourteen largely narrative episodes, 'Circe' reverts to the dramatic style of *Exiles*, and – like the drama – stages erotic conversations in order to contrast various attitudes towards the power over life" (95). Recalling Catherine MacKinnon's comments that jurisprudence is a theory of the relation between law and life, we see here Streit's contention as a codicil to this, suggesting that this relation is complex – that power over life comes in many forms. Law is implicated in this polyphony, not merely as one of the many voices, but as a polyphonic entity itself. This makes the liberal democratic principle of the rule of law somewhat more porous than a purely theoretical form of positivism, and points to problems, again, with accessing the legal imperative of truth.

The style in "Circe," therefore, is a revelation of the hidden polemics behind the printed law. The law, in this way, represents itself in the dramatic style of "Circe." Andrew Gibson makes a similar point as he explains the differences that "Circe" exhibits in contrast to most of the other episodes: "Like 'Wandering Rocks,' but unlike all the other later chapters in *Ulysses*, 'Circe' does not chiefly rework English (or Anglo-Irish) discourses that are traceable to printed texts. Fragments of a variety of the kind of discourses I've described appear in the chapter. But it is not primarily a treatment of them. For 'Circe' is a chapter of voices" (183). Gibson ties history and politics to the aesthetics of *Ulysses*, and he enumerates the discourses of colonialism and something he calls "hysterical nationalism." "Circe," according to Gibson, does not simply "treat" the printed texts that inscribe these discourses, as, one might argue, occurs in "Oxen of the Sun," but instead creates a multi-directional dialogue, loosely similar to that of the courtroom and its participants.

But even the participants themselves often do not behave in the ways we expect. Gibson speaks of a kind of ventriloquist act, where figures shed their colloquial speech and adopt the dominating discourse of the law: "People in 'Circe' often don't sound like themselves. The most improbable figures may suddenly drop into an uncharacteristically English-sounding idiom: the jurors, for example" (188). In this example, and in yet another kind of inversion, the enumerated list of jurors drop their Irish idiomatic speech and answer in strange unison, "Most of us thought as much" (595). The response comes after "The Nameless One," described as a jury member with a "featureless face," joins the attack on Bloom. Here, in front of Bloom and the open, carnivalesque court, the ideal juror acts in the most inappropriate ways, giving odds and employing the rhetoric of horse racing in his comparisons with Bloom. Yet all of this, again, rests at least in part on the difference between the portrayal of the voices in dramatic conversation and the satiric, or at least parodic, styles of "Oxen of the Sun."

The importance of this, especially to a critic such as Robert Spoo, cannot be overstated. Spoo describes two binaries dividing literature from drama and history from life: "To literature-and-history Joyce opposed drama-and-life in his 1900 address: 'Drama,' he claimed, 'has to do with the underlying laws first, in all their nakedness and divine severity, and only secondarily with the motley agents who bear them out'" (151). Spoo justifies reading Joyce from Joyce's perspective. Yet it is Spoo's addendum of literature and history that allows him to make his authorial claim to this dichotomy. That is to say, Joyce's sensitivity to drama as dealing with "underlying laws" goes to a kind of Derridian reading of "truth." If the truth is inaccessible, we move closer to a different idea of truth the more we approach its polyphonic nature. History, Spoo would argue, because it privileges the voice of the historian, lacks this kind of truth. Spoo furthers this argument: "Reader response to 'Oxen' and 'Circe' has tended to agree with Joyce's prejudicial ranking in 'Drama and Life' (drama-and-life above literature-and-history), for many critics have judged that in 'Circe' Joyce returned to his proper haven of psychological expressiveness and evocation of essential, if disturbing, truths, after an increasingly questionable odyssey of style that culminates, or dead-ends, in 'Oxen'" (153). Although I do not wish to broach the topic of what the proper haven of psychological expressiveness might be, I do take issue with reading the truths expressed in the dialogues as "essential, if disturbing." Here, Spoo's argument seems somewhat counterintuitive. How Joyce's style, which quite clearly uses drama as its vehicle in this episode, reveals the essential nature of truths is terribly unclear, unless we return to the idea that, essentially, there is no essential. There is no crystalline truth in the polyphonic style of "Circe"; rather, the style questions the very ability of psychological deliberations to yield even a belief in truth. The actors, especially Bloom, end up with little by way of conventional justice through their carnival-court. Instead, the drama unfolds akin to Bloom's psychomachia.

This is not to say that the episode should be read as occurring entirely within Bloom's psyche, but simply that it could be. Other critics have suggested the hallucinogenic characteristics of the episode; I merely want to add that much of the style of "Circe" concerns itself with exploring the interiority of Bloom's mind. In effect, the episode devotes itself largely to revealing Bloom's *mens rea*, or lack of it, in the commission of the alleged offences. There are as many accusers as there are excuses in this episode, and Bloom's style of denial often begs the question of his guilt. "Gentlemen of the jury," begins Bloom at one instance, "let me explain. A pure mare's nest. I am a man misunderstood. I am being made a scapegoat of. I am a respectable married man, without a stain on my character" (583). He then gives some details of his life to prove these claims. Yet his speech equivocates. He acknowledges the complexity of the situation, and then proposes a simple solution. But his inability to halt his reasoning belies his argument that this is all a simple misunderstanding. The style, instead, becomes a kind of inverted confession, pleading with the gallery to think of him as one of their own. The style is as one pleads or beseeches, not as one argues. The style makes Bloom seem a man found out, and divests him of his claims to innocence. Before pursuing this matter further, I want to contextualize the style of "Circe" in the historical moment from which it sprang, in order to establish a foundation for examining the trial and its traumatic challenges to both the epistemology and ontology of the narrated trial proceedings.

If the dramatic style Joyce uses in "Circe" challenges the first fourteen episodes through its polyphony and narrative indirection, Joyce is going beyond even the most internalized kind of indirect interior monologue as he implicates everyone and everything possible in this circus of sexual, national, and colonial shame. Nevertheless, the framework that holds these spinning tops of narrative together is the law. Joyce was no stranger to the intricacies of trial procedure, as he both followed and participated in legal cultural events. He had much sympathy for Wilde, not only on nationalist grounds, but also because of the violence he saw inherent in Britain's courts, as Joseph Valente makes clear: "Bloom's trials in 'Circe' take the notorious trials of Oscar Wilde as a background context for parodying the evidentiary procedures and declamatory rhetoric of the British courtroom, showing them to be little more than a legitimating mask of ideological violence, the vehicles whereby the received stereotypes of patriarchal and imperialistic discourse become the stuff of apparently rational judgement" (245). Valente's ideas frame nicely the relations at play in Joyce's most legalistic episode. Wilde's ghost walks the streets of nighttown, where Bloom and Stephen meet. Although Wilde's trials concluded over a quarter-century before the publication of "Circe," British consciousness was much affected by Wilde's media scandal and its accompanying challenges to decorum and sexuality. Wilde was vilified and tortured in the trial process and the press, to be sure, yet the massive news coverage afforded to the event opened British consciousness to alternative sexuality. Although the initial reaction, real to many and feigned by others, was revulsion, Wilde's trials were, regardless, a way of initiating and "normalizing" a nonheterosexual sexuality. Many critics, such as Marvin Taylor, trace the history of the construction of "homosexuality" to Wilde. Although sex between men was nothing new, Wilde's publicity helped beget a national awareness of what, until the 1890s, had dared not speak its name, simply because it hadn't one.[14]

Anti-Semitism, British Colonialism, and Nationalist Ireland

Although sexuality and its treatment by the law are two of the most prominent features of the "Circe" episode, I want to examine the ways the cultural context of this episode is enriched by what I conceive as a triangulation of Englishness, Irishness, and Jewishness. Joyce made Bloom Jewish as a foil to Irish nationalism and Bloom's accusers predominantly Irish as a foil to the English colonial courts. He also made the English courts intolerant. That is to say, the representation of English patriarchy through law recognizes neither the Jewish nor the Irish identity, but seeks, instead, to assimilate those individuals willing to conform and to punish and discard those unwilling to do so; we have already seen this in the jurors, whose language shifts to conform to the state-imposed legal apparatus. To begin, I investigate the relationship between Jewishness and the fictional representation of the law in "Circe."

Bloom's position as a Jew in Dublin is more complex than simply subjection to racist sentiment held towards Jews in nationalist Ireland. A kind of ideological bigotry, so clearly focused on homosexuality with Wilde, was rife in the judiciary and its treatment of Jews. Ira Nadel details England's anti-Semitic consciousness at the turn of the twentieth century in a most notable figure: Sir Frederick Falkiner, the Recorder. Nadel remarks on Falkiner's having made numerous and continual "racist remarks in his sentencings," for which he was forced to apologize. He then relates Falkiner's relapse into unadulterated and unabashed anti-Semitism: "[I]n 1902 [Falkiner] resorted to new slanders: to a Jew guilty of breaking windows in Dublin, he charged 'You are a specimen of your race and nation that cause [*sic*] you to be hunted out of every country'" (59). Nadel then compares this historical figure to the episode in "Circe": "At the trial of Leopold Bloom in 'Circe,' Sir Frederick, in a mockery of Moses, the lawgiver, sentences Bloom, telling the court that he will 'rid Dublin of this odious pest'" (59). Scorned by the Irish as an outsider and a threat to Irish nationalism, persecuted by the Anglo-Irish imperial court system as a scourge to humanity, the Jew in Ireland occupied a tormented position.

But the force of law was not only directed against Jewish identity. The English imperial project was also seeking to transform the Irish consciousness, and of this Joyce was particularly wary. Gibson gives extensive treatment to the colonial aspects of English domination in Ireland and Joyce's retaliatory rhetoric. His chapter on "Circe" details the ways Joyce creates a double voice as it satirizes the language of Imperial England and simultaneously recognizes its authority. As I have noted, characters at once acknowledge and emulate the Anglicized idioms in efforts to attain standing and authority in the system, but they often slip back, consciously and unconsciously, into Irish idioms that challenge the language of the colonizer. But the ideological imperialism takes on a concreteness far beyond lexical or rhetorical representation.

Britain's military presence in Dublin was, for Joyce, a physical manifestation of colonial violence. Gibson describes how "the British presence in Dublin's 'nighttown' encloses the chapter. That the soldiers are in 'nighttown' at all is significant. In the first few years of the century, Maud Gonne and others had been protesting about Irish girls consorting with 'enemy soldiers' (often as prostitutes)" (184). Soldiers, according to Gibson, not only threaten the Irish identity; they also represent a threat to Irish girls. In yet another kind of inversion, we see rhetoric similar to that of the Contagious Diseases Act played out as against the English colonial presence. The soldiers, both for their repressive and violent nature and for their dubious sexual practices, were linked to Irish political problems. The same rhetoric employed to malign English women in sexual service to English soldiers now shifts blame towards the English soldiers who procure Irish sexual partners. "But 'Circe,' argues Gibson, "is primarily concerned not with a military or political but with a cultural English presence barely noted by critics" (185). Yet it is not merely the militarism that frightens us in "Circe," but its connection to the authorized violence of the state and the cultural framework in which it operates.

Myriad kinds of power are at play in this theoretical framework; the law is, again, fundamental. Gibson attaches law to the power politics of Freemasonry rhetoric in "Circe": "'Circe' repeatedly emphasizes the connections between Freemasonry and power, privilege, affluence, status, and influence (especially legal influence)," he argues (190). Joyce plays with this idea in what seems a parodic representation of Wilde, drinking champagne wearing a "blue Masonic badge in his buttonhole" (574). Bloom later gives hand signals that represent inclusion in the secret society, in what seems an effort, again, also to prove his inclusion in the legal system that views him as the Other. For the law and Freemasonry seem interrelated to Bloom, as he perceives both as mysterious brotherhoods. Belonging, for Bloom, becomes his only means of circumventing his legal persecution. He concentrates more on proving his place in British society than on pursuing some kind of justice. Bloom's is the rhetoric of the desperate man, searching for Freemasonry footholds, or any other form of inclusion, to persuade the colonial court to have leniency.

Before analysing the episode's trial scene, I want to explain two further historical influences on Joyce's textual production. The first deals with the murder of his colleague; the second outlines Joyce's particular personal collisions with the law. Richard Ellmann describes the effects on Joyce of the murder of Francis Sheehy Skeffington, who had published Joyce's "The Day of the Rabblement" in 1901. On 24 April 1916, during the Easter Rising, Skeffington "was arrested while trying to keep the Dublin poor from looting." The British officer who arrested him had him shot without trial. Although the officer was later found guilty of murder, he was judged insane. He offered Skeffington's widow indemnity, but, against the advice of George Bernard Shaw, she refused (Ellmann 399). Joyce followed these events with much interest and dismay. The colonial presence and its amenability to state-sanctioned violence were taking a new turn. The military was now judge, jury, and executioner, and the law forgave such injustices in ways that drove Joyce to fits of anger.

Two years after the Easter Rising, Joyce found himself involved in judicial proceedings of a different sort. Although they were much less significant than murder, Joyce was nonetheless enraged by what he considered the injustice he suffered at the hands of the law. On 29 April 1918, Joyce opened his first production of *The Importance of Being Earnest* at the Theater zu den Kaufleuten, in Zurich (Norburn 82). Making a significant connection between himself and oppressed Irish writers, and during the applause at the performance's close, Joyce called out "Hurrah for Ireland! Poor Wilde was Irish and so am I" (Ellmann 426). Joyce and his colleague, Claud Sykes, had collaborated to produce English-language plays in Zurich, where they were conspicuously absent. Sykes was to direct while Joyce was to manage the business affairs (Ellmann 423). The company, called the English Players, employed Henry Carr as its Algernon Moncrieff. The relations between Joyce and Carr were less than amicable, and they fought two days after the opening of the play. Carr felt underpaid and, further, wanted money for a costume allowance; Joyce gave Carr twenty tickets to sell, for which Carr returned money for only twelve. The dispute ended in a shouting match in which Carr, quoted by Joyce, exclaimed, "You're a cad. You've cheated me and pocketed the proceeds. You're a swindler. If you don't get out, I'll throw you down stairs. Next time I catch you outside I'll wring your neck." Ellmann notes that Joyce thought these "monstrous injuries inflicted on his honour," especially as they were shouted at the British consulate (Ellmann 427).[15] Two days later, Joyce attended the offices of Konrad Bloch and initiated two actions against Carr: for money owing on the tickets and for libel. Carr counterclaimed for what he thought his fair share of the company's profits or, in the alternative, an elevated acting fee from what originally had been agreed, plus his costume expenses.

Ellmann argues that "Joyce had always been litigious and saw the incident as another example of his war with authority, represented on this occasion by a British consular official" (428). Perhaps this contributed to, or more likely drove, Joyce's lawsuits, especially as the claim for money owing on the tickets amounted to approximately $5 in 1918, or $65 in contemporary terms. After a failed settlement conference at Joyce's request on 13 May, and after a postponement of the trial on 8 July due to his iritis, Joyce finally got his day in court on 15 October. Vindicated by the court's findings, Joyce was awarded the full 25 francs he claimed as proceeds for the ticket sales, and Carr's countersuit for acting fees and costume expenses was dismissed (Norburn 82–4). To this, the court added 39 francs in costs and 60 francs for Joyce's expenses, bringing the grand total to something like $325 in current currency (Ellmann 445). This must have further fuelled Joyce's litigiousness, as he proceeded with his libel suit against the advice of many of his cooler-headed advisors. Perhaps Joyce felt that, on this small scale, he was correcting the wrongs of British Imperial power, so brutally suffered by those like Wilde only twenty-three years earlier. Yet Joyce, like Wilde, refused to contemplate the consequences of a trial for libel and the implications it ultimately would have for all parties involved. Joyce was ideologically blind to the institutionally sanctioned violence that the court might commit upon its litigants.

On 11 February 1919, two months after Joyce's poor initial hearing, the trial proceeded. Bloch had repeatedly urged Joyce to withdraw his action, yet Joyce chose to ignore the advice of his counsel. Not until the trial was under way and Joyce could see the inevitability of his defeat did he instruct his lawyer to abandon the action (Ellmann 452). Like Wilde, Joyce waited until it was too late. Driven by his sense of natural justice, Joyce was blind to the evidentiary needs of the liberal democratic judiciary.[16] From the initial hearing of the matter, Joyce knew it would be his word against Carr's. Yet he proceeded on the assumption that his story would be more convincing, that he was indeed publicly libelled by Carr's statements, and that the court, realizing these facts would, just as in the case of the tickets, find in his favour and vindicate his reputation. When Joyce finally realized how badly the case was going, he instructed Bloch to withdraw; Bloch did so, arguing that the usual indemnification due to defendants in such cases be waived, as Carr both caused the quarrel and prolonged the proceedings. These arguments held little, if any, sway, and the judge ordered Joyce to pay costs of 59 francs and damages of 129 francs (Ellmann 452). Joyce refused, and the court had no alternative than the remedy of distraint. Sometime after Joyce's return from Locarno in mid-May, an officer of the court appeared at his residence to seize whatever goods might make up the sum owed. Told the furnishings were rented, the official proposed taking first Joyce's books and then his typewriter. Arguing necessity in both cases, as an author and as one with eye trouble, Joyce managed to deter seizure. Instead, the officer asked to see the money Joyce had on his person and relieved him of half of it (Ellman 457).[17]

Parody, History, and the Idea of Justice

Joyce's trials played out, in parodic microcosm, those of Queensberry and Wilde, not only because the libel suits ended by punishing the initiators, but also because the press and publicity took over once the judicial proceedings were finished. Joyce wanted to publicize both his shoddy treatment and that of his English Players at the hands of the British consulate, which was now supporting Carr and causing difficulties for Joyce's play company. Grossly inflating the value of the stakes to 10,000 francs, Joyce reported his financial plight and the circumstances surrounding it to influential friends in Dublin, publisher friends in New York, the British Foreign Office in London, and the Irish-American mission in Paris (Ellmann 456). This eventually led to large amounts of money being sent to Joyce from various sources, some anonymous. Unlike Wilde, Joyce used his fall from English grace to create a media scandal in his support. Using his connections and charisma, Joyce managed to quell what he saw as an attack on Irishness and on dramatic licence. This was, of course, a comparatively easy task when contrasted with Wilde's circumstances. Wilde's charm, class, social status, and even connections could not suppress the raging antihomosexual morality at the heart of English society and its judiciary. Although Joyce escaped this kind of ruin, his dealings with the courts made him acutely aware of their impact on the ontology of the individual, which he details in his trial in "Circe."

In *Ulysses* Joyce depicts Bloom as a compromised civil subject. Throughout his wanderings, we realize his ignominy towards his impure thoughts and position as a cuckold, his precarious position as an alienated Jew in nationalistic Ireland, and his abhorrence of, and anxiety about, sanctioned violence. Each of these contributes to, and interacts with, Bloom's psyche as he undergoes his trial in "Circe." Nighttown becomes the courtroom in which sex, nationalism, and violence all interact. Through bringing together these challenges to Bloom's ontological status at the locus of the law, Joyce both criticizes and reworks traditional thinking about legal procedure and its treatment of the civil subject in ways that emphasize the connection of culture to law. The civil subject is at once inundated by the law (internalizing its authority) and creating the law (interacting with the external juridical systems to influence the progression of jurisprudence). More than Wilde, Conrad, or Ford, Joyce writes with an understanding of the law as culture.

The style of Joyce's prose in "Circe" is connected to the work this episode performs on the reader. Ann L. Ardis argues that Joyce's contemporaries worked to hide the sexual, and especially the homosocial, aspects of *Ulysses* by praising his style. "Pound adopts the same strategy," notes Ardis, "praising Joyce for his 'clear hard prose' and his capacity to 'deal with subjective things' without succumbing to 'sloppiness' and 'softness'" (69). But this, she argues, is merely an attempt to mask Joyce's connections with Wilde and his treatment of the violence he suffered in and after the trial process. Because *Ulysses*, like *The Waste Land*, brought high modernist style to the forefront of literary discussions about texts, style was also a useful device, in Ardis's eyes, for hiding the inherent sexuality of the text's content. Yet, if this were true, it would be difficult to find reasons the book was banned. If Joyce's contemporaries were trying to prevent this, they clearly failed. Rather than merely asserting the style in *Ulysses*, and especially "Circe," to be intrinsically subjective, Ardis convincingly argues for the connection of style to judicial violence.

If we use Ardis as a point of departure, our next queries should investigate the purpose and effects of connecting legal style to juridical violence in this way. For critics such as Joseph Valente, for instance, there is a natural correlation between Joyce's use of humour and the inner workings of the trial process. For Valente, "Joyce does not link the juridical and the comical so much as juxtapose them as a way of demystifying the principle of humor already at work as a structural possibility of the solemnity of the law. He also remarks as much in the 'Circe' trial" (248). Valente argues that using the style of dramatic dialogue allows for an in-between space where the messages of "Circe" are neither purely humorous nor purely authoritarian. When J.J. O'Molloy pulls on his barrister's wig and stuffgown to prepare for his duties as Bloom's defence counsel, he speaks in "a voice of pained protest" and declares, "We are not in a beargarden nor at an Oxford rag nor is this a travesty of justice. My client is an infant, a poor foreign immigrant who started scratch as a stowaway and is now trying to turn an honest penny" (Joyce 558–9). Valente sees this as Joyce's way of vitiating binary thinking, at once asserting clichéd legal rhetoric while undercutting it with humour. He argues: "Why doesn't [O'Molloy] declare 'This is a travesty of justice'? Unless in the textual unconscious of 'Circe,' where the repressive reign of logical binarism collapses, O'Molloy inevitably speaks both the conventional sacredness of the law and its underlying impropriety to itself" (248). The law's impropriety to itself, as Valente puts it, is, in a sense, the self-reflexive dialogue among judges, lawyers, and legal combatants. But if each of the participants plays a role in the making of law, then the law is not merely authoritarian, but also vulnerable to shifts in meaning.

It is the internal operation of parody, within the law and its language, that makes the trial in "Circe" both comical and self-reflexive, argues Valente. Parody, he says, is at once improper yet natural to judicial proceedings: "If judicial procedures are never supposed to fall into mere parodies of themselves, travesties, and yet the law is parodistic at its core, in the manner I have outlined, then travesty, improper self-parody, is strangely interior to these procedures, an improper constituent of their being" (248–9). For Valente, speaking of travesties of justice is as natural to the language of the law as is the actual pursuit of justice. But if we take his argument to heart, we can take the idea of justice no more seriously than we can the idea of legal rhetoric staged to challenge the idea. That is to say, even clichéd legal language, like that used by O'Molloy, is useful in troubling the most sacred ideas the law holds dear, or at least in troubling our conviction that we might access these scared ideas. For Valente, as for Joyce, justice is a slippery endeavour.

To this point in his explanation, Valente's observations are sound and well argued. Yet his ultimate conclusions about the relevance of parody to conceptions of jurisprudence seem rather contorted in some ways. He proceeds as follows:

> Joyce's representation of a trial like Bloom's, which is to say his parody of a trial like Wilde's, would seem to suggest that liberal jurisprudence rests not on a fixed set of oppressive values but on the repressive dissimulation of the relativity of all values. Such an ideological formation, being inherently defensive, is tremendously vulnerable to comic parody at one level. But because the truth of parody is also the hidden truth of jurisprudence, because the repressive dissimulation of relativity is itself based on that relativity and so can take any and all forms, can undergo the most protean self-revision, this ideological formation is at another level quite immune to comic parody. Liberal jurisprudence can always be parodied, but the parody must be done incessantly and on an always different footing. (249)

The jumps Valente makes are rather uncomplicated to conceive in a continuum, but his conclusion is one with which I struggle. As others have argued, Joyce's trial in "Circe" contains many elements of parody, which hearken back specifically to Wilde. Moreover, Joyce's portrayal of the "Circe" trial does indeed suggest that liberal jurisprudence rests on the relativity of values, not merely on a specific fixed set of repressive values, although the authority of the law often makes this seem otherwise. This point again underlines the importance of the rule of law as a responsive ideological framework, not just as a fixed idealistic oppressor. The law, in its seeking the ideal of "truth," necessarily commits a "dissimulation of the relativity of all values," as there is no doubt a real sense of authority in the pursuit of epistemological certainty. Cloaking the relativity of values at play privileges the authority of the law and the lawmaker. Again, Wilde's two trials for gross indecency illustrate the gross travesties of justice committed upon an individual at the hands of a paternalistic and anti-homosexual legal regime.

Valente's next assertion, that "the truth of parody is also the hidden truth of jurisprudence," is where the argument unstitches itself, if we hold any other than a purely defeatist opinion of the law. This unstitching begins with his assertion regarding a further proposition: that the law's representation of relativity is dissimulative. That there is really any relativity in the values of the law at all, he maintains, becomes immune to parody because it "can take any and all forms," and thus is always ready to conceal the internal values at play. In this ideological framework, the law dissimulates relative positions to assert its own and final position. These arguments are the basis for further ones about the failure of liberal jurisprudence to recognize an individual's rights in favour of either another individual or a group of individuals. This again points to the internal failure of jurisprudence, of which both Joyce and Valente seem equally aware. Yet, after saying that the law's dissimulation of the relativity of all values makes it on one level "immune to comic parody," Valente concludes that the law is always vulnerable to this parody, although the change in footing for these parodic affronts is crucial to countering the intrinsic dissimulation.

Valente then uses Linda Hutcheon's *A Theory of Parody* to further explain his position. He seeks to define the entire history of jurisprudence within an ideological framework of parody, for which he offers an equally broad treatment. Ironically, Hutcheon states, at the beginning of her exploration of parody, that "in [her] focus on twentieth-century art forms, [she] hope[s] to suggest that there are probably no transhistorical definitions of parody possible" (10). I suggest the same conclusion applies to liberal jurisprudence, if for no other reason than the shifting authority of the rule of law. Although Valente might convince us that the law uses dissimulation to obscure relativity, this is only possible when the culture of argument, which is equally important in legal procedure, fails. Liberal jurisprudence, like parody, has no transhistorical ideal, no tablets from which we can glean certain and precise access to right and wrong. Rather, it engages the dialogues of the culture it governs, and decides what is right and wrong under the law using precedent – the same use of precedent an artist employs in his or her parodic constructions. It seems strange to argue that the law is in any way immune from parody, as both law and parody are clearly dependent on the historical circumstances from which they come.

There is, perhaps, one further stipulation necessary in addressing Valente's theory of parody as it applies to law. Although he momentarily invokes Hutcheon's ideas of parody, he neglects any discussion of the ways parody is fundamentally linked to both irony and satire (61–8). If we talk about the trial in "Circe," we necessarily have to speak not only of the parody and the work it performs upon the reader's ideas of liberal jurisprudence, but also of the ways satire and irony inflect this discussion.

Returning to the example Valente cites, O'Molloy's declaration that "[t]his is not a travesty of justice" – especially in the context of his proving that Bloom's circumstances are indeed that which he negates – brings into the discussion the very reliability of legal language. We must wonder whether O'Molloy's comment is intentionally scornful, mocking, or respectful. Equally questionable is whether the comment, in context, actually poses or, rather, begs the question of Bloom's guilt. This kind of dialogue makes impossible the dissimulation that Valente suggests. That is to say, although even a majority might read "Circe" or, for that matter, the trials of Wilde with paternal and anti-homosexual sentiment attached to their interpretations, it is the very culture of argument in the courts that allows alternative positions to be voiced. We might be able to hear these voices only in hindsight, as the values that infuse themselves in the law, in fact, might strive to dissimulate competing values, yet there is always the ability to return, to go back to the transcripts, to the archival record of the dialogue that addressed the issues at trial. Parody, therefore, is but one way in which any serious critique of the law might proceed.[18] Satire, irony, and parody are not new to literature on law, but they are the ways Joyce, especially in "Circe," chose to inflect his understanding of liberal jurisprudence with the cultural critique with which we still regard the law, and that make his work so pertinent to contemporary jurisprudence.

More Sex on Trial: Bloom's Conduct and the Public Microscope

Style and context aside, "Circe," also raises issues of confession, violence, and intention. Felman's ideas of trial as traumatic incident and Brooks's notions of testimony as performance are again of the utmost importance. These concepts guide my own thinking about Bloom's ontology, and help clarify for me much of what occurs in "Circe." Recall that Felman looks at the ways legal procedure concurrently contains and exacerbates trauma. She posits that the trial itself searches for "legal conscious terminology" (5) to assuage somehow the traumatic events it ultimately judges. The law, in effect, tries to provide a language that might translate the events into a legally acceptable formula and thus contain the violence in the criminal act. Yet this procedure, argues Felman, fails in the end, as, instead of containing the trauma within a legal rhetoric, it creates a platform from which the traumatic events might find a wider audience.

For Felman, the failure of judicial procedure to contain the trauma amounts to the traumatic events actually "reclaiming the trial" (5). She calls this phenomenon "judicial blindness that unwittingly reflects and duplicates the constitutional blindness of culture and of consciousness toward the trauma." She then speaks about the trial as acting and re-enacting the trauma it seeks to end, and continues: "like society itself and despite its conscious frames and rational foundations, the law has quite conspicuously and remarkably its own structural (professional) unconscious" (5). Felman thus uncovers a paradox at the root of court-room procedure: the pursuit of truth and justice often sanctions harm against individuals by the *state* in the interest of curtailing further harm between the *individuals* at trial.

Brooks, as we have seen, connects trauma and the judicial process, but he does so by talking about the specific instances of forced confession. He also comments upon the links between the judicial process and the literary canon as a space for exploring the relations between the judicial process and guilt. Again, Brooks's key concept is that the true individual personality is somehow validated by the sincerity and authenticity of confession. And again, trial always pursues the confession of the accused, which necessarily challenges the "truth of the individual personality" or, as I interpret this, the individual's ontological status as a civil subject. In effect the confessional act *produces*, rather than *exposes*, the guilt of the accused.

"Circe" opens at "[t]he Mabbot street entrance of nighttown," and envisages for its readers the stuff opium dreams are made of: "red and green will-o'-the-wisps" dancing among the "danger signals" and "rows of flimsy houses with gaping doors" (561). This seems an unlikely place for a trial, but only a short distance down the street Stephen already encounters the strong arm of the law in Privates Carr and Compton, although at this juncture they merely foreshadow the violence to come. Those familiar with the court proceedings between Carr and Joyce note the added contemptuous detail when Carr first opens his mouth and emits a "volleyed fart" (563). Their British soldier's "redcoat" uniform is "bloodbright," their demeanour is boorish, and they are drunk. They intimidate everyone around them with their colonial authority, and use churlish threats to exercise it.

But the first act of physical aggression, surprisingly, does not come from them. Instead, it is shortly after Bloom's first appearance in the episode that we encounter physical manifestations of violence. We initially see Bloom stuffing his pockets with bread and chocolate (565). Next, he moves along Mabbot street and procures some meat from the butcher (566). These events are significant especially for the frenzied way in which Bloom carries them out. His somewhat languid saunter in other chapters is replaced at this juncture by a run. Shortly out of breath, he proclaims, "Stitch in my side. Why did I run?" (566). This bubbling-up of motion makes the first act of violence against Bloom that much more obvious. As he wades through the crowds that impede his progress, it is "a sinister figure" who is "injected with dark mercury" and who "regards [Bloom] with evil eye" who eventually "bars his path" (567–8). He engages the figure in an awkward dance to see him pass, but, failing in this, he pleads: "I beg" (568). He manages to blunder by, but only seconds later, as he slips back into his interior consciousness, Tommy Caffrey "runs full tilt against Bloom" (568). It is here that "he halts" (568). Again, the whirlwind of motion is constantly encumbered by people seeking his stillness. Stillness, in this instance, is very much a kind of confinement. Much as Wilde, Jim, and Edward Ashburnham all reflect on the helplessness of bearing witness to one's own actions, this episode in *Ulysses* also confirms the feeling of suspension, the limited and restrained space in which the trial proceeds. Bloom's confinement is a metaphorical dock.

One of the strangest and most disconcerting juxtapositions at this stage in the narrative is the appearance of Rudolph, Bloom's father. He accuses Bloom of drunken debauchery and notably inquires, "have you no soul?" (569). These are perhaps the slightest challenges to Bloom's character, but they initiate the chain of accusations that lead, finally, to the arrest and trial scenes in which Bloom suffers attacks on his ontological status as a good civil subject. It is no coincidence, in my view, that the first of the accusers is both literally and metaphorically paternal. To make this even clearer, Rudolph provides a lineage for Bloom back to Abraham and Jacob. The reminiscences begin; Rudolph speaks of all the ills Bloom committed as a boy; at the same time, the famous wardrobe changes begin. Again, these signify different historical moments in Bloom's life, but they also suggest the onset of the ontological crisis now just over the horizon.

The next accuser comes as "a handsome woman in Turkish costume" (570). A short blazon follows, the conclusion of which reveals she is Bloom's wife, Molly. Her exoticized Orientalist description makes her somewhat of a double figure: she is at once a fetishistic object of Bloom's desire and a cross chastiser of his "cold feet" (570). Her figure as a dominatrix, linked both to pain and suffering and to sexual pleasure, brings his pending trial more within the arena of sexuality and perceived perversion, and circumscribes Bloom further within his shrinking sphere of self-confidence. When she "fiercely slaps [her camel's] haunch" and "scold[s] him in Moorish," Bloom's proximity to this act of violence brings him to a position of submission as he then follows the camel's lead in what he thinks an awaiting game of leapfrog (570–1). Instead the exchange eventually ends with Molly disdainfully sauntering away, "humming the duet from Don Giovanni" (571). This signifies Bloom's position as a cuckold on at least two levels. First, the irony of Molly's walking away when she sings the duet, translated most literally as "there we will entwine our hands," clearly excludes Bloom, and signifies instead her affair with Blazes Boylan. Second, her retreat leaves him sexless within nighttown's brothel district, more alone and ever more anxious, increasingly falling into the district's hellfire.

Gerty MacDowell[19] and Mrs Breen both make a short appearance and accuse Bloom of sexual misconduct, the first praising his misadventures with her, the second using language of a far more indictable tone: "Mr Bloom! You down here in the hunts of sin! I caught you nicely! Scamp!" (573). This is the first accusation that goes further to suggest not only past malfeasance, but current misconduct. Being caught in some proverbial act of sexual misdemeanour lends this moment in the episode its first taste of legal rhetoric. Sin, sex, and legal transgression all mix at this point, creating still more tension in Bloom's consciousness. Continuing her accusatory dialogue, Mrs Breen next threatens to reveal Bloom's whereabouts to Molly, and then demands an accounting: "Account for yourself this very minute or woe betide you!" (573). Apart from the legal imperative of answering the accusations posed, there is also a strange implication of business and finance. Bloom resists this demand for the moment, but the force of law, through legal language, continues to seep into the episode.

As if the language of legal inquisition were not clear enough, Joyce begins bringing unmistakably legal objects within the episode's frame. Richie Goulding appears with a "black legal bag of Collis and Ward on which a skull and crossbones are painted in white limewash" (576). The law is thus linked to the secret society of Freemasonry, which, in turn, brings questions to our minds regarding the opacity of the law's procedures. Linking the secret society to the law in this way makes representations of the law that much more amorphous. For Bloom, however, the bag is only a foreshadowing of his trial, and he must again engage with Mrs Breen and her demand for an explanation for his presence in the neighbourhood. Bloom, at this point, agrees to explain all, but suggests that they walk. Mrs Breen agrees, and they move away from the bawd, disgruntled at having lost a customer. Walking gives Bloom an escape. As he tells Mrs Breen a protracted story, ostensibly to explain himself, he instead moves Mrs Breen's memory to times past, to emotions they had for each other. As Bloom prattles on about past events, he puts Molly in the background, and hints further and further that at the end of his story it will be Mrs Breen to whom he makes a confession. He has her breathless with anticipation as he moves towards an admission: "and you asked me if I ever heard or read or knew or came across …," to which she eagerly replies, "Yes, yes, yes, yes, yes, yes, yes" (578). Here Mrs Breen "fades from his side" (578). Bloom's ability to free himself from her clutches rests on his ability to walk, to free himself from the physical boundaries imposed on him, and to talk, to free himself from the mental impediments imposed on him.

The Watch make their first appearance in the chapter moments later, as each lays a hand on Bloom's shoulder. Much akin to Joseph K in his arrest in Kafka's *The Trial*, Bloom puzzles the circumstances surrounding their accusations: "Caught in the act. Commit no nuisance" (581). This is a repetition of the prior accusation, and he immediately begins to defend his character: "I am doing good to others" and "[t]he friend of man. Trained by kindness" (581). These are the first utterances he makes under these verbal threats. Yet they do little to dissuade First and Second Watch from their duties as interrogators. They inundate him with accusations, unleashing the bureaucratic fury available only to those in positions where self-importance grossly eclipses actual power. Nonetheless they begin to read something like a criminal information against Bloom: "Henry Flower. No fixed abode. Unlawfully watching and besetting" (582). Immediately afterward, a demand for an alibi follows. Bloom's attempts at misdirection seem at first to work, but he is then ordered to the station. At this point, all of Bloom's avoidance tactics fail, and he is put squarely in the position of an accused on trial, with no escape from either the physical or the mental violence this entails.

The Watch are only part of the judicial machinery in this episode, as the witnesses to Bloom's crimes come quickly and repeatedly. Martha, the first woman actually to demand legal recourse in her dealings with Bloom, once the Watch arrest him, demands that he "[c]lear [her] name" (583). Bloom replies, among other things, "You remember the Childs fratricide case," and "I am wrongfully accused," but then adds: "Better one guilty escape than ninetynine wrongfully condemned" (583). For Bloom, answering the accusations before him is akin to fratricide, as he uses this case as a precedent to his own. The mention of fratricide, moreover, readies the reader for other kinds of familial violence: making answer to his accusations equates to a metaphoric paternal murder, as Bloom feels the pressure of the paternalism of law. This is also perhaps the first instance where Bloom's statements not only mimic – and twist – notions of liberal jurisprudence but also point to the inherently compromised position he suffers in making answer to the accusations before him. His testimony pleads his innocence, while, arguing in the alternative, as a lawyer would, he recognizes that, if he is condemned, he should still be let free based on the liberal tradition of ensuring that no innocent person be punished for crimes he or she did not commit. Of course, he gets the legal idiom wrong, but it nonetheless exemplifies Bloom's connection to and – somewhat skewed – understanding of liberal jurisprudence. It is shortly after this first witness gives her evidence against Bloom for his alleged "breach of promise" that he adopts the language of the barrister.

His statement, "Gentlemen of the jury, let me explain" (583), becomes, as Felman might reason, an effort to contain the violence of his sexual thoughts and actions in the judicial consciousness; his rhetoric is the courtroom's rhetoric. He bears witness to his own character, and assures the triers of fact that he is "a respectable married man, without a stain on [his] character" (583). The accusations quickly turn, however, to questions of nationalism. Bloom proudly announces his membership in the royal Dublins and is quickly censured as a turncoat. He regroups and makes an emotional appeal based on his father's affiliation with Britain, while claiming, "I'm as staunch a Britisher as you are sir," and further, "I did all a white man could" (584). Here the courtroom acts as a microscope with which to further scrutinize Bloom's character and, in this case, his patriotism. Again, as in the accusations directed towards his sexual misconduct, Bloom reacts with fawning, deferential spinelessness. Yet this weakness does little to diminish our sympathy for him. Instead, and again much in the manner of Joseph K, we sympathize with the man who is doing all he can with the weight of the legal machinery of trial crushing down upon him. It is this disconnection of the reader from the legal machinery that signals the trauma of the individual giving testimony, especially when the mind of that individual begins to doubt the innocence of the actions of which he is accused.

Further complicating the nationalistic conundrum in which Bloom finds himself, a voice from the gallery exclaims, "Moses, Moses, king of the jews, / Wiped his arse in the Daily News" (586). Bloom's efforts to identify himself as a member of the citizenry are constantly thwarted not only by the rampant racism he faces, but also by the allowances the judicial system makes for these persecutions. He succumbs to the pressures of the trial and, as Neil Davidson argues, tries to undermine his Jewish heritage by claiming the injustice of not being treated as an individual, but instead as a member of an ethnic group: "Cast in the position of the accused, Bloom fortifies his own defense with malapropisms of Judaism – 'shitbroleeth' – and traditional stereotypes – 'I am being made a scapegoat of.' In his closing arguments, O'Molloy reinforces Bloom's self-defense by referring first to Hebraism – 'The Mosaic code has superseded the law of the jungle,' and then to scapegoating – 'when in doubt, persecute Bloom'" (Davison 223). By his malapropisms,[20] Bloom performs an act that both connects him with and distances him from Judaism. That he uses a Hebrew word at all necessarily suggests his inclusion in the ethnic group; because he uses it wrongly, however, it suggests he is trying to maintain some detachment from being clearly labelled a Jew. As Davidson notes, though, Bloom is willing to accept his Jewish heritage so long as it aids in his legal defence. By the repeated references to scapegoating, Bloom and his counsel attempt to place him outside the stereotypical confines created by nationalistic Britain. Bloom argues that he is innocent, and accused of crimes only because of his membership in an ethnic group. Bloom's rhetoric invokes the liberal jurisprudential tradition on individualism and rights. Although he is neither ashamed of nor reticent about his Jewish heritage in other moments in the novel, here Bloom must at least appear dissimilar to the stereotypes rampant in Joyce's contemporary society; he is, in effect, avoiding a kind of racial profiling. But while he waffles and dissociates himself, he calls attention to the British nationalism that so infects, and thus inflects, the court system. The paternalism inherent in its operation carries with it a vigorous dose of racism. Bloom's individual identity is subsumed within his ethnic character.

But this is not necessarily a terrible rhetorical position from which to argue points of nationalism. If we return to contemporary ideas of law as culture, the legal historical moment seems to echo some of Joyce's work in "Circe." Joyce links Bloom's identity to the past and to history; Bloom is "handcuffed to history" (Rushdie 9). But, in so confining him, Joyce creates a dialogue between the historical Jewish identity and the individual. For Ira Nadel, this adhesiveness of history and the individual has a twofold effect, both linking and freeing the individual: "Ironically, the inability to lose one's identity or past, both imprisons and frees the individual as the 'Circe' episode of *Ulysses* demonstrates in its fantasy recreation of the pasts of Bloom and Stephen" (24). In effect, the created pasts of individuals can rework the historical moments from which they spring. Although the law works to uncover the inaccessible "facts" of the past and tries to narrativize and confine the identities of the persons accused of a crime, Joyce questions the liberal notion of monologic legal rhetoric. The law's voice, authoritarian as it might be, is still only one voice, even within the confines of the courtroom. For Nadel this reworking of history helps revitalize the idea of facts and historical meaning: "But in mythologizing history, most notably in 'Cyclops,' 'Circe' and the *Wake*, Joyce solves the dilemma of the emptiness of fact and the poverty of historical meaning. By turning fantasy, fiction and repetition – in short, myth – into history, Joyce not only revitalises history but gives new energy to myth." Nadel concludes that Joyce recognizes that "specific events cannot define man" (43). If we take this line of argument, it becomes clearer that this authoritative definition is the very project the law tries to encourage. As Felman notes, the courtroom is a stage on which events are recreated specifically to find the elusive "truth," but where, instead, violence re-enacts itself. Joyce, according to Nadel, refuses this kind of relationship among individuals, history, and the law. Joyce, in these respects, is one of the first cultural critics of twentieth-century jurisprudence.

But the inclusive and exclusive nature of nationalism is only one of the lines of attack the law aims against Bloom. "The afterbirth of 'Oxen of the Sun,'" notes Streit of "Circe," "in whose linguistic chaos Bloom dissolves, is transformed into a fertile protoplasm that reconstitutes and expands sexuality, as it does Bloom, as well as other characters and plot elements of the foregoing text. Compelled to tell 'all,' the episode becomes the text's confessional" (95). Confession and sexuality ground most of the rest of Bloom's trial. As a line of women appears to bear witness to Bloom's immoral sexual practices, Mary Driscoll's curiously humorous allegations of being "surprised in the rere of the premises" precede what the clerk of the Crown calls Bloom's "making a bogus statement." The stage direction further pre-emptively eviscerates Bloom's statements by describing them as "a long unintelligible speech" (587). As Streit puts it, "[t]he episode's plot is structured in accordance with Bloom's fascination with, and Stephen's aversion to, confession. This movement begins in the trial scene, in the course of which Bloom must testify even though his speech has already been branded a lie" (96). Ultimately, and again acting in a way that diminishes the rhetorical effect of Bloom's words, we do not hear the speech, but only the paraphrased stage direction of these self-defences. Bloom is silenced in the narrative that demands his confession. O'Molloy appears to act on Bloom's behalf, but his defence of his client amounts, instead, to more character assassination. He begs the court's forgiveness for his client's possible hereditary atavism and somnambulism, rather than denying the actions of which his client is accused (589). Further accusations against Bloom's sexual character come from Mrs Yelverton Barry, Mrs Bellingham, and The Honourable Mrs Mervyn Talboys. But throughout the entire sordid affair, Bloom never confesses his guilt.[21]

Let me return to traditional liberal jurisprudence and the idea that guilt, for criminal offences such as those levelled against Bloom, requires the satisfaction of the two conditions of *actus reus* and *mens rea*. Although Bloom often admits to his actions, not even obloquy and coercion at the hands of the judicial process make him admit his guilty intentions. In this case the forced confession fails. Brooks explains the significance of the confession regarding its reliance upon manufacturing guilt in the speaker of the confession:

> As de Man suggests, the speech act of confession is double. In the terms of J.L. Austin's famous distinction, there is a constative aspect (the sin or guilt to which one confesses) and a performative aspect, precisely the elusive and troubling *action* performed by the statement "I confess." When one says "Bless me Father, for I have sinned," the constative meaning is: I have committed sins, while the performative meaning is: absolve me of my sin. The confessional performance of guilt always has this double aspect, and since it does, it opens the possibility that the performative aspect will produce the constative, create the sin or guilt that the act of confessing requires. That is, the verbal act that begins "I confess" entails guilt, which is already there in the act of confessing, so that the referent – this particular guilt – may merely be a by-product of the verbal act. (21)

In his trial, Bloom is physically subdued, mentally tortured, and publicly humiliated. His character suffers continued attacks based on his physical frailty, his faulty nationalism, and his alleged sexual deviancy. Yet even though he is silenced, the state and its apparatus fail to exact a confession.[22] But this small triumph seems somewhat less satisfying at the end of the episode. It is the fictionalized judicial process itself that manufactures these feelings of victimization in the minds of the participants of this trial procedure. Brooks again offers insight into the ways the judicial process produces a disconnection between its dual purposes of seeking truth and administering justice. He argues that "[t]he effort to produce the confessional truth would seem, in very many cases, to produce as the very condition of its production a state of abjection that undercuts the very claim of voluntariness on which the definition of truth reposes, and beyond that, the very notion of human agency that the law must promote in order to do its judging" (81).

For Bloom *is* the abject. He is neither accepted as a civil subject nor desired as a sexual object. His already compromised position and self-perception, once publicly scrutinized at trial, suggest further challenges to his ontological status. But for all of these confrontations and for all of the public scorn, Bloom manages to refuse the confession the law so vehemently pursues. Unlike Joseph K, Bloom lives to wander another day. In effect, it is not Bloom on trial, but the trial procedure itself. The reproduction of the events at the locus of the trial, moreover, works in a self-reflexive way with the rest of the text. As Streit argues, the inaccessibility of the truth, even in the staged situation of a courtroom confession, leads to a re-examination of the apparatus that creates the story, and allows for a more polyphonous retelling of events: "The adaptation of the confessional form, which can never reach the ultimate truth of the bodies, and the hyperbole, which can always be pushed one step further, suggest that this rewriting does not claim to be the only possible version of the events. Instead, the text generates the *virtual–textuality* version of the continuation of the 'pre-"Circe"' episodes of *Ulysses* – merely *one* of the possible plot variants" (95–6). Streit rightly connects confessional to self-reflexive textual disintegration. I submit that this same loosening of meaning is inherent when we connect testimony to the impossibility of epistemological truth at trial. The participants in a trial are in much the same position as Bloom, where all exterior influences, including the judge, jury, witnesses, and even the witness box, play roles in determining the ontological status of the testifying subject.

Robert Spoo argues a similar position in his look at James Joyce and the language of history, where he links historical experience to human identity: "Just as 'Oxen,' which Budgen described as 'a parade of costume styles,' interrogates historical experience, 'Circe' puts in question the authenticity of human identity. If 'Oxen' explores the problem of literature-and-history, 'Circe' reminds us that drama-and-life are no less problematic because no less constructed" (154). Here Spoo returns to the idea that literature is fundamentally linked to historical telling, and drama is fundamentally linked to life. Although this might be too rigid a dichotomy, if we accept this premise for a moment, it is clear that "Circe" does not neatly fit this mould. History is implicated both privately and publicly, and, for Spoo, this means a reworking of the ways we think about historical authenticity: "In 'Circe' history is what hurts, the private pain of individuals like Stephen and Bloom who experience guilt not only for sins of commission and omission but also for desires and unconscious wishes; even thoughts they *may* have entertained are treated with legalistic thoroughness and wild exaggeration" (155).

History, in this treatment of "Circe," is as much the private and imagined lives of its participants as it is the public and enacted lives that are so terribly inflected by historical events. This is, of course, exactly the same assertion I put forward about the law. Law and legal procedure, just like history, inflect the individual and his or her unconscious in such profound ways that a kind of legal ideology becomes part of the individual's ontological structure. In "Circe," for instance, Bloom's subjection to all his accusers' allegations, as I have described it, plays out in his unconscious, and there is often little to delineate whether an action in this episode is occurring externally or internally for Bloom. In effect Bloom's *mens rea* is never clearly established, as it inflects, and is inflected by, all the people involved in the trial. In this manner, and even though the episode is clearly in the dramatic style, an indirect interior monologue is still working in the text. Only "monologue" does not work in this instance; it would be better to call it indirect interior dialogue. Blurring the lines of Bloom's consciousness and that of those around him, Joyce creates a synthesis between interior and exterior, between self and other, one necessarily implicating the next.

Spoo's further arguments about the proprietary nature of history, I believe, are equally applicable to the study of law and culture, as Joyce implicates legal practice as a part of history, as a part of human experience. Spoo argues that, "to know the shameful details of Bloom's past, whether real or fictional, actual or potential, suggests that history is no longer the official tale of the tribe but rather a protean property of the community, woven and rewoven on the looms of gossip, a delight to the talebearer and a reproach to the victim" (155). Although this reading might be a bit too cynical when applied to legal procedure, in that we must hope that what occurs in a court of law is something more than "gossip," there is still a culture of argument at work that delights the tale-maker and reproaches the accused.

Ronald Dworkin, in *Taking Rights Seriously*, explains the culture of argument in the law as he focuses on what he calls "hard cases" that, in turn, reveal for him the polyphonic texture of the law (80–130). An increasing number of hard cases arises in social and political situations not anticipated by the current law; in effect the law fails to account adequately for all situations, especially in rapidly changing times.[23] In situations where the law gives way, the culture of argument surrounding the ill-defined legal issue provides, for Dworkin, insight into both the case at bar and the legal institutions that host this argument. In the world Joyce creates in "Circe," the accused's voice is one thread of yarn in the loom of legal procedure, woven and rewoven within the rhetoric of sexuality, sin, nationalism, and liminality.

All of these arguments draw from my discussion of the ways we might alter our thinking about traditional ideas of liberal jurisprudence, and they are, I think, influenced by the schools of cultural criticism. Yet it seems to me that we cannot simply abandon ideas of the individual, regardless of how mediated he or she might be. As the nightmare trial in "Circe" depicts, Bloom is at the mercy of a public anxiety based on xenophobia and fears of sexual irregularity, much of which is itself inflected by religion. There is, thus, a need somehow to demarcate the ways the law chooses to interact with individuals so as to create rights that trump mob rule. Failure to do this results, for Bloom, as for any accused, in trial by majority opinion, morality, or even whim. My reading of "Circe" suggests that the law's operation demands emendation. For Joyce that elusive objective of justice is possible only if the spirit of the individual is preserved free of the paternalism, racism, and gender discrimination that seem so prevalent in the legal machinery. Recognizing, rather than prejudicing, an individual's connections to community becomes the project that confronts liberal jurisprudence.

Chapter Four

Conclusion: Manufacturing Individual Identity

Modernist culture's collisions with the law are histories that guide the ways we continually engage with ideas of the law. Descriptive and normative interpretations of legal systems are crucial to our understanding. Although the law governs us every day, there is also much bewilderment about how we actually engage with the legal system. Although the liberal tradition of jurisprudence in practice leaves much to be desired, our critical interpretations of this practice must offer something to the normative understanding of what the law is for; otherwise, the law is a dead ideological state apparatus, not a lived practice in our lives. Julie Stone Peters foresees the death of interdisciplinarity resulting in a study that asserts the hyper-reality of the objects under study, but then posits this hyper-real space as the means to affect change. Regardless of the fact that the hyper-real does not exist, we can still use it to change the real. We see that, in a similar manner, to treat the law as a system, in full knowledge of the system's porosity, is the only way to improve it. The British moderns used violence and trauma in the trial process to underscore the need for court reform. The interplay between legal and literary discourses surrounding the interiority of the civil subject offers analysis of the liberal tradition of trials and testimony.

Shifting Ontology: Legal Personhood Meets Literary Identity

Stephen Gordon, in *The Well of Loneliness*, assumes a Christ-like character in the final paragraphs of Radclyffe Hall's 1928 novel. She hears the voices of her persecuted brethren and, employing a kind of Keatsian full-blown-rose rhetoric, adopts the position of the forsaken saviour. The voices call: "'Stephen, Stephen, speak with your God and ask Him why He has left us forsaken!'" (446). Hall's narrator continues sewing this religiously inflected thread and, as in the biblical stories of Jesus, Stephen becomes a conduit between humanity and God. Alluding to the story of Matthew, she offers up her own plea: "'God,' she gasped, 'we believe; we have told You we believe … We have not denied You, then rise up and defend us. Acknowledge us, oh God, before the whole world. Give us also the right to our existence!'" (447).[1]

The persecuted for whom Stephen Gordon pleads are lesbians, and the cultural context that saw the novel banned was not much evolved from that in which Wilde, Conrad, Ford, and Joyce wrote. Many levels of irony were at play. First, the novel was published in the same year the British government enacted universal suffrage for persons over age twenty-one. Second, that same government banned the book. Chief Magistrate Sir Chartres Biron's judgment found the book to defend what the court thought of as unnatural practices between women. Third, although Virginia Woolf's *Orlando* and Compton Mackenzie's *Extraordinary Women* also dealt with lesbianism, they did not attract the censure of the British courts. The reason Hall's treatise attracted so much attention, argues Adam Parkes, was that it advocated, in earnest, a position the others could be interpreted as putting forth either as fanciful or in jest (434). Parkes connects this earnest plea for lesbian acceptance to the government's proposed legislation extending the definition of gross indecency: "A proposal to extend to women the 1885 Labouchère Amendment, which outlawed 'acts of gross indecency' between men, ran aground in the House of Commons in 1921 because [as Samuel Hynes speculates], 'men found it [lesbianism] too gross to deal with'" (Parkes 434). This is the reasoning Parkes uses to assert that "'sexual inversion' (as it was then known) was not legally recognized in early twentieth-century Britain" (434). Yet another level of irony is working in this cultural context: Hall's text advocates recognition of lesbian culture, but the law, in failing to recognize it at all, fails to make this sexual preference criminal. In a sense Hall might have been saved some of the ignominy Wilde suffered, although her disgust with the legal system, which so blatantly ignored her identity, seems to parallel the disgust Wilde felt towards his persecution, first by Queensberry, then by the legal system. She, unlike Wilde, was never tried personally for her sexual preference; instead, like *Ulysses*, *The Well of Loneliness* was banned and its ideas suppressed.

This situation brings my discussion of the British moderns and their cultural circumstances full circle. Hall's characters' struggle for recognition uncovers yet another instance where liberal jurisprudence fails in its project of equality. "You will see unfaithfulness, lies and deceit among those whom the world views with approbation. You will find that many have grown hard of heart, have grown greedy, selfish, cruel and lustful," notes Stephen Gordon as she contemplates her relationship with her partner, Mary (304). She continues: "[A]nd then you will turn to me and will say: 'You and I are more worth of respect than these people. Why does the world persecute us, Stephen?' And I shall answer; 'Because in this world there is only toleration for the so-called normal'" (304). Identifying the hypocrisy of a homophobic culture that did not even recognize same-sex relationships between women and that abided a far more troubling list of deadly sins within its legal structure, Hall attempted to fracture the liberal foundation of justice – a justice turning, supposedly, on tolerance. What is tolerated and what is not becomes the focal point of her critique of liberal jurisprudence: the concepts of rights, autonomy, and justice do not apply to her, as she is not an individual or, at least, not an individual who counts under the law.

As I have argued, however, this kind of legally sanctioned discrimination flows from failures in liberal systems of justice, not from failures in liberal philosophy. The law's decision to ignore a person over whom it has jurisdiction amounts to ontological nullification. Rather than promote the liberal project of toleration, the courts in the era of the British moderns chose to challenge the existence of certain identities, making it impossible for lesbians to assert arguments based on rights, autonomy, or justice simply because they had no legal standing and could not participate in the culture of argument that is the law. Attempts to bring this kind of sanctioned discrimination to light ultimately failed. At the end of Wilde's trials, for example, Alfred Douglas wrote a letter to editor W.T. Stead.[2] "Perhaps you are not aware that 'Lesbianism' exists to any extent in London," wrote Douglas. Asserting its presence in the upper echelons of British society, he continued: "I can assure you that it does, and though of course I cannot mention names, I could point out to you half a dozen women in society or among actresses who would be considered as 'dangerous' to young girls as Oscar Wilde will I suppose henceforth be considered to boys" (Hyde 343).

Stead refused to publish Douglas's letter based on what Hyde calls its "spirited defence of homosexual conduct" (344). The paradox of being socially prevalent yet legally irrelevant points to the heart of the conflict between the liberal and cultural studies' views of the law's project. For cultural studies critics, the law is either ignorant or wilfully blind. For liberal jurisprudence, the law is not concerned with this particular kind of situation. In either case the result is suppression. Ironically, however, if the law were concerned with lesbian identity, the result would have been the same kind of discrimination that confronted homosexual men. The lack of a legal identity saved many lesbians from criminal prosecution, although there were those for whom legal martyrdom would have been an agreeable price to pay for pushing the law towards equal rights for all homosexuals.

My intention here is not to investigate the historical modernist legal landmarks of lesbianism; rather, I am more interested in showing the ways these kinds of legal cases emphasize the nature of legal identity. I have discussed the ways Wilde, Conrad, Ford, and Joyce all interacted with and wrote about the law and its formation of identity. In each case, I have tried to show that the law's practice of giving testimony necessarily provides challenges to the ontological certainty of individual identity. Yet this demonstration seems to privilege the position that there is, at core, some unshakable individual identity.

Ironically, however, the law's project of challenging individual identity often manufactures guilt. In each of the representations of trial I have discussed, a pattern emerged concerning changes in the mental state of the individual on trial. Whether the individual goes to trial feeling innocent, regardless of having committed a crime at law or not, or feeling guilty for the crimes of which he or she is accused, the accused often takes on the identity suggested by the law.

This kind of ontological shift integrates legal identity with personal identity. That is to say, the kinds of suggestions made in the search for epistemological certainty at law necessarily influence the self-image of the civil subject. The legal identity attributed to the subject, whether criminal, negligent, or not guilty, affects the ontology of the subject and alters self-perception. In cases where the law utterly fails to recognize legal subjectivity, as it did for Radclyffe Hall, there is an equally traumatic challenge to the ontological status of the individual. In all of these cases, the hyper-conflicted nature of the individual at trial suggests that "individualism" itself is a legal fiction, although liberal jurisprudence suggests otherwise. But this does not trump liberal ideas of rights, autonomy, and justice. Just because we acknowledge that these concepts are also theories – that we may never approach autonomy, justice, or even rights without acknowledging their theoretical natures – does not render them inoperable in the ultimate liberal pursuit of equality under the law.

"The Reasonable Man" Makeover: The Contribution of
Cultural Studies to the Legal Landscape

The theoretical nature of the legal individual is perhaps nowhere more obvious than when it is compared to the proverbial "reasonable person" in law. Criminal, tort, and administrative law rely on the precedent-based theory of what, until recently, was commonly referred to as the "reasonable man." In each instance, the conduct of an accused or a defendant is compared to that of the reasonable person, a precedent-based depiction from a collection of judicial decisions. A judge, in fashioning his or her decision, narrates the events of the case at bar alongside an ideal set of events in which the reasonable person plays the leading role. In so doing, the competing narrative of the judicially conceived reasonable person becomes the standard that regulates the conduct of the accused.

Mayo Moran's *Rethinking the Reasonable Person* offers a broad historical analysis of the concept, while arguing for a kind of egalitarian conception of this professed objective standard. Comparing accepted notions of the reasonable person in case law to the problems of capacity in mentally challenged individuals and children, Moran acknowledges the pitfalls of the proposal of an objective standard of reasonable behaviour. Yet in later chapters she argues that the search for an objective standard, while practically unobtainable, is still essential to the project of egalitarian treatment under the law: "[A]bandonment of the objective standard is not an appealing egalitarian response" (275–6). She turns, instead, to recent feminist law reforms regarding sexual harassment as the basis for her proposed solution.

Following these debates, Moran broaches the idea of a "reasonable woman" standard (276–81). She ultimately concludes that this kind of standard is of little help, as it is more, as Kathryn Abrams puts it, "a matter not of innate common sense but of informed sensibility [that] can be cultivated in a range of women and men" that will, for Moran, make a difference (280). The key to creating an objective standard based on toleration, not on accepted bias, however, lies in faith that the judiciary is able to apply a liberal standard of toleration – that it is able to see the difference between "what is reasonable and what is customarily done" (315). This is, I believe, one way we might allow for recognition of the individual's connections to the community without making them the basis for judicial decision. Ultimately, argues Moran, the objective standard is still a useful, if troubled, legal perception.

Revisiting the Moderns: Characterization and Clues to Legal Interpretation and Identity Politics

I want to make parallel arguments here regarding my discussion of the individual and legal identity. The British moderns I explored each engaged with their legal culture in representing trials in which not only the actions of individuals, but also the very identities of individuals were put on trial. In the instances of Wilde, Ford, and Joyce, the sexual conduct of the represented individual ultimately caused gross and dire alterations to his ontological status. Wilde's was clearly the most traumatic case, as his trial led to his bankruptcy, literary ruin, incarceration, and death. From his representations of his life at the time of the trial, we see his utter despair at confronting a legal system that proscribed conduct that, for Wilde, was not ethically or morally wrong.

Wilde believed that sexual relations between consenting adults should not attract the law's interest, while the morality of the day imagined otherwise. In Moran's theoretical framework, the judge, in order to apply a kind of egalitarian theory of the objective standard of the reasonable person, would have to question the custom of censoring homosexual conduct, and consider whether the rights afforded to heterosexual behaviour should also flow to homosexual behaviour. That is to say, should the rights of equality extend so far as to trump the ingrained legal bias and paternalism operating in precedent? Again this supposes a fairly enlightened judge, and would have been a more difficult project in the modernist legal climate. But recalling Wilde's two criminal trials, we see, even then, that there was real sympathy for his position and that both the first jury and the first judge, Justice Charles, saw holes in the prosecution's case. Tactical shifts between the two trials mended these holes, not with expert advocacy, but with brute rhetorical prejudice. The question of evidence became completely secondary to the question of how much harm homosexual conduct might inflict if left unchecked. Wilde's specific circumstances and his individual conduct became secondary to the law's project of curtailing behaviour it considered customarily immoral.

In Conrad's *Lord Jim*, in contrast, we see a representation of an individual who cannot recall either his actions or his intentions. Regardless of his honest attempts at reconstructing the events, he falls terribly short of the epistemological certainty required by the law. The trauma of the events, of leaving his human cargo, weighs heavily on Jim, and he stands trial in an almost self-destructive kind of mental state. Here, counsel plays on his weakness, exploiting his confusion and undermining his attempts at telling the most accurate version of the events he can recall. The events are further made traumatic for Jim through the exoticized courtroom and the colonial trappings of admiralty authority. In this kind of environment, it is difficult to imagine how the nautical assessors in charge of trying Jim might have applied an egalitarian objective standard of what might be reasonable in the circumstances, even if the events were not as muddled as Conrad has Marlow describe them. Having the events mediated through Marlow further emphasizes the problems with reaching for objectivity, although the narrative does not abandon this possibility completely. Instead, as it shows Jim both earnestly attempting to recreate the "truth" and also failing terribly in his efforts to grasp his actions and intentions, Marlow's reconstruction actually leaves open the question of whether Jim acted in a reasonable manner. Having been stripped of his first mate certificate, Jim becomes a wandering, broken character, and is, for years, unable to assert any kind of individual identity not encumbered with the shame of criminality.

Again the inherent trauma in giving testimony obscures the project of deciding whether Jim's conduct was reasonable. But this situation also demonstrates the need for recognition of Jim's connections to his community also to be recognition of his individualism. This might seem paradoxical in my articulation. Yet, in this way Jim might have still been punished, but he would not have been outcast. Even if the assessors proved his conduct unreasonable in the circumstances, it is the act of stripping Jim of his ties to the nautical community that is the most traumatic for him, and the most significant aspect of the law as Conrad represents it in *Lord Jim*. It creates a relationship between the law and the individual that lays bare the indelible marks of legal process on the psyche of the individual – marks that suggest that the law can be entirely fallible when the pursuit of truth usurps the protection of the individual from harm. *Lord Jim* is yet another example of the difficulty in balancing these two competing projects.

Ford's literary representations of the law also confront sexuality and paternalism as sites for discovery. His personal circumstances before the courts left him somewhat bewildered as to the relationships between trauma and punishment. Although he felt anxiety over his actions in eloping – and then exposing the private matters of the court to the public press – and although he fully expected the court to find him in contempt, the court, showing deference to his social status and his self-professed literary prowess, chose instead to allow him to escape any real judicial punishment. His second encounter with the law, which saw him imprisoned for refusing to pay his wife directly the support he was already paying through an intermediary, again left him bewildered, unable to see the justice in the court's acting on such a technicality and unable to understand the harsh punishment for what he saw as such a meagre affront to the law. In *The Good Soldier*, Edward Ashburnham becomes the embodiment of Ford's legal anxieties. His tale, like Jim's, comes mediated through a third person. As Dowell relates Ashburnham's legal stumblings, we see a parallel instance of a character unable to grasp the gravity of the offences he has committed in the theoretical framework of the jurisprudential process. The pain he feels grows as he recounts the events over and over, and it is through this telling and retelling of the narrative that we come to a better understanding of Ashburnham's sexual conduct. Again Moran's work on rethinking reasonableness seems helpful in its insistence on revisioning the standard by which we judge individuals.

Based within a narrative that clearly shows the ways the law privileges paternalism and allows aggressive sexual behaviour, Ford's story makes clear the law's bias in favour of social status. The suggestion seems to be that Ashburnham, in the court's eyes, overstepped his bounds but in no really significant way, as he might have been merely avuncular, not libidinous. The law sees his conduct as reasonable in the circumstances, but only marginally so. Here we see the law's reliance on custom and paternalistic bias. Because it was customary to allow aggressive sexual behaviour, the law continues this custom without any serious questioning of whether this was particularly reasonable. Reasonableness, again, needs to be held to a higher standard of philosophical debate. Ashburnham's concupiscent behaviour escapes the legal censure it deserves, and this is yet another failure in the law's project to protect an individual from the harmful interference of another. Ford's narrative of the law becomes an almost cautionary tale of the law's propensity to lapse into routine bias and to find reasonable that which is merely customary.

For Joyce, as for Conrad, perceptions of the legal system were inextricably linked to conceptions of colonialism. His personal experience with English officials left a sour taste in his mouth. His later experiences with the English Players, and with Henry Carr in particular, led to court appearances that had parallel, although less severe, engagements with the law to those of Wilde. For Joyce, nationalism, racism, paternalism, and gender were all components of legal bias, and Bloom's trial in "Circe" invariably and vigorously critiques legal culture for these multifarious sites of prejudice. Bloom's varied trouncing at the hands of the law enunciates Joyce's disdain for court procedure and its inability to move swiftly to justice, or at least Joyce's idea of justice. Joyce's representation of the judicial system creates a dialogue of disparate voices, most of which are oppressive and few, if any, of which champion Bloom's defence. Both Bloom and his lawyer make disparaging remarks about his case, and the parade of witnesses seeks to eviscerate at least Bloom's credibility, if not also his conscience.

In Joyce's hallucinogenic trial, the grounds on which we attempt to understand the proceedings constantly shift beneath our feet, and we are left only with the perception of a legal system of chance and randomness. This arbitrariness, and the associated guilt we see Bloom internalize, still fails to convict Bloom in any serious way. He leaves the trial altered ontologically, yet he is neither incarcerated nor fined. It might seem that any discussion of a new egalitarian theory of an objective standard for reasonableness is impossible in these circumstances, but I think, in this case, it is quite the contrary. Joyce's trial, where everything seems unreasonable and where Bloom is subjected to constant and indiscriminate legal censure, accentuates the need for some kind of narrative of reasonable behaviour. The trial, in its utter lack of a reasonable standard by which it might judge Bloom, further shows the necessity of creating such a standard. It is through this kind of parallel narrative that Bloom, as an accused, might have been able to judge the error of his ways. Yet in the carnivalesque courtroom of nighttown, the reasonable person is more an absolute fiction than a legal one. Bloom is tried on cultural customs, which Joyce paints as the most harmful and odious characteristics of his society. If bigotry and bias are allowed to infiltrate the law's project of protecting those with whom it is concerned, the result, for Joyce, is not unlike the mayhem he creates in "Circe."

Hanging on to the idea of an individual creates at least some semblance of responsibility. If all actions are attributable to cultural factors, we have to give up completely ideas not only of freedom and autonomy, but also of legal accountability. Holding on to the idea of a reasonable person must continue to facilitate an egalitarian perception of these ideas. Although this person must be refigured to expose precedent-based bias, and must reflect the multivariate nature of ethnicity, religion, gender, nationality, and economic factors of human life, the project of reconstruction must continue. This is, indeed, a grand project, but one with which the British moderns struggled. Their literary works reflect the deep suspicion with which they regarded legal procedure. Their personal experiences informed these representations in many intricate ways that contemporary scholarship has yet to uncover. Through my initial discussions of the law and the British moderns, I hope to stimulate further enquiry into these literary works and their legal connections, and the ways these representations prefigure much of the legal theoretical debate in which we are now engaged. Although our court systems are still profoundly flawed with systemic bias, I think there are real arguments for reform in the writings of Wilde, Conrad, Ford, and Joyce.

In *Literary Criticisms of Law*, Guyora Binder and Robert Weisberg talk about the power of myth in mobilizing citizens in circumstances of oppression in a way that, I think, relates to this kind of literary critique. In their text they recount the situation of parents who are told they have a physically challenged child. This "authoritative announcement of deviance" triggers similar responses in the parents, making them mythic champions in the legal and educational systems that often prejudice their children. "[P]articipation in social myth," argue Binder and Weisberg, "helps build communal strength among parents," as it provides reinforcement in legal standing; it creates a group from which their voices seem less isolated and more focused (249). For Binder and Weisberg, this all leads to greater ability to participate in the legal conversation: "Culturally available narratives play a role in determining who will assert themselves in institutional areas and to what ends. Thus, one role for narrative scholarship is to make available narratives that can help mobilize participation by recovering and emphasizing aspects of historical experience that prevailing institutional narratives ignore" (249). My arguments here attempt to underscore this point. Rarely does a work of literature single-handedly change the way a government operates or legislates,[3] but it is far more useful to think about literary representations of British trial procedure as mobilizing documents – texts in which we might find a culturally available narrative of which we were previously ignorant.

The role of the press in these kinds of literary/legal conversations inflected my arguments to accentuate the historical context surrounding the authors I chose. Yet as my research and writing progressed, I saw the potential for an entirely new investigation, centred upon the British press and the ways it further mediated legal and literary representations. The press, too, creates mobilizing documents, but these often participate in myth-making, which prejudices the individual and creates its own kinds of harmful myths. Beginning with the press coverage of Wilde's trials, and moving towards the formation of the British Broadcasting Company (later, Corporation) in 1922, I see shifting mandates in the roles of the media.

Further Questioning: Focus on the Press and the BBC

As I look forward to new conversations in law and culture, I can see future lines of inquiry following a similar path to my discussion here of Wilde, Conrad, Ford, and Joyce. Although not every British author found him- or herself in the clutches of the courts, most found themselves represented in the press. That is not to say that we need to shift away from focusing on the law, however – merely that this opens new opportunities to study those involved more tangentially with the law. E.M. Forster, for instance, championed the PEN movement at its inception, and although he never found himself the direct object of court proceedings, he campaigned against the suppression of Radcylffe Hall's *The Well of Loneliness* and appeared as a witness for the defence in the trial of D.H. Lawrence's *Lady Chatterley's Lover*. But to close my examination here, I want to revisit the authors with whom I have spent so many of these pages, and offer some points of departure for further contemplation.

Ironically, like the man famous for his paradoxes, the representation of Wilde in the press was bitterly paradoxical considering that, only months before his trial, his plays had been lauded as works of genius in that same press and, more so, because he had been writing reviews for the *Times*, one of the papers that later censured his conduct. The sensationalism was not limited to the most reputable dailies, of course. Publications such as the *Illustrated Police News* ensured that even those with limited literacy could, through pictorial representations and simplistic text, grasp the events surrounding the trials. As the excerpt I used as an epigraph at the beginning of this study makes clear, only the number of papers reporting the events limited the media coverage available. Adding to the irony, two of Wilde's plays were running concurrently with his trials, and were enjoying great success. After the press reports, however, the theatres faced increasing social pressure to cease performances of the plays. The court proceedings that branded Wilde with committing acts of gross indecency, in suggesting that his plays must be equally immoral, had force outside the legal community.

Wilde's trials, equally paradoxically, supplanted his plays as the spectacle for which he was most noted. By the time Wilde was released from prison, British theatre dared not speak his name. Future examination of these events should focus on the ways the media reported the courtroom events – specifically, on the way the spectacle enacted in the confines of the courtroom became almost carnivalesque. As Michel Foucault suggests in *Discipline and Punish*, the courts were far from the last judge in this series of events: the press manufactured guilt far beyond the courts' mandate. That is to say, although the courtroom proceedings necessarily attempted to limit the "facts" brought to trial, the media, with almost no formal limitation on reportage, had a field day "bringing to justice" every imaginable aspect of Wilde's character. Although we are used to these media circus events in contemporary culture – one need only look at the O.J. Simpson trial to appreciate the significance of courtroom media coverage capabilities – one must also remember that, prior to 1922, there was no public electronic media in Britain.[4] The literate, instead, read to the illiterate, enacting and re-enacting the events of the trial, while creating yet another public venue of transmission.

And it was not only matters of "gross indecency" that attracted the attention of the media.[5] Newspapers during the modernist era, according to R. Brandon Kershner, served three major functions: they reported the news, they purveyed ads, and they listed "known transgressors." Although the first two purposes are rather self-evident, the last was, perhaps, broader than might be expected. Generally, the "transgressors" included those engaged in the courts for actions in divorce, bankruptcy, and breach of promise. A review and explanation of the ways each of these offences affected the people with which they dealt might then usefully turn to Ford Madox Ford. As I have outlined, he was forced into chambers for his acrimonious relations with his various partners. Each of the women with whom he became romantically involved eventually censured his infidelity and infantile behaviour, and some of them took him to court. He absolutely abhorred the process, and was all too aware that adding to his disgrace was the inevitable newspaper coverage. The treatments of Ford in the papers and the subsequent allusions to them in his work could ground much of the discussion in looking at the rise of the media during this period.

This kind of examination could also look at Joyce and his collisions with the press. Focusing on the derogatory and downright perplexing representation of the daily news in the "Circe" section of *Ulysses*, one might argue that Joyce was not only aware of the power of the press, but abhorred its authority. For Joyce the press was an object of both fascination and disgust. Although he was an avid reader of papers and his attraction to their stories was undeniable, he also feared their influence. He worked as an editor, reviewer, and reporter early in his literary career, and gained a reflective understanding of the workings of the press. Comparing "A Painful Case," to some of the stories Joyce read in the press of the time could clarify his conflicted relationship with the press. By further comparing these pieces to the mentions of the press in the trial scene of "Circe," we might conclude that Joyce, very much in the vein of contemporary critical cultural and legal scholarship, exposes the damaging influence the press could unleash when teamed with the equally damaging spectacle of trial.

The shift from total reliance on the printed press to the introduction of radio is another fulcrum of modernist balance. Nineteen twenty-two was a watershed year in British modernist history, as it saw not only the publication of *Ulysses* and *The Waste Land*, but also the creation of the British Broadcasting Company, a new conglomerate of broadcasters that was given unparalleled power through its ability to communicate with the mass public. A look at the formation of this company and the cultural and political forces that mobilized the new technology is of utmost importance. The mandate given to John Reith, the BBC's first general manager, and his moulding of the company "according to a moral vision whose traces are discernible even today" (Crisell 18) is equally crucial to the discussion. Although most accounts of these events focus on their technological significance and economic impact on capitalist endeavours, we need to posit a theory that, contrary to many interpretations, the BBC was, at least in part, an effort to curtail much of the spectacle that the press so ardently promulgated. Using Mark Hampton's discussions about the educational versus the representational aspects of the media and the "New Journalism," we might imagine the creation of the BBC as government policy to curtail the denigration and sensationalism so prevalent in print media and initiated, in many instances, by courtroom proceedings.

Ultimately the media become purveyors of what citizens take as the unmediated truth. Reporting the legal facts surrounding a trial is a delicate business, as reporters must select those details of the events that encapsulate the daily proceedings. Invariably, however, it is the most sensational details that find the greatest audience. The elegance of counsel's rhetorical turn and the minutia of a judge's reasoning are rarely the subject of reportage. Instead the subjects on trial, already subjected to public ontological trauma, see themselves represented in the media, larger than life, in an exaggerated, grotesque portrait of the court's making. This is, perhaps, yet another instance of how the British media still operate today, since, for everyone other than lawyers and judges, the media offer the only access citizens have to the legal conversation, and few people have the time or energy to read legal reports, much less legal transcripts. I am not suggesting that we should all sit and watch C-SPAN or CPAC daily, or attend regularly the courts of our local jurisdiction, but I do find it deeply disturbing that we entrust so much to something of which we know so little or, at least, know only in this kind of abstraction. If we trace British modern literary production from the inception of the BBC, especially by authors such as Forster and Lawrence, we begin to see that the modern media play a crucial role in determining the ways conversations among law, literature, and the media evolve.

Notes

Introduction

1 That X-rays actually changed the tissue the rays observed was neither discovered nor discussed until a year later. The effect, beyond trauma, of legal procedure on testifying individuals, on the other hand, was not widely studied before cultural and critical legal studies turned its focus to liberal jurisprudence. That is to say, although it might be obvious that both X-rays and legal procedure are invasive, it is less obvious that legal events such as trial actually change the ontological structure of individual identity.

2 The large stylized "S," was used in the first authorized American edition of *Ulysses*, published by Random House in 1934. The edition also included Judge Woolsey's exoneration and his full decision, which lifted the Federal Customs ban on the text. I use it here in homage to that first edition. Although the circumstances of Wilde's trials are familiar and much debated in literary criticism, they serve as an excellent point from which to begin thinking about the issues I raise.

3 This was a notable sign of the gravity with which Wilde treated the trial, and was in austere contrast to the more ostentatious dress he sported at the first and second Magistrate's Court proceedings.

4 There is some contention over the exact words on the card. The phrase, as I discern it, is my deciphering of Queensberry's rather inchoate hand (Holland xiv, Hyde 98). This is a matter of some importance, and I address this issue in following chapters.

5 Jonathan Grossman goes so far as to argue that "the novel, in becoming the ascendant literary genre of the nineteenth century, played an active role in a process through which a reinvented criminal trial supplanted the spectacle of the gallows as the culmination of justice" (4). Although his focus is

primarily narrative form and the law courts as a forum for storytelling, my
claims, rather, go to the ways personal legal events in the lives of authors
affect the understanding of interiority of a testifying subject.

6 Lumping cultural studies and critical legal studies into one group
invariably will trouble theorists in each field and invite criticism for
generalizing what are both broadly discussed and complex subjects. I will
discuss various scholars and texts from both schools in turn, and thus wish
only to create the CCLS acronym for brevity and ease of use here.

7 See also Andrew Altman's slightly more recent "liberal critique" of CLS.

8 Julie Stone Peters's article demonstrates, rather sadly, yet precisely, the
difficulties law and literature face as an interdisciplinary practice. Sad,
because a movement that has been in the making for thirty years is still
internally conflicted along the legal/humanities boundary, which, Peters
argues, amounts to "grave disappointment" from both schools when
they meet (443). The nature of the conflict relates to the inability of each
discipline to acknowledge the kinds of subject positions the other proffers.
Law's preoccupation with the individual impedes social change from
the perspective of the humanities, while the focus on ideological change,
from the law's perspective, lacks practical power to implement social
programs. Peters briefly traces the "three major projects" in law and
literature from humanism in the early 1970s (which, for people such as
Richard Weisburg, was supposed to remedy the rift between legal thought
and practice and to bring the "real," or the humanity, back to the practice
of law) to hermeneutics in the early 1980s (which, taking into account
French deconstruction and literary theory that questioned the "truth" and
the "real" in literary texts, proposed the law as a site for enacting political
change to which the old literary humanism could no longer lay claim)
to narrative in the late 1980s (which, beginning with concurrent feminist
thought, explored the potential of storytelling inside the courtroom as a
means to challenge and oppose the master narratives driving the law and
to give voice to those previously unheard) (444–8). Peters's conclusions
pronounce a new optimism, however, that "allows us freedom from
interdisciplinary longing," while also allowing "disciplinary tourism," the
effect of which is to "ponder the new terms we've erected as touchstones
of our common project, and to offer richer readings of those real (and
sometimes hyperreal) objects of our study" (451).

9 Most at odds with current ideologies in literary and cultural studies
approaches are some of the foundational tenets of liberal jurisprudence.
Liberalism, nicely summarized by Ted Decoste, is a political morality based
on the moral equality of individuals that insists on the priority of justice

over power and that individuals be treated equally despite differences of power, affiliation, and attribution. This political morality takes form in a theory of the state according to which the state exists to guarantee equality by enforcing negative tolerance through a regime of rights. Liberal definitions of law insist that the law is subversive of power because it requires power to respond in terms other than power itself. Liberal law, in effect, sides with the vulnerable in service of equality (otherwise its proclamation of the priority of justice over power carries no weight). Liberal jurisprudence claims that the law approaches power with "deep suspicion" because the law thinks that all power needs justification in terms of "universality and equality." The law, in this formulation then, is corrosive of collectivities in which power consolidates because the law is first and last a commitment to the moral and political significance of individuals. In this pronouncement, the rule of law, individual autonomy, and rights all become pillars on which formulations of liberal jurisprudence rest.

10 Whether ordinary fact or expert witnesses, the challenges to the witness remain the same.

11 We might contrast this to legal pragmatism, which, as the name suggests, is outcome focused. Although positivism relies on theory to produce law, pragmatism puts more stock in the adjudicator.

12 The concept of *mens rea* was already inaugurated by the Early Modern period, but it was not until 1753 that William Blackstone inaugurated a private course on the common law. Before that date Roman law was taught at Oxford and Cambridge, and barristers and solicitors then apprenticed and trained while attending the Inns of Court. By the turn of the twentieth century, however, the legal profession was already using expert witness testimony more frequently to speak to the accused's state of mind.

13 See Roth and Roth, where they relate these seemingly arbitrary situations:

Anglo-Saxon law was based on trial by ordeal, in which the accused were exposed to physical dangers supposed to be harmless to the innocent ... But these early Germanic legal procedures came in two parts: Before the actual ordeal, there was a proceeding to hear the two sides, decide if there was need for a trial and pinpoint the actual issues involved. Defendants or plaintiffs could bring along friends to verify oaths. This was not to corroborate any testimony, but only to pledge that the oath taker was sincere. Eventually, it seems, these people began not only to attest to an oath, but to speak in favour of their friends. (22)

See also John Briggs's account of trial by compurgation, where "the jury or *juratores* (those sworn), usually numbering twelve, were summoned to swear to the truth of the submission of the defendant or complainant. They did so on the basis not of evidence presented in court but of their knowledge of the disputants and the alleged offences. It was … a form of arbitration with a tendency towards compromise" (5). See also Sadakat Kadri's discussion of early witnesses acting also as jurors (71–2).

14 See Robert Popper's historical account of the evolution of testimony, particularly the ways the right to testify developed in both England and America.

15 See M.H. Abrams for a thorough discussion of interior monologue. He differentiates between interior monologue and "stream of consciousness" by stating, "'Interior monologue' is then reserved for that species of stream of consciousness which undertakes to present to the reader the course and rhythm of consciousness precisely as it occurs in a character's mind" (299). Although he reserves interior monologue as a stripe of nonauthorial intervention, others have found it useful to divide narration of this kind between direct and indirect. Direct interior monologue is purely the character's course and rhythm of consciousness, while indirect allows for some authorial intervention.

16 The number of reported English cases that deal with intentionality and states of mind at the turn of the twentieth century grows rapidly. More important, the attention to the relationships between intention and identity become more intricately explored by the judiciary.

17 I use the word trauma here and throughout my discussion in a sense somewhat removed from classical trauma theory. I bring out these distinctions as my discussion of the moderns and their experiences with the law progresses, and further define these terms in Chapter 1.

18 Richard Ellmann, celebrated and equally criticized biographer of Joyce, offers a rather prodigious account of Joyce's activities between 1914 and 1918. Yet he still maintains that Joyce remained essentially neutral, and that almost any contact with these important yet external events was treated as an intrusion (339–447).

19 Although critics such as Melanie Williams and Jan-Melissa Schramm have begun these kinds of inquiries, my focus travels beyond looking at subjectivity as a historiographic artefact and argues for a revitalization of liberal jurisprudence as an addition to cultural theory in understanding the complexities of the literary/legal fault line.

20 Legal reporting series, much like literary publications, must choose what to publish. Only those cases that the editors deem important changes to

the law or that are precedent-setting make their way into a reporter. For this reason, most cases go unreported, although trial transcripts often remain archived within the court that heard the case.

21 See Peter Goodrich's treatment of the poem in *Law in the Courts of Love*. Similarly, his discussion of the overlap between legal traditions carries weight here. For example, when he speaks of peasants removing their hats before the courts, he suggests that "that norm of civil honour or secular reverence was not an accident of custom or of local practice, it was a recognition, although perhaps only a partial one, of the historical transmission of spirituality and of 'ghostly power' from natural to positive law" (26).

22 The stark contrast between descriptive and normative in liberal jurisprudence is exactly the dichotomy I want to trouble in my writing here. The history of law's normativity, and perhaps even objectivism, is best reworked through using the porosity between law's objective aims and critical aims in the humanities.

23 A useful point of departure into a history of the interaction between law and literature might begin with Daniela Carpi's *Shakespeare and the Law*, a collection of essays dealing with the life and works of Shakespeare as legally interpreted and as legal interpretation. Another, more focused anthology is Cedric Brown's *Law in Shakespeare*, as its essays focus primarily on the rise of the professional class during the Early Modern period and on the intersection of dramatic and legal language. For a first-hand account of these interactions and his rather acrid responses to them, see John Donne's "Satire 2."

Chapter 1

1 It was not until 1967, following the British government's consideration of the 1957 Wolfenden Report, that new legislation permitted homosexual acts in private between consenting men age twenty-one and older.

2 Hyde's potential reasons for Wilde's "abnormal" sexual preference include abnormalities like an excessively large pituitary gland, inherited from his mother, a similar inheritance of her artistic nature, and the exposure to his father's sexual promiscuity (and possible rape of his medical patients under chloroform) (50–2).

3 His Chapters 4 and 5, which deal with the cultural climate of "heterosexism and homophobia as historical constructs" and "theorizing Wilde's identity and desire," are especially illuminating in providing historical context for the climate surrounding Wilde's actions during this period.

4 *Ulysses* was one of the first books to be put on trial. Previously, censors attacked publishers or the authors themselves. See also *United States v. One Book, Entitled "Contraception," by Marie C. Stopes*, 51 F.2d 525 (S.D.N.Y. 1931), and *United States v. One Obscene Book Entitled "Married Love,"* 48 F.2d 821 (S.D.N.Y. 1931).

5 That is not to say that Wilde's testimony was without falsehood. He was first asked about his age, and most unwisely lied (Holland 64). This was not, of course, the last or only evasive manoeuvre Wilde undertook. His efforts to undercut the court's authority were, however, always met by Carson's retributive attacks.

6 This will become abundantly clear in my discussions of Ford Madox Ford.

7 This distinction, between the "private" civil law and the more socially concerned criminal law, is more pronounced in English jurisprudence. See Lindsay Farmer's "Reconstructing the English Codification Debate" for descriptions of the ways English criminal law differs from the Anglo-American tradition of criminal law, where it is "largely treated (and taught) as an adjunct of private law; that is, it is concerned primarily with the definition and protection of private rights and interests. It only considers the limitation of state power as this might be understood to be naturally limited by the existence of a pre-existing sphere of private autonomy" (398).

8 The "harm principle" in civil procedure underlies the liberal philosophy of jurisprudence. Only defined harms are actionable in tort. This is not the same principle underlying criminal procedure, where harm can manifest itself outside individual harms. For instance, assault is a harm recognized by both criminal and civil procedure, each of which defines the harm in its own terms. Vandalism of a public statue, for example, is a harm that attracts only criminal procedure. Civil harms are *in personam*, or against the person; criminal harms are *in rem*, or against the world.

9 Agreeing with Hyde and Foldy, I believe that, had Wilde pursued legal measures before this time, he might well have been successful. Many of Queensberry's actions constituted verbal and written threats upon Wilde, and criminal proceedings for assault, rather than libel, which would not have implicated Wilde's personal life by shifting the burden of proof, might have been a more effective way to deal with the harassment.

10 There is, of course, a plethora of differences between civil and criminal trial procedure, but for the sake of my argument, I limit the discussion to intent and its effects on determining guilt. The distinctions in ideas of intent are important when considering the trials of Ford Madox Ford and James Joyce, to which I turn in subsequent chapters.

11 There is another persuasive reason for doing so: Bracton's treatise on the law was exceptionally rare. That is to say, there were remarkably few treatise writers on English law in medieval England, a tradition that continued through most of the Early Modern period. The principal reason for this was the common law's concern with judge-made law and its avoidance of codification; the law was an instrument of judges, and the rule of law was an extremely porous – or, perhaps better, ambiguous – entity. The reliance on precedent and the vast amount of unwritten material judges had to commit to memory made monographs on the law a protracted endeavour, to say the least.

12 See Sayre's discussion of the lack of a "line between murder and manslaughter" and the concept of voluntarism (994–5).

13 The Year Books report the law of medieval England. The earliest examples are from around 1268, and the last in the printed series is for the year 1535. The Year Books are the principal source materials for the development of legal doctrines in these years. The common law developed into recognizable form in this period.

14 See Sayre's detailed analysis of the progression of *mens rea* in homicide cases, which elucidates their ideological, jurisprudential, and procedural history beginning in the thirteenth century (994–8).

15 Although a discussion of defences to criminal liability opens an entirely new avenue for critical inquiry, perhaps it deserves a small mention here. In the twelfth century, defences to criminal acts, like insanity, infancy, or compulsion, also relied on the accused's choosing between good and evil, not on whether the accused had a specific purpose behind his or her actions. This, too, changed in the seventeenth century, when defences became increasingly reliant on specific intent (Sayre 1004).

16 See also Lisa Rodensky's introduction in *The Crime in Mind*, which nicely elucidates some of the intricacies between intention and *mens rea*.

17 Perhaps Chief Justice Coleridge's powers of reason were equally suspect in his tautological finding: "With the object of protecting women and girls against themselves the Act of Parliament has made illicit connection with a girl under that age unlawful; if a man wishes to have such illicit connection he must wait until the girl is sixteen, otherwise he breaks the law" (712).

18 See Hyde's Chapters 4 and 5 for detailed and accurate accounts of Wilde's criminal trials. Hyde's accounts are based not only on newspaper and first-hand reports of persons present, but also on what he purports to be unexpurgated and unpublished shorthand reports. The *Central Criminal Court Sessions Papers*, the usual source for these court reports, declined to print any of Wilde's trial proceedings, as it deemed them unfit to publish.

Hyde also uses Mason and Grolleau as historical texts, which, from my perusal, support the accounts from the newspaper sources. For an excellent summary of Hyde's work, along with interesting notes from the *Daily Telegraph* and the *Star*, see Foldy's Chapter 1.

19 Again this sort of rhetoric goes to the moral outrage that this specific magistrate felt in regard to the offence, and certainly not to the statutory regime in England at the time. Wilde's offence carried a maximum sentence of two years with hard labour, as his was a misdemeanour, not a felony. Some of the most odious felonies carried the death sentence or life imprisonment. The abstract/absolute does violence to the particular here, as moral outrage replaces statutory interpretation. This, of course, also says nothing about how the judge might interpret the gravity of aggravated assault, rape, or murder.

20 Hyde, Foldy, Mason, and Grolleau refer to the tactical disadvantages Wilde suffered under the new judge, prosecutor, and severance of the action between Wilde and Taylor. Each of these three changes reflected the Crown's drive to convict Wilde at any cost, which was supposed to quell the growing social unrest associated with the trial and the publicity surrounding its "indecent" content.

21 Lockwood's strict attitude to the letter of the law would not leave, thought the prosecution, any room for sympathy for Wilde's position, as Gill's prosecution clearly had.

22 See Foldy for a more extensive summation of these differences and their effects.

23 A chess position in which one is forced to move, yet any move will only further compromise one's position.

Chapter 2

1 See especially Lecture XI, in which Austin discusses most particularly the distinction between the constative and performative aspects of utterances (133–47).

2 John Searle, in his book *Speech Acts*, summarizes what he sees as the intrinsic importance of these utterances: "The reason for concentrating on the study of speech acts is simply this: all linguistic communication involves linguistic acts. The unit of linguistic communication is not, as has generally been supposed, the symbol, word or sentence, or even the token of the supposed, the symbol, word or sentence, or even the token of the symbol, word or sentence, but rather the production or issuance of the symbol or word or sentence in the performance of the speech act" (16).

3 Wilde began serving his sentence, after conviction on 25 May 1895, in
Pentonville Prison. On 4 July he was transferred to Wandsworth Prison,
for unknown reasons, although Hyde speculates it was so that the
Reverend W.D. Morrison might keep a particular watch on him (284). On
21 November Wilde was again transferred, this time to Reading Gaol, after
his bankruptcy proceeding saw him again in court in August and early
November, a process that, combined with hard labour, brought him near
the edge of both mental and physical breakdown.

4 The fate of the manuscript, handed to Wilde's friend and later literary
executor Robert Ross on 19 May 1897, the day of his release from
prison, was no less fractious and fraught with tribulation than the trials
themselves. Lord Alfred Douglas sought its destruction or, if impossible,
the copyright. Ross had copies made, and donated the original manuscript
to the British Museum. Douglas's efforts to keep copies suppressed
saw him launch an action for libel against Arthur Ransome, who used
the manuscript in his study of Wilde. Douglas lost, and Ransome was
awarded costs. See Vyvyan Holland's introduction, Hyde's accounts
(297–306), and Ellmann's chapter, "letter writing" (510–16).

5 See Lecture XII for Austin's summary of this position (148–50).

6 This is, of course, another iteration of a foundational tenet of legal
positivism in Chapter 1.

7 Recall here Hart's ideas about the rules of recognition and secondary rules.
Wilde, like Hart, searched for a rational foundation otherwise lacking in
fin de siècle jurisprudence.

8 How the autonomy of the individual relates to his or her assertion of
rights and, of course, to a just decision is again paramount here. Wilde
was not tried on the facts, but on evidence such as possible lurid messages
in his writing. In this case, autonomy and rights were suspended, a
position that is simply unconscionable in modern liberal democratic
jurisprudence.

9 Some of these things include instances such as Wilde's comment that he
would not kiss Walter Grainger "because he was ugly" (which sparked
an uproar as the gallery and judge missed completely the wit and focused
on the implied converse) and testimony from "rent boys" such as Charles
Parker, who, although discredited by the court as blackmailers and
witnesses for hire, were still allowed to testify to alleged sexual encounters
with Wilde.

10 Save, perhaps, Ellmann's assertion that one might confess another's
transgressions. From the discussion so far, it should be fairly clear that
my understanding of confession is that it is necessarily self-reflexive

and internalized, and cannot take into account the ontology of another. Although the confession itself is externalized through language, it is impossible to know the mental states of another, and thus only the person confessing can ever know whether the *mens rea* of the confession is real.

11 This, of course, again raises the question of authenticity, with which Brooks is much concerned. If confession and testimony are to bear a special stamp of authenticity, what Wilde said in the dock and wrote in *De Profundis* challenged these assumptions of the legal system in a most adversarial manner. Confession, for Wilde, as a weapon of censure and scorn, could only assert a kind of authenticity that would be in diametric opposition to the morality of the law. In this way, the authenticity of the law is not shared with the authenticity of the subject. In effect, there exist competing "authenticities."

12 Jeffrey Meyers, for example, comments on Conrad's Jamesian narrative techniques (156–9), while equally emphasizing his influence on Eliot (238), Ford (403), Gide (261), Hemingway (245), and Mann (394).

13 See Brian Artese's discussion of narration and the importance of the characters in *Testimony on Trial*. When considering Marlow, Artese argues that there "was no incertitude as to facts" (30). He further states that "all the novel's questions … would have remained questions without Marlow's participation" (31). Focusing on the characters' contributions to the narrative, rather than on the shifts in narration itself, Artese offers a thoughtful alternative to traditional interpretations of Marlow's voice.

14 Ash's work is tied strongly to psychoanalytic criticism. *Writing in Between* explores relationships between Conrad's constructed subjectivity, in his world, and the fictional narratives he creates. Her ideas about "shared social experience," which she knowingly takes from psychoanalytic historian Peter Homans and psychoanalysts Heinz Kohut and Didier Anzieu, re-evaluate what Homans calls "the universal human, spontaneous sense of and wish for 'the whole'" (Ash 6). In a world of increased mechanization and industrialization, Ash argues, the shared human experience becomes dislocated, and the self becomes less accessible as an isolated entity. These ideas, of course, also relate particularly well to my discussion of rights and autonomy of the civil subject in a liberal democracy. These ideas drive what I see as Conrad's more complex understanding of the civil subject and his or her inability to access the "whole" or "core" individual that the law so demands in its search for ontological certainty.

Chapter 3

1 Ford also appeared as counsel for a soldier under court martial proceedings
  in 1918, and in 1935 attended, on behalf of the Associated Press, the trial
  of Bruno Hauptmann for the 1932 kidnapping and murder of Charles
  Lindbergh's son (Saunders 2:47, 478).
2 Although Joyce's encounters with the courtroom were far more pronounced
  in *United States of America v. One Book Called "Ulysses,"* for example, Joyce
  was not actually on trial.
3 In Wilde's case, it was not for these reasons, as his was definitely a
  precedent-setting cause of action. Instead the courts chose to suppress the
  reporting of the proceedings, as the subject matter was thought too indecent
  to report. Compare this decision to Ford's, where Elsie Martindale's father
  makes an application to protect his daughter from Ford.
4 Fordian scholarship is silent regarding discussions of this judicial
  decision. Although biographers and critics both discuss the circumstances
  surrounding this trial, there has not been, to date, any real attempt to
  connect the legal report of this case to Ford's life. Although we know that
  Justice North censored Ford, the intricacies of the case are wholly neglected.
5 See *Andrew v. Raeburn* [L.R.] 9 Ch. App. 522–4.
6 See *Mellor v. Thompson* 31 Ch. D. 55–6.
7 See *Badishche Anilin und Soda Fabrik v. Levinstein* 24 Ch. D. 156–76.
8 In addition to reports in the *Star*, which emerged on the same afternoon
  as the morning hearing, further accounts hit the dailies the following
  mornings. On 7 June, the *Pall Mall Gazette* published a similarly touting
  paragraph, adding the falsity that the proceedings were in open court, and
  on 8 June this paragraph appeared in *People* (195) under the headline, "A
  Young Novelist's Romance":

> A romance which has excited much interest in certain literary and artistic
> circles in *London* became more widely known yesterday as forming the
> subject of an action in Chancery Court No. 2, before Mr. Justice *North*. The
> cause was *In re Martindale*, and the action taken to prevent the marriage
> of a Miss *Martindale*, a minor and a ward in Chancery. When the case
> came on it was found out that there was no longer a Miss *Martindale* to
> be protected, and an adjournment had to be made. In fact, the lady had
> three weeks before been married to the lover who it was sought to bar –
> Mr. *Ford Madox Hueffer*. Mr. *Hueffer* has already made a certain mark in
> fiction. He has also published a book of verse, and his last book, "The
> Queen who Flew," is illustrated by Sir E. Burne-Jones. Mr. *Hueffer* is

son of the late *Dr. Hueffer*, the champion of *Wagner* and the well-known musical critic, and grandson of the late *Ford Madox Brown*.

 9 Here Justice North refers to Ford's counsel's argument that Ford was both looking out for Elsie Martindale's best interests and acting on her instructions when he sent the information to press. The "line" defence counsel put forward was that the publication of the *in camera* proceedings was to Elsie's advantage, as it otherwise would appear she was living with Ford out of wedlock. Ford's motivation for publication, counsel argued, was "for the protection and benefit of the ward" and Ford "had no intention of disclosing anything prejudicial to his wife" (197–8).

10 After describing the metanarrative of justice, which Dimock convincingly argues dominates Western philosophical thought, she begins to lay the foundations of her own argument, where she argues that justice is "first and foremost a set of cognitive postulates … not infrequently, dissolving the world in the very act of describing it" (2). She seeks to trouble the metanarrative by pointing to the very philosophical and argumentative frameworks that underpin both jurisprudential and literary conceptions of justice as "corrective, distributive, compensatory, or revolutionary." Instead, she argues, justice is "one particular virtue, one virtue among others" (5). Dimock rejects ideas of justice as self-evident, arguing instead its conditional nature. Central to her arguments is her attack on "commensurability" within the language of justice. Dimock abandons commensurability, seen as inadequate, in favour of the incommensurate, "understood as the operative conditions and possibly as the operative limits of justice … of what remains unredressed, unrecovered, noncorresponding" (6).

11 The *Throne* case took place on 7–8 February 1913, and Ford started *The Good Soldier* in March. By 22 July Ford was in bankruptcy court on Elsie's petition. Her counsel adjourned the proceedings to pour further over his accounts, but Ford was again noticeably shaken (Saunders 1:389). "An imagist poem will produce little effect upon [a] man who is going through the bankruptcy court," remarked Ford shortly thereafter (391).

12 At least in contrast to Martindale, for instance, where her father initiates the proceedings.

13 The 5 shilling fine in 1915 was equivalent, in 2006, to approximately £14, or $35.

14 The *Oxford English Dictionary*, for example, cites the first printed usages of "homosexuality" and "homosexual" in English in 1892, and applies the term to both men and women. It was first used in the context of a form of psychosis.

15 See Rushing for an in-depth analysis of the events between Joyce and
    Carr, along with a balanced appraisal of both sides of the dispute. See, in
    particular, where Rushing cites the actual order of Division I of the Circuit
    Court of Zurich, which states, "plaintiff brought a libel action against
    the defendant" (384). Why this was treated as libel and not slander is
    unknown, as neither Rushing nor other scholars since have raised this
    legal issue.

16 See Adrian Hardiman's article, which nicely illustrates Joyce's
    preoccupation with the legal system and his doubt of its effectiveness.
    Hardiman explains: "the doubt that Joyce expresses about the official
    version of these sensational trials anticipates the epistemological concerns
    that he manifests about various Irish cases to which he refers in Ulysses
    and Finnegans Wake, and vindicates in quite a dramatic way the validity
    of philosophical (and judicial) doubt where certainty is not properly
    attainable" (3).

17 Richard Ellmann reports this sum as 50 francs, Norburn as 40.

18 I do not mean to suggest that Valente is ignorant of these facets of the
    text, but merely that any study of the ethical and political aspects of
    Ulysses is seriously impoverished without considering the ways justice
    necessarily connects not just with style, but also with its historical context.
    As it stands, Valente's argument neglects the historical in favour of the
    rhetorical.

19 See Ellmann (451) for a discussion of what he sees as Joyce's affairs
    providing the historical background to the encounter with Gerty.

20 See the shibboleth story in Judges.

21 Streit claims that "Bloom's degradation in the confession drastically
    brings to the text's surface Foucault's statement that Western man
    has become a 'confessing animal,'" but bases this upon the "linguistic
    staging of sexual practices that the text distributes among various female
    speakers" (96). This, I argue, is a misreading of the scene, as the parade
    of witnesses who testify against Bloom does not equate to Bloom's own
    confessional act.

22 The closest Bloom comes to a criminal confession is his admission, after
    Mrs Mervyn Talboy's long rant about Bloom's invitation to her to whip
    him, that "[he] meant only the spanking idea. A warm tingling glow
    without effusion. Refined birching to stimulate circulation" (593–4). Even
    here, however, he lacks the *mens rea*, or at least testifies that he lacks the
    mens rea, for the act of which he is accused. Further complicating this
    admission, Bloom's statement is so utterly humorous that it is difficult to
    regard it as little more than rhetorical play.

23 Technology and regulation of the Internet, for example, are together
perhaps one of the most topical contemporary cases. I argue later that the
BBC was also a result of the need for government intervention resulting
from the legal institution's culture of argument surrounding spectacle in
the press. The Internet, in its present context, mirrors many of the same
issues the British government faced at the turn of the twentieth century as
it dealt with popular sensationalism.

Chapter 4

1 Matthew 27: 45–6.
2 After his release from prison for the Eliza Armstrong fiasco, and now
editing a new journal he called the *Review of Reviews*, Stead continued to
monitor and criticize the government and its laws and policies (Hyde 340).
3 Harriet Beecher Stowe's *Uncle Tom's Cabin* might be one such literary work.
4 Shoshana Felman's *The Juridical Unconscious* includes a thorough discussion
of the Simpson trial, where she argues that a legal memory corresponds to
the Freudian idea of "a return of the repressed." In effect, the law's memory
comes by precedent and by "a forgotten chain of cultural wounds and by
compulsive or unconscious legal repetitions of traumatic, wounding legal
cases" (57). This theory of legal repetition emphasizes, in the Simpson
events, the exigencies of gender and race relations in the United States, as
well as the archiving of these traumas.
5 See Asa Briggs and Peter Burke's *A Social History of the Media* for an
informative discussion of the revolutions in print culture and electronic
communication. The term "media," in fact, is somewhat anachronistic, as it
entered into common use only in the 1920s (1). This is, of course, significant
to later discussion, especially in reference to the BBC.

Works Consulted

Abrams, M.H. *A Glossary of Literary Terms*. Ithaca, NY: Cornell University Press, 1999.

"Actus reus." In *A Dictionary of Law*. Edited by Elizabeth A. Martin. Oxford: Oxford University Press, 2002. Available online at http://www. oxfordreference.com.myaccess.library.utoronto.ca/views/ENTRY. html?subview=Main&entry=t49.e61.

"Actus reus." In *Oxford English Dictionary*. Edited by John Simpson. Oxford: Oxford University Press, 1989. Available online at http://dictionary.oed. com.myaccess.library.utoronto.ca/cgi/entry/00296619?single=1&query_ type=word&queryword=actus+reus&first=1&max_to_show=10.

Adams, James Eli. *Dandies and Desert Saints: Styles of Victorian Manhood*. Ithaca, NY: Cornell University Press, 1995.

Admiralty Offences (Colonial) Act. 1849. 12 and 13 Vict. c. 96.

Altman, Andrew. *Critical Legal Studies*. Princeton, NJ: Princeton University Press, 1990.

Andrew v. Raeburn. [L.R.] 9 Ch. App. 522–4.

Ardis, Ann L. *Modernism and Cultural Conflict*. New York: Cambridge University Press, 2002.

Aristodemou, Maria. *Law and Literature: Journeys from Her to Eternity*. Oxford: Oxford University Press, 2000.

Artese, Brian. *Testimony on Trial: Conrad, James, and the Contest for Modernism*. Toronto: University of Toronto Press, 2012.

Ash, Beth Sharon. *Writing in Between: Modernity and Psychosocial Dilemma in the Novels of Joseph Conrad*. New York: St Martin's Press, 1999.

Auden, W.H. "Law Like Love." In *Collected Poems*. Edited by Edwart Mendelson. New York: Vintage, 1991.

Austin, John. *The Province of Jurisprudence Determined*. Edited by W.E. Rumble. Cambridge: Cambridge University Press, 1995.

Austin, J.L. *How to Do Things with Words*. Edited by J.O. Urmson and Marina Sbisà. 1962. Reprint, Cambridge, MA: Harvard University Press, 1975.

Badishche Anilin und Soda Fabrik v. Levinstein. 24 Ch. D. 156–76.

Bailey, Derrick Sherwin. *Homosexuality and the Western Christian Tradition*. London: Longmans, 1955.

Baker, J.H. *An Introduction to English Legal History*. London: Butterworths, 1979.

Banerjee, Bharati. *The Chutneyfication of History*. Heidelberg, Germany: Universitätswerlag C. Winter, 2002.

Barleben, Dale. "Judging *Ulysses*: Censorship and Evidence in the Trials of 'One Book.'" Paper prepared for the Republic and Letters Panel, Creativity and the Law Colloquium, University of Toronto, 21 January 2006.

Batchelor, John. *Lord Jim*. London: Unwin Hyman, 1988.

Beebe, Maurice, ed. *Ford Madox Ford. Modern Fiction Studies* 9, no. 1, special issue (1963).

Benstock, Bernard, ed. *James Joyce: The Augmented Ninth*. Syracuse, NY: Syracuse University Press, 1988.

Berlin, Isaiah. *Four Essays on Liberty*. Oxford: Oxford University Press, 1969.

Berlin, Isaiah. *Liberty*. Oxford: Oxford University Press, 2002.

Berlin, Isaiah. *Two Concepts of Liberty*. Oxford: Clarendon Press, 1962.

Billy, Ted, ed. *Critical Essays on Joseph Conrad*. Boston: G.K. Hall, 1987.

Binder, Guyora, and Robert Weisberg. *Literary Criticisms of Law*. Princeton, NJ: Princeton University Press, 2000.

Bracton, Henry. *De Legibus Et Consuetudinibus Angliæ*. "Bracton Online." Available at http://bracton.law.harvard.edu/, accessed 15 November 2006.

Briggs, Asa, and Peter Burke. *A Social History of the Media*. Cambridge, UK: Polity, 2005.

Briggs, John, et al. *Crime and Punishment in England*. New York: St Martin's Press, 1996.

Brooks, Peter. *Troubling Confessions: Speaking Guilt in Law & Literature*. Chicago: University of Chicago Press, 2000.

Brown, Cedric C., et al., eds. *Law in Shakespeare*. New York: Palgrave Macmillan, 2006.

Buggery Act. 1533. 25 Hen. VIII c. 6.

Butler, Judith. *Excitable Speech*. New York: Routledge, 1997.

Butler, Judith. *Gender Trouble*. London: Routledge, 1990.

Carpi, Daniela. *Shakespeare and the Law*. Ravenna, Italy: Longo, 2003.

Carrithers, David W., et al., eds. *Montesquieu's Science of Politics*. Lanham, MD: Rowman & Littlefield, 2001.

Coke, Edward. *The Selected Writings and Speeches of Sir Edward Coke.* Indianapolis, IN: Liberty Fund, 2003.

Coke, Edward. *The Third Part of the Institutes of the Laws of England: Concerning high Treason, and other Pleas of the Crown, and Criminal Causes.* 4th ed. London: A. Crooke, 1669.

Coleman, Jules. *The Practice of Principle.* Oxford: Oxford University Press, 2001.

Colonial Laws Validity Act. 1865. 28 and 29 Vict. c. 63.

Conrad, Joseph. *Lord Jim.* Edited by John Batchelor. 1900. Reprint, Oxford: Oxford University Press, 2000.

Contagious Diseases Act. 1864. 27 and 28 Vict. c. 85.

Coombe, Rosemary J. "Critical Cultural Legal Studies." *Yale Journal of Law & the Humanities* 10, no. 2 (1998): 463–86.

Cover, Robert. *Narrative, Violence, and the Law.* Edited by Martha Minow, Michael Ryan, and Austin Sarat. Ann Arbor: University of Michigan Press, 1995.

Cover, Robert. "Violence and the Word." *Yale Law Journal* 95, no. 8 (1986): 1601–29.

Criminal Law Amendment Act. 1885. 48 and 49 Vict. c. 69.

Crisell, Andrew. *An Introductory History of British Broadcasting.* New York: Routledge, 2002.

Crotty, Kevin M. *Law's Interior.* Ithaca. NY: Cornell University Press: 2001.

Culleton, Claire A. *Joyce and the G-Men.* New York: Palgrave, 2004.

Culver, Keith, ed. *Readings in the Philosophy of Law.* Peterborough, ON: Broadview Press, 1999.

Daggers, Jenny, and Diana Neal, eds. *Sex, Gender, and Religion: Josephine Butler Revisited.* New York: Peter Lang, 2006.

Davidson, Neil R. *James Joyce, Ulysses and the Construction of Jewish Identity.* Cambridge: Cambridge University Press, 1996.

Decoste, Ted. "Torts Lecture." Given at the University of Alberta Law School, Edmonton, 6 October 1994.

Delbanco, Nicholas. *Group Portrait: Joseph Conrad, Stephen Crane, Ford Madox Ford, Henry James, and H.G. Wells.* New York: William Morrow, 1982.

Derrida, Jacques. *Speech and Phenomena.* Translated by David B. Allison. 1967. Reprint, Evanston, IL: Northwestern University Press, 1973.

Derrida, Jacques. "Ulysses Gramophone." In *James Joyce: The Augmented Ninth.* Edited by Bernard Benstock, 27–75. Syracuse, NY: Syracuse University Press, 1988.

Dimock, Wai Chee. *Residues of Justice.* Berkeley: University of California Press, 1996.

Dimock, Wai Chee. "Rethinking Space, Rethinking Rights: Literature, Law, Science." *Yale Journal of Law & the Humanities* 10, no. 2 (1998): 487–504.

Dimock, Wai Chee. "Rules of Law, Laws of Science." *Yale Journal of Law & the Humanities* 13, no. 1 (2001): 203–25.

Dolin, Kieran. *Fiction and the Law*. Cambridge: Cambridge University Press, 1999.

Donne, John. "Satire 2." In *The Complete English Poems*. Edited by A.J. Smith. Toronto: Penguin, 1996.

Dworkin, Ronald. *Law's Empire*. Cambridge, MA: Harvard University Press, 1986.

Dworkin, Ronald. *Taking Rights Seriously*. Cambridge, MA: Harvard University Press, 1978.

Eliot. T.S. "The Love Song of J. Alfred Prufrock." In *Collected Poems 1909–1962*. 1963. Reprint, New York: Harcourt Brace, 1991.

Ellmann, Richard. *James Joyce*. Oxford: Oxford University Press, 1984.

Ellmann, Richard. *Oscar Wilde*. New York: Knopf, 1987.

Englander, David. *Poverty and Poor Law Reform in 19th Century Britain, 1834–1914*. London: Longman, 1998.

Farmer, Lindsay. "Reconstructing the English Codification Debate: The Criminal Law Commissioners, 1833–45." *Law and History Review* 18, no. 2 (2000): 397–426.

Felman, Shoshana. *The Juridical Unconscious: Trials and Traumas in the Twentieth Century*. Cambridge, MA: Harvard University Press, 2002.

Ferguson, Rex. *Criminal Law and the Modernist Novel*. Cambridge: Cambridge University Press, 2013.

Fitzpatrick, Peter. *Modernism and the Grounds of Law*. Cambridge: Cambridge University Press, 2001.

Foldy, Michael S. *The Trials of Oscar Wilde*. New Haven, CT: Yale University Press, 1997.

Ford, Ford Madox. *The Good Soldier*. Edited by Thomas C. Moser. 1915. Reprint, Oxford: Oxford University Press, 1999.

Forman, F.N. *Constitutional Change in the United Kingdom*. London: Routledge, 2002.

Foucault, Michel. *Discipline and Punish*. Translated by Alan Sheridan. 1975. Reprint, New York: Vintage, 1995.

Frank, Jerome. *Law and the Modern Mind*. Gloucester, MA: Peter Smith, 1970.

Fuller, Lon L. *The Morality of Law*. 1964. Revised ed., New Haven, CT: Yale University Press, 1969.

Gibson, Andrew. *Joyce's Revenge: History, Politics, and Aesthetics in Ulysses*. Oxford: Oxford University Press, 2002.

Gillespie, Michael Patrick, and A. Nicholas Fargnoli, eds. *Ulysses in Critical Perspective*. Gainesville: University Press of Florida, 2006.

Glendon, Mary Ann. *Rights Talk*. New York: Free Press, 1991.

Goodrich, Peter. *Law in the Courts of Love*. New York: Routledge, 1996.

Gordon, John. *Joyce and Reality: The Empirical Strikes Back*. Syracuse, NY: Syracuse University Press, 2004.

Grolleau, Charles. *The Shame of Oscar Wilde: From the Shorthand Reports*. Paris: privately printed, 1906.

Gross, Ariela Julie. *Double Character*. Princeton, NJ: Princeton University Press, 2000.

Grossman, Jonathan H. *The Art of the Alibi*. Baltimore: Johns Hopkins University Press, 2002.

Hale, Matthew. *The History of the Common Law of England*. Edited by Charles M. Gray. 1713. Reprint, Chicago: University of Chicago Press, 1971.

Hale, Matthew. *Pleas of the Crown*. Edited by P.R. Glaxebrook. 1678. Reprint, London: Professional Books, 1972.

Hall, Radclyffe. *The Well of Loneliness*. 1928. Reprint, London: Virago, 1982.

Hampson, Robert, and Tony Davenport, eds. *Ford Madox Ford: A Reappraisal*. International Ford Madox Ford Studies 1. Amsterdam: Rodopi, 2002.

Hampton, Mark. *Visions of the Press in Britain, 1850–1950*. Urbana; Chicago: University of Illinois Press, 2004.

Hardiman, Adrian. "Joyce, Great Wyrley and the Necessity of Judicious Doubt." *Dublin James Joyce Journal* 5 (2012): 1–15.

Harris, Frank. *Oscar Wilde, His Life and Confessions*. New York: Horizon Press, 1974.

Hart, H.L.A. *The Concept of Law*. Edited by Penelope A. Bulloch and Joseph Raz. 1961. Reprint, Oxford: Clarendon Press, 1994.

Hoffmann, Charles G. *Ford Madox Ford*. Boston: Twayne, 1990.

Holland, Merlin. *The Real Trial of Oscar Wilde*. New York: Perennial, 2004.

Holland, Vyvyan. "Introduction." In *De Profundis and Other Writings*, by Oscar Wilde, 91–6. Edited by Hesketh Pearson. New York: Penguin, 1986.

Holmes, Oliver Wendell, Jr. "The Path of the Law." *Harvard Law Review* 10, no. 8 (1897): 457–78.

Hutcheon, Linda. *A Theory of Parody*. Chicago: University of Illinois Press, 2000.

Hyde, H. Montgomery. *The Trials of Oscar Wilde*. New York: Dover, 1962.

In re Martindale. [1894] 3 Ch. 193–203.

Jordan, Jane. *Josephine Butler*. London: John Murray, 2001.

Joyce, James. *Ulysses*. Edited by Seamus Deane. 1922. Reprint, Toronto: Penguin, 2000.

Judd, Alan. *Ford Madox Ford*. London: Collins, 1990.

Kadri, Sadakat. *The Trial: A History, from Socrates to O.J. Simpson*. New York: Random House, 2005.

Kafka, Franz. *The Trial*. 1915. Reprint, Oxford: Oxford University Press, 2009.

Kahn, Victoria. "Early Modern Rights Talk." *Yale Journal of Law & the Humanities* 13, no. 2 (2001): 391–411.

Kairys, David, ed. *The Politics of Law*. New York: Basic Books, 1998.

Kelman, Mark. *A Guide to Critical Legal Studies*. Cambridge, MA: Harvard University Press, 1987.

Kennedy, Duncan. "Critical Labor Law Theory: A Comment." *Industrial Relations Law Journal* 4, no. 3 (1981): 503–6.

Kennedy, Duncan. "Legal Education as Training for Hierarchy." In *The Politics of Law*. Edited by David Kairys, 54–75. New York: Basic Books, 1998.

Kerr, Margaret H. "R. v. Hawisa, R. v. Alan the Miller, and William Son of John v. Walter Son of Ralf Hose: Three Murder Trials in England c. 1200." In *Crime and Punishment in the Middle Ages*. Edited by Timothy S. Haskett, 87–111. Victoria, BC: University of Victoria, 1998.

Kershner, R. Brandon, ed. *Cultural Studies of James Joyce*. New York: Rodopi, 2003.

Kershner, R. Brandon, ed. *Joyce and Popular Culture*. Gainesville: University Press of Florida, 1996.

Kershner, R. Brandon. "Ulysses and the Daily Press." Presentation to Popular Culture Panel, International James Joyce Symposium, Budapest, 14 June 2006.

Knowles, Owen. *A Conrad Chronology*. London: Macmillan, 1989.

Lacey, Nicola. *A Life of H.L.A. Hart*. Oxford: Oxford University Press, 2004.

Larmore, Charles. *Patterns of Moral Complexity*. Cambridge: Cambridge University Press, 1987.

Lawrence, Karen. "Paternity as Legal Fiction in *Ulysses*." In *James Joyce: The Augmented Ninth*. Edited by Bernard Benstock, 233–43. Syracuse, NY: Syracuse University Press, 1988.

Libel Act. 1843. 6 and 7 Vict. c. 96.

Lindberg-Seyersted, Brita, ed. *A Literary Friendship: Correspondence between Caroline Gordon & Ford Madox Ford*. Knoxville: University of Tennessee Press, 1999.

Lindberg-Seyersted, Brita. *Pound/Ford: The Story of a Literary Friendship*. New York: New Directions, 1982.

Locke, John. *Two Treatises of Government*. Edited by Ian Shapiro. 1689. Reprint, New Haven, CT: Yale University Press, 2003.

Ludwig, Richard M., ed. *Letters of Ford Madox Ford*. Princeton, NJ: Princeton University Press, 1965.

MacKinnon, Catherine A. *Towards a Feminist Theory of the State*. Cambridge, MA: Harvard University Press, 1989.

Manderson, Desmond. *Kangaroo Courts and the Rule of Law: The Legacy of Modernism*. New York: Routledge, 2012.

Mason, Stuart. *Oscar Wilde: Three Times Tried*. London: Ferrestone Press, 1912.

Melaney, William D. *After Ontology: Literary Theory and Modernist Poetics*. New York: State University of New York Press, 2001.

Mellor v. Thompson. 31 Ch. D. 55–6.

"Mens rea." In *A Dictionary of Law*. Edited by Elizabeth A. Martin. Oxford: Oxford University Press, 2002. Available online at http://www. oxfordreference.com.myaccess.library.utoronto.ca/views/ENTRY. html?subview=Main&entry=t49.e2274.

"Mens rea." In *Oxford English Dictionary*. Edited by John Simpson. Oxford: Oxford University Press, 1989. Available online at http://dictionary.oed.com. myaccess.library.utoronto.ca/cgi/entry/00305931?single=1&query_type= word&queryword=mens+rea&first=1&max_to_show=10.

Merchant Shipping (Colonial) Act. 1869. 32 and 33 Vict. c. 11.

Meyers, Jeffrey. *Joseph Conrad*. London: John Murray, 1991.

Mill, J.S. *On Liberty*. 1869. Reprint, London: Everyman, 1973.

Minow, Martha. "Politics and Procedure." In *The Politics of Law*. Edited by David Kairys, 79–96. New York: Basic Books, 1998.

Mizener, Arthur. *The Saddest Story: A Biography of Ford Madox Ford*. New York: World Publishing, 1971.

Montesquieu, Charles de Secondat, baron de. *The Spirit of the Laws*. Edited by Anne M. Cohler et al. 1748. Reprint, Cambridge: Cambridge University Press, 1990.

Moran, Mayo. *Rethinking the Reasonable Person*. Oxford: Oxford University Press, 2003.

Moser, Thomas, ed. "Introduction." In *The Good Soldier*, by Ford Madox Ford, vii–xxvii. Oxford: Oxford University Press, 1999.

Nadel, Ira B. *Joyce and the Jews*. Gainesville: University Press of Florida, 1989.

Norburn, Roger. *A James Joyce Chronology*. Houndmills, UK: Palgrave, 2004.

O'Donnell, Bernard. *The Old Bailey and Its Trials*. Westport, CT: Greenwood, 1952.

Offences Against the Person Act. 1861. 24 and 25 Vict. c. 100.

Parkes, Adam. "Lesbianism, History, and Censorship: The Well of Loneliness and the Suppressed Randiness of Virginia Woolf's Orlando." *Twentieth Century Literature* 40, no. 4 (1994): 434–60.

Peters, Julie Stone. "Law, Literature, and the Vanishing Real: On the Future of Interdisciplinary Illusion." *PMLA* 120, no. 2 (2005): 442–53.

Plowden, Alison. *The Case of Eliza Armstrong*. London: British Broadcasting Corporation, 1974.

Poor Law Amendment Act. 1834. 4 and 5 W. IV. c. 76.

Popper, Robert. "History and Development of the Accused's Right to Testify." *Washington University Law Review* 1962, no. 4 (1962): 454–73.

Post, Robert. *Law and the Order of Culture*. Berkeley: University of California Press, 1991.

Potter, Rachel. "Waiting at the Entrance to the Law: Modernism, Gender and Democracy." *Textual Practice* 14, no. 2 (2000): 253–63.

The Queen v. Tyrrell [1894] 1 Q.B. 710–13.

Rawls, John. *Political Liberalism*. New York: Columbia University Press, 1993.

Rawls, John. *A Theory of Justice*. Cambridge, MA: Harvard University Press, 1971.

Reichman, Ravit. *The Affective Life of Law*. Stanford, CA: Stanford University Press, 2009.

Representation of the People Act. 1832. 2 and 3 W. IV. c. 45.

Representation of the People Act. 1867. 30 and 31 Vict. c. 102.

Representation of the People Act. 1884. 48 and 49 Vict. c. 3.

Rodensky, Lisa. *The Crime in Mind*. Oxford: Oxford University Press, 2003.

Ross, Stephen. *Conrad and Empire*. Columbia: University of Missouri Press, 2004.

Roth, Andrew, and Jonathan Roth. *Devil's Advocates: The Unnatural History of Lawyers*. Berkeley, CA: Nolo Press, 1989.

Rousseau, Jean-Jacques. *The Social Contract*. Edited by Susan Dunn. 1762. Reprint, New Haven, CT: Yale University Press, 2003.

Rushdie, Salman. *Midnight's Children*. Toronto: Vintage Canada, 1997.

Rushing, Conrad L. "The English Players Incident: What Really Happened?" *James Joyce Quarterly* 37 (2000): 371–88.

Said, Edward W. "Conrad: The Presentation of Narrative." In *Critical Essays on Joseph Conrad*. Edited by Ted Billy, 28–46. Boston: G.K. Hall, 1987.

Sarat, Austin. "Going to Court: Access, Autonomy, and the Contradictions of Liberal Legality." In *The Politics of Law*. Edited by David Kairys, 97–114. New York: Basic Books, 1998.

Sarat, Austin, and Thomas R. Kearns, eds. *Law in the Domains of Culture*. Ann Arbor: University of Michigan Press, 1998.

Saunders, Max. *Ford Madox Ford: A Dual Life*. 2 v. Oxford: Oxford University Press, 1996.

Saunders, Max, and Richard Stang, eds. *Ford Madox Ford: Critical Essays*. New York: New York University Press, 2004.

Saussure, Ferdinand de. *Course in General Linguistics*. Edited by Charles Bally and Albert Sechehaye. New York: Philosophical Library, 1959.

Saussure, Ferdinand de. "The Cultural Lives of Law." In *Law in the Domains of Culture*. Edited by Austin Sarat and Thomas R. Kearns, 1–20. Ann Arbor: University of Michigan Press, 1998.

Sayre, Francis Bowes. "Mens Rea." *Harvard Law Review* 45, no. 6 (1932): 974–1026.

Schauer, Frederick. "(Re)Taking Hart." Presentation to Legal Theory Workshop, Faculty of Law, University of Toronto, 14 October 2005.

Schramm, Jan-Melissa. *Testimony and Advocacy in Victorian Law, Literature, and Theology*. Cambridge: Cambridge University Press, 2000.

Searle, John R. *Speech Acts*. Cambridge: Cambridge University Press, 1969.

Secor, Robert, and Marie Secor, eds. *The Return of the Good Soldier: Ford Madox Ford and Violet Hunt's 1917 Diary*. English Literary Studies 30. Victoria, BC: University of Victoria Press, 1983.

Sedgwick, Eve Kosofsky. *Between Men*. New York: Columbia University Press, 1985.

Seidman, Louis Michael, and Mark V. Tushnet. *Remnant of Belief*. New York: Oxford University Press, 1996.

Shapiro, Scott. "Massively Shared Agency." Presentation to Legal Theory Workshop, Faculty of Law, University of Toronto, 8 September 2006.

Sherard, R.H. *Bernard Shaw, Frank Harris & Oscar Wilde*. New York: Greystone Press, 1937.

Sherard, R.H. *The Life of Oscar Wilde*. London: T.W. Laurie, 1911.

Singer, Joseph. "The Player and the Cards: Nihilism and Legal Theory." *Yale Law Journal* 94, no. 1 (1984): 1–70.

Smith, Patricia. *Feminist Jurisprudence*. Oxford: Oxford University Press, 1993.

Spoo, Robert. *James Joyce and the Language of History*. Oxford: Oxford University Press, 1994.

Spurr, David. *Joyce and the Scene of Modernity*. Gainesville: University Press of Florida, 2002.

Stafford, Ann. *The Age of Consent*. London: Hodder and Stoughton, 1964.

Stang, Sondra J., and Karen Cochran, eds. *The Correspondence of Ford Madox Ford and Stella Bowen*. Bloomington: Indiana University Press, 1993.

Stevens, Wallace. *Selected Poems*. London: Faber and Faber, 1953.

Stoppard, Tom. *Travesties*. New York: Grove Press, 1975.

Streit, Wolfgang. *Joyce/Foucault: Sexual Confessions*. Ann Arbor: University of Michigan Press, 2005.

Taylor, Marvin. *Reading Wilde: Querying Spaces*. New York: New York University Press, 1995.

Thurston, Luke. *James Joyce and the Problem of Psychoanalysis*. Cambridge: Cambridge University Press, 2004.

Thomas, Brook. *Civic Myths*. Chapel Hill: University of North Carolina Press, 2007.

Unger, Roberto Mangabeira. *The Critical Legal Studies Movement*. Cambridge, MA: Harvard University Press, 1986.

United States v. One Book, Entitled "Contraception," by Marie C. Stopes. 51 F.2d
    525 (S.D.N.Y. 1931).
United States v. One Obscene Book Entitled "Married Love." 48 F.2d 821 (S.D.N.Y.
    1931).
Valente, Joseph. *James Joyce and the Problem of Justice.* Cambridge: Cambridge
    University Press, 1995.
Vicinus, Martha, ed. *Suffer and Be Still.* Bloomington: Indiana University Press,
    1973.
Weeks, Jeffrey. *Coming Out: Homosexual Politics in Britain from the Nineteenth
    Century to the Present.* 1977. Rev. ed., London: Quartet, 1990.
Welsh, Alexander. *Strong Representations.* Baltimore: Johns Hopkins University
    Press, 1992.
Williams, Melanie. *Empty Justice.* New York: Routledge-Cavenish, 2002.
Williams, Melanie. *Secrets and Laws.* Portland, UK: Cavendish Publishing,
    2005.
Wigmore, John H. "Responsibility for Tortious Acts: Its History." *Harvard Law
    Review* 7, no. 6 (1894): 315–37; 7, no. 7 (1894): 383–404; 7 no. 8 (1894): 441–63.
Wiesenfarth, Joseph, ed. *History and Representation in Ford Madox Ford's
    Writings.* International Ford Madox Ford Studies 3. Amsterdam: Rodopi,
    2004.
Wilde, Oscar. *De Profundis.* Edited by Hesketh Pearson. 1905. Reprint, New
    York: Penguin, 1986.
Wilde, Oscar. *The Soul of Man under Socialism.* Edited by Linda Dowling. 1891.
    Reprint, New York: Penguin, 2001.

Index